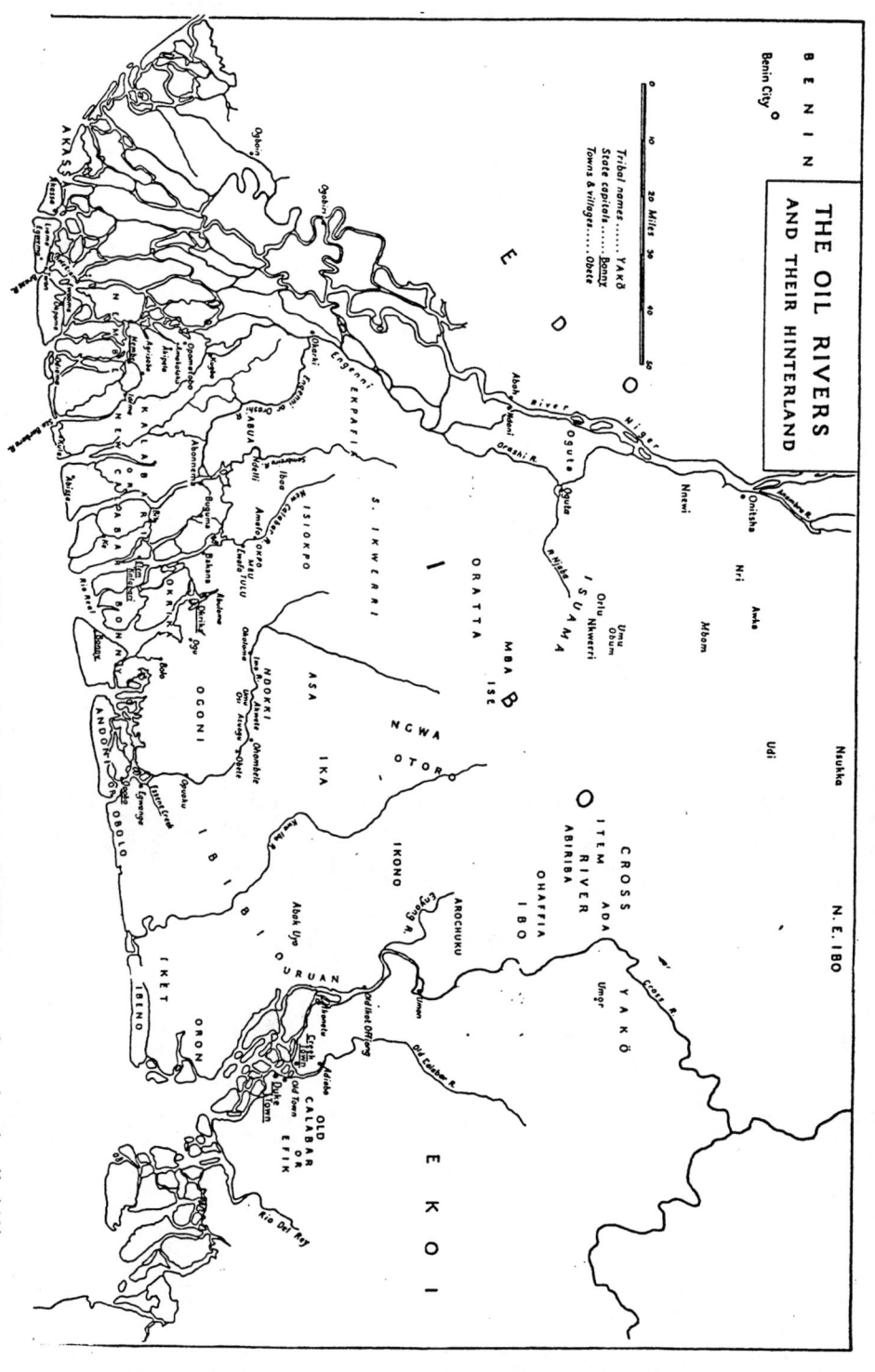

The Oil Rivers Protectorate was proclaimed in 1889. Its capital was Bonny. In 1893 it was enlarged and called Niger Coast Protectorate. The capital was Calabar. Reproduced by courtesy of The International African Institute London.

By the same author:

*Fundamental Human Rights During
a Period of Emergency*
Jonn Okwesa Ltd. Commercial Estate
Yaba, Lagos, Nigeria. 1963

*No Condition is Permanent*
Galago Publishers Ltd. Palace Grove,
Bromley, England.1989

# NIGERIA
## Foundations of Disintegration

**Aliyi Ekineh**

NEW MILLENNIUM
292 Kennington Road, London SE11 4LD

Copyright © 1997 Aliyi Ekineh

All rights reserved. No part of this publication may be reproduced in any form, except for the purposes of review, without prior written permission from the copyright owner.

British Library Cataloguing in Publication Data.
A catalogue record for this book is available from the British Library.

Printed by Roadkings Ltd. Ruskin Road, Southall, Middx.
Issued by New Millennium*
ISBN 1 85845 175 2
*An imprint of The Professional Authors' & Publishers' Association

To my loving wife, Florence, who encouraged me to undertake this work

CONTENTS

Page

| | |
|---|---|
| Preface | ix |
| Introduction | 1 |
| Chapter 1. How Colonization Began (outline) | 15 |
| Chapter 2. Thirty Years of Peace 1914-1945 | 29 |
| Chapter 3. Emergence of Tribalism | 37 |
| Chapter 4. Dreams of Self-Government in Southern Nigeria | 43 |
| Chapter 5. 1945-1947 The Crises Begins | 47 |
| Chapter 6. In Search of a Constitution for Peace | 59 |
| Chapter 7. The Road to Independence | 65 |
| Chapter 8. Independence | 77 |
| Chapter 9. First Two Years of Independence | 81 |
| Chapter 10. Three Stormy Years 1962-65 | 87 |
| Chapter 11. 1966, The Coup Begins | 97 |
| Chapter 12. The First Military Regime – General J. T. Aguiyi-Ironsi | 113 |
| Chapter 13. The Military Regime the East Refused to Recognise | 127 |
| Chapter 14. Search for Reconcilliation | 145 |
| Chapter 15. The Drift to Civil War | 151 |
| Chapter 16. The Civil War 1967-1970 | 159 |
| Chapter 17. The Peace After the War | 181 |
| Chapter 18. The Third Military Regime | 191 |

Chapter 19. Preparation for Return to
   Civilian Government  203
Chapter 20. The Second Civilian Regime:
   1979-1983  217
Chapter 21. A Military Regime that Harried
   Politicians  225
Chapter 22. The Regime with a Star-Crossed
   Election  233
Chapter 23. A Civilian Government that
   was not Elected  245
Chapter 24. The Failing Struggle  249
Chapter 25. The Military's Final Solution
   Against Ogoni  261
Chapter 26. 'Judicial Murder' that Provoked
   World Anger  269
Chapter 27. Conclusions  273
Chapter 28. The Commonwealth Failed Nigerians  287
Chapter 29. Dedication to Wasted Lives  291
Appendix I   Lord Lugard's account and report of
   the amalgamation 1914 to the British
   government in 1919  293
Appendix II  Maps showing the progressive creation
   of new states as each tribe struggles for
   a secure place  301
Index  311

# Preface

In 1992 as I listened to the discussions and the debates on the Maastricht Treaty and the objections that were being expressed about integrating twelve of the most advanced communities in the world into the European Union, even on a federal basis, my thoughts went to poor Nigeria. She was created at the turn of the century by Great Britain merging more than two hundred different and unrelated tribes without their knowledge. At that time, many of them did not even know of the very existence of many of the others. Unlike the twelve nations of the European Union, the two hundred Nigerian tribes did not have much in common; not even a basic religion,* from which their morals, arts and culture might have evolved. Their early administration as one country did not even sow the seeds of democracy.

Yet in June 1993 many around the world seemed surprised to hear that the "country has been practically ungovernable during the past fifty years" (commentary by foreign press). But Nigeria has outlived the former Soviet Union and Yugoslavia. Both of these countries had fewer different indigenous communities than Nigeria. Their communities had more than one thousand years of related histories. They were also much more highly advanced and were sophisticated enough to appreciate the advantages of a union.† Even so, they collapsed while Nigeria still slogs on; albeit under the iron grip of her own military which does not allow democracy to take root and grow.

* Unlike Asia, Africa has no ancient religion such as Buddhism or Hinduism common to large communities and areas.
† The European Union was formed and developed more slowly and cautiously during a period of more than twenty years, while the Nigerian tribes were merged more hastily and less thoughtfully like the Soviet Union and Yugoslavia.

How much longer can the country trudge on, while it now regresses fast, is difficult to forecast. Some observers who claim to know the country well, insist that it would be extremely difficult *ever* to build Nigeria into one united and peaceful democratic nation, because of its complex tribal composition and the incompatibility of Northern Nigeria and Southern Nigeria. The two territories were separate Dependencies or colonies of Great Britain at the close of the last century. In order to colonise them more conveniently and profitably, the two were merged. In official parlance, AMALGAMATED, in 1914. This notwithstanding the fact that one is a massive Islamic region and the other contains a huge wholly Christian area. Each of them consists of more than one hundred different and separate tribes, each of which speaks a totally different language. Probably no other country in the whole world has half these types of peculiarities and problems. Some scoffers see Nigeria as an experiment in building a Nation of Babel. And the incessant, sudden, bloody and violent changes of government by military action since 1966, also cause unimaginable misery that have made millions of Nigerians subhumanly passive.

In June 1997 the British Foregin Secretary, Robin Cook, said "Nigeria should be the second richest country in Africa. What holds it back is a corrupt regime and a very poor standard of government."

But Nigeria's unending crises as well as its instability, corrupt regime and poor standard of government, are all the direct consequences of its creation as a reckless mixture of disparate tribes and warring fundamental religions. For this, many blame earlier British Governments.

This book discusses the long chain of crises from their very beginning in 1945 to the period of the sixth military regime when the country became the first to be punished with suspension in the Commonwealth. It also discusses the efforts that have been made since that time, to the present time, in order to solve these crises. The opening chapters narrate in outline, the origin of the colonial system in both Northern Nigeria and Southern Nigeria and also the amalgamation of the two. Lord Frederick Lugard's own report on the amalgamation appears as the first appendix.

I would like to thank the British Library for allowing me to use their facilities. I would also like to thank my friends Abel Esien, F. Inko-Dokubo and Michael Bongilli with whom I often discussed the topics that widen my understanding of Nigeria's problems and crises. I would also like to thank many other friends, some living in Nigeria, others living abroad, who have been helpful to me by sending me press-cuttings and other materials, but who do not want their names to appear "in a book like this which may be offensive to this military regime engaged in brutal repression".

However, despite such understandable fear, the territory must quickly take a form that will enable its people to progress and board the fast train moving into the next century that casts shadows of heavenly peace and breathtaking technology.

Aliyi Ekineh.

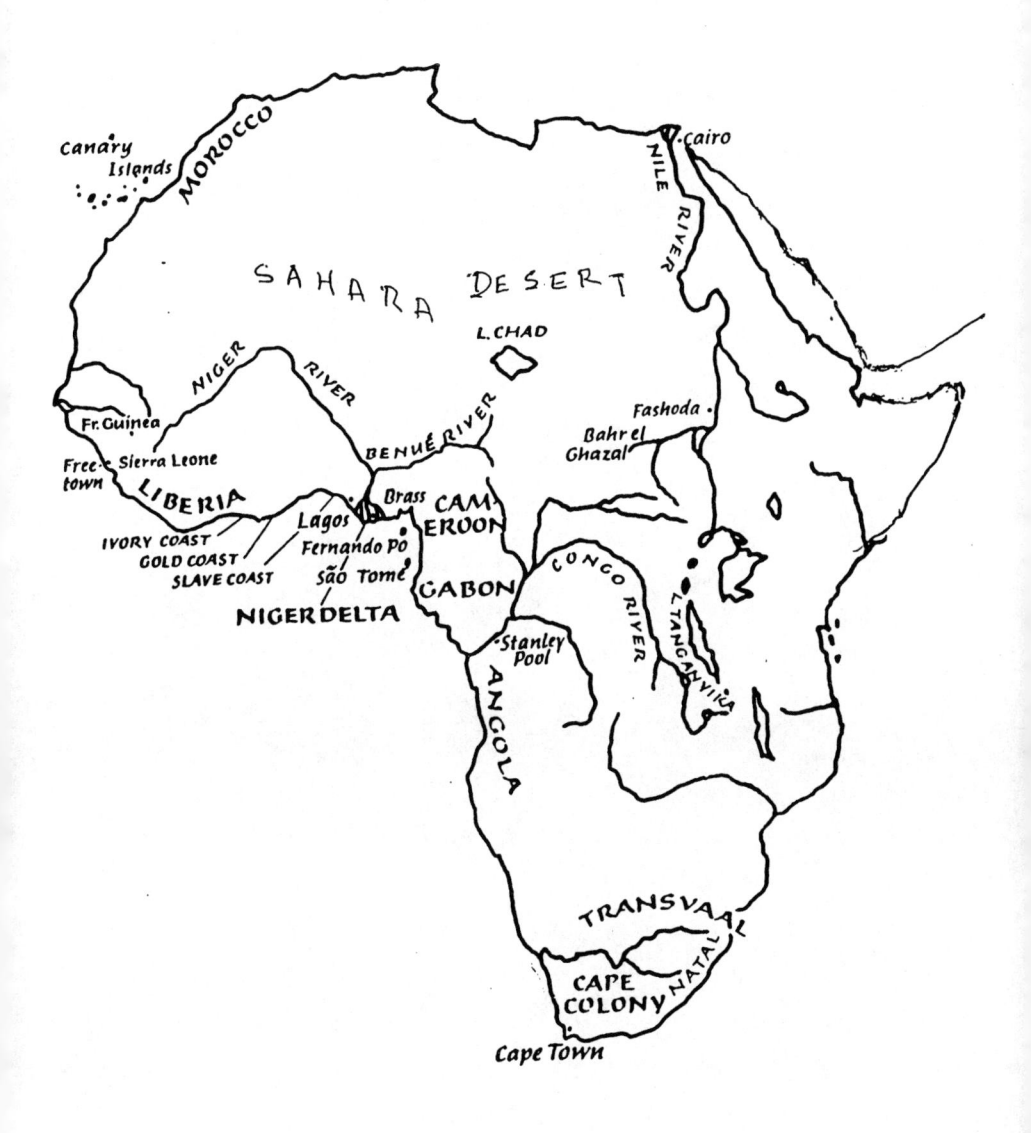

The map of Africa before the final partition 1884, shows no country or national boundaries as there were none.

NIGERIA

# Introduction

For several centuries obstacles of nature prevented the communities of Africa south of the Arab region from contact with the nations around the Mediterranean and north of it. The great civilizations that spread from these areas, particularly Egypt, Greece and Rome, to every corner of the European continent did not bear upon any of the communities of Africa south of the Arabs. It was the European colonial system, pursued vigorously in the nineteenth century that ended the exclusion of most of Africa.

By the beginning of the present century the colonial system was at its highest peak, and it continued well into the century as if it was unstoppable. African communities suffered the brunt of its brutality; but it enabled the new nations it created out of collections of heterogeneous tribes to bounce speedily into the modern world of democracy and technology. However, in many cases, because the new nations contained too many different and unrelated tribes, and the people were ill-prepared in the practice of self-rule, the sudden change to nationhood, caused protracted trauma, and a sort of apoplexy among the unspoiled communities.

Also it was unlucky for Africa that independence came during the hottest period of the Cold War between Capitalism and Marxism. As the imperial powers got ready to quit, the fear of Marxist elements taking over worried them. In some cases, they installed stooges and nincompoops who soon developed a penchant for sybaratism that led to corruption and later to repression. In the few places where "Nationalists" took over, they were so inexperienced that they could not maintain a balance as each side of the Cold War powers pulled them to its own side. They too ended up being undemocratic and repressive.

The result in many cases has been widespread communal disturbances, genocide and even civil wars and prolonged conflicts that have been difficult to end. Nigeria is a typical example. It was created by Great Britain at the turn of the century by merging together more than two hundred heterogeneous communities or tribes. Many of them at the time did not even know of the very existence of many of the others. Their differences as well as their respective ethnic aspirations were suppressed until the Imperial Government announced its intention to grant them independence as one nation.

It was trade mainly in palm oil and the suppression of the slave trade in the early years of the last century that motivated Great Britain to the coastal areas. She began by appointing consuls for the districts for the welfare of her own citizens trading in the area, and for those of the emancipated slaves housed in Lagos 400 miles West of the Niger Delta. At that time the Niger Delta was the centre of the palm oil trade.

Before long the consuls got involved in the politics of the communities. It was the consul's interference between the warring contenders to the throne of Lagos that hastened Lagos to become the first British colony in the area.

In the Niger Delta, as trade progressed, the consul made treaties of protection with the several different communities there; and later in the hinterlands, far up almost to the confluence of the river Niger and its main tributary, the river Benue.

Then came the Berlin Conference in 1884-85. By virtue of it, and of the several treaties made between the consuls and the several independent communities in the area, Great Britain proclaimed Protectorate over the vast area bordering the French colony of Dahomey in the West, and the German colony of Cameroon in the East. Southwards the area extended to the Atlantic coast; and Northwards it bordered a few miles South of the confluence of the Niger and the Benue. It was called the Niger Coast Protectorate. Calabar became its head quarters or capital. It contained more than 100 ethnic groups, including Yoruba, Ibo, Benin and Ijaw.

Henceforth, all inter-tribal wars ended; the slave trade stopped; modern administration with all departments was introduced; Christian missionaries were encouraged to rush in and open schools, colleges, hospitals and other institutions. More honourable trade replaced the slave trade; and English became the lingua franca. Later the name was changed to Colony and Protectorate of Southern Nigeria.

Earlier in 1886 as trade in the Niger Delta became more competitive, George Taubman Goldie, a former Royal Engineer in East Africa, obtained a royal charter for the Niger Company. The charter empowered it to acquire territories outside the jurisdiction of the consul appointed by the Foreign Office, and to administer such territories.

Within ten years of the grant of the charter, the Royal Niger Company had acquired lots of bits and pieces of territories around the river Benue and North of it as well as around the river Niger and North of it, to the Islamic areas. The company called these territories Niger Territories. But it soon got into difficulties with the French, who, supported by their own government, were also searching for territories and spheres of influence in the area.

On the advice of Sir George Goldie, the company invited Captain Frederick Lugard from East Africa to come to the area and settle the company's territorial claims with the French, and also to establish a military presence for the company in the area. Notwithstanding Lugard's successes in these regards, the

British government settled the territorial claims with the French by the Anglo French Convention of 1887. In consequence of the settlement, the British government took over the company's territories and later proclaimed protectorate over them as they did with the Southern communities. But here, they had to fight wars of conquests over the large territories bordering the Sahara and including the Sokoto and Bornu emirates, which were under Arabic-Islamic influence. From being Niger Territories, they became Niger Sudan and later Protectorate of Northern Nigeria.

Then came the AMALGAMATION, 1914. It united the two territories and called it Colony And Protectorate of Nigeria. Unlike in the South, in the North, Christian missionaries were not allowed to open schools and hospitals, with the result that educated Southerners assisted British officials in the administration of the whole country. This system continued until the end of the Second World War in 1945; and there was never any clash between Northerners and Southerners, although the two groups did not live on a mixed basis throughout the country.

In the aftermath of the war, as European colonial powers scrambled to quit Africa perfunctorily, Great Britain, too, decided to leave Nigeria. To this end, the then governor, Sir Arthur Richards, suddenly announced that the country would be a federation of three autonomous regions or states. Northern Nigeria would be one region or state and Southern Nigeria would be split into two regions, namely Western Region and Eastern Region. Each region contained one large tribe and about eighty smaller tribes. There was to be a central legislature in Lagos.

The announcement caused panic in the South as every Southerner, wherever he lived, became apprehensive about the future. The North announced its determination 'to take its rightful place' in the central legislature and to partake in the public services at once, and with no conditions, even as to educational qualifications. Also, it would not allow Southerners and women to engage in politics within its jurisdiction.

It was a very poor country with hardly any industry or business that employed up to one hundred workers, except in the government-owned utilities and undertakings such as the electricity supplies and the railways. The literate work force was less than ten percent of the population estimated, at the time, to be about thirty million. As Sir Richards' announcement gradually materialised, every individual as well as every tribe in every region was faced with the imminent realities of the termination of the colonial authority. That authority created the country; and it maintained peace by suppressing, without force, tribalism, nepotism and ethnic aspirations for thirty two years from 1914.

But that peace was only superficial and protected. Now that the safeguard would be off, the worms of hateful distrust would surface and afflict the country with inter-tribal antagonism and hostility. Every individual and every tribe in every region began the struggle for a secure position in the new situation. That produced a storm of conflicts aggravated by religion, as every tribe accused the others of wanting to dominate it.

In order to avert a 1990 Yugoslavian type of situation in her largest African dependency, Great Britain arranged conferences in Nigeria and the United Kingdom to enable Nigerians to resolve the conflicts; but the conferences failed and the conflicts continued beyond independence in 1960. With independence, Great Britain terminated her concern over Nigeria and the conflicts intensified, though the celebrations of independence wore a facade of peace that effectively misled the world.

The first five years of independence were marked by

widespread rioting and other violent disturbances caused by ethnic and political conflicts in every region. Unstoppable, they progressed to genocide more gruesome than many the world have seen. In the Western region a whole faction of the leadership was imprisoned on the evidence that they went to Ghana for military training in order to overthrow the elected Federal Government. In the Eastern region, Isaac Adaka Boro led an armed revolt for seceding the Niger Delta 'from Ibo domination'. In the Northern region the Nigerian military were engaged in fighting the Idomas, the Tivs, Gbokos and others, struggling for separate regions or states.

In January 1966, even as Commonwealth Prime Ministers were concluding their conference on Ian Smith's Rhodesia, held in Nigeria, a group of Southern Nigerian troops staged a coup and wiped out the top Northern Nigerian politicians and their 'Southern collaborators'. They also killed several Northern soldiers in different parts of the country. Those Northern politicians killed included Sir Ahmadu Bello, the Sardauna of Sokoto, who was the Premier of the Northern region. He was also the leader of the Northern People's Congress which controlled the Federal Government. Religiously, he was the spiritual leader of the predominantly Islamic North. Also killed was his deputy in the party, Sir Abubakar Tafawa Balewa, who was the Prime Minister of the whole country by virtue of his Party's, the N.P.C's control of the Federal Parliament.

The killing of their political leaders and spiritual rulers angered the North bitterly. But almost every one in the South glorified the coup. At least no one in the South openly condemned it in writing or words. Instead, every organisation and group jubilantly extolled it as a 'God sent miracle to save the country from ruin'. Southern troops then set up a military regime, the first in the country.

Five months into a period of extreme tension, apprehension and instability, particularly in the North, where thousands of Southerners had assisted British colonial officers in the administration. Northern troops planned, what Eastern Nigerians later called, 'their mini jihad'. It was their revenge. And it began on the 29th of May. From dawn that day, Northerners went wild killing Southerners in their homes, offices, churches, schools, railway stations, lorry parks and everywhere conceivable. With no one able to stop them, they continued their killing for several days and nights until they were exhausted. Easterners suffered the brunt of the killing, because most of the troops that staged the January coup were Easterners and all Christians. At the beginning, Northerners did not know that there were ethnic differences in the South. When they later knew, they concentrated their killing on Easterners if they could pick them out.

After a phoney respite of some weeks, on the 29th of July, Northern troops began the killing again. This time they went farther to army barracks in the South for their slaughter which continued on civilians in the streets of Lagos. And they ended up staging a coup and setting up a military regime; the second in the country. Then they considered secession of the North; but later dropped the idea.

As the conflicts developed, and as the North did not secede, the Ibos who are the largest tribe in the East and therefore controlled its government, decided on secession of the whole of the Eastern region. But the non-Ibos in the East, including the Niger Delta area and the Cross River district, which are not Ibo speaking, rejected secession. These occupied the coastal part of the East as well as the border with the Cameroons. The two groups had been fighting since 1945 for separate regions or states of their own: and in the case of the Niger Delta, there had been an attempted secession from the Region. Yet the Ibos could not secede alone; because without the non-Ibos joining them, they would be surrounded by what would be left of Nigeria.

In the maze of conflict, the Northern military, now in control of the Federal Government, agreed to cancel all three Regions that were created by the Richards' Constitution in 1945. In their places, they would create twelve states. These would be six in the North and six in the South. In the Eastern Region there would therefore be three states in which the Ibos would occupy one, and the Niger Delta one, and one also for the Cross River area. Every community, except the Ibos, accepted the new arrangement. Thereupon, the conflicts developed to a civil war following the declaration of secession by the tribally divided Eastern Region, as Biafra. The war raged from 1967 to 1970.

The civil war ended suddenly and without a negotiated settlement. While Easterners were still feeling wretched by it, the country was blessed with an oil boom that brought in lots of unexpected money into the treasury. But the situation seduced many in the army to imagine the wealth and the power they could command in a totalitarian regime such as a military one that had been on for four years. The deep tribal divisions in the country, the irrelevance of the Easterners and the fawning traits of the educated caste, could secure such a regime. And so the coups began again; albeit, for different reasons.

In 1975, a military coup led by General Murtala Mohammed ousted the regime of General Gowon who led the country through the war. The following year, General Mohammed himself was killed in an attempted coup, which failed to topple his regime, following street fighting by opposing factions of the country's own military.

The survivors of General Mohammed's regime quickly introduced an American style civilian regime in 1979. But it was impeded by ethnic clashes, confrontations and continuing corruption, until it was toppled in a coup by another General Mohammed in 1983. But this regime did not last. It was overthrown by yet another coup, the fifth successful coup, in 1985.

By this time, because all the successful coups since July 1966 had been by Northern troops, the spectre of Northern domination reappeared to haunt Southerners, this time more sorely. The military promised to introduce a democratically elected government of the American type, but in June 1993, even as the results of the Presidential election was being announced, the military stopped the announcement, and then annulled the election, which, in the opinion of international observers, was quite fair. At the time of the annulment, Chief Abiola, a Southerner of Yoruba ethnic group, was said to be ahead of his Northern opponent, Alhaji Tofa.

Abroad, the annulment of the election was strongly condemned by world leaders. In Nigeria, Southerners, particularly the Yorubas, the ethnic group of Abiola, countered the military, nearly beginning another bout of civil war, as other tribes also agitated that it was their turn to have a member of their own tribe as president.

Despite the stormy situation, another coup by Northern troops succeeded to establish the sixth military regime in November 1993. Death always followed those who attempted coups but failed, and there have been umpteen failed coups, followed by execution by firing squad. To the successful coup makers, the country's treasury, enriched with oil money, is the trophy. While the stake is so high and it seems quite easy to stage a coup, later to be supported by a crawling elite, no measure has been devised to stop military coups.

The long period of military rule and the incessant, sudden and violent changes of government caused severe trauma on the people. Inflation rose dizzily as foreign businesses withdrew in large numbers. Instability and frustration heightened and every institution fell along with the rapidly collapsing economy.

The more pro-democracy activists, though generally sustained on tribal lines, agitate for the end to military rule, the more repressive the military becomes. On account of the deep tribal divisions in the country, no issue has ever cut across tribal appeal, not even independence – that came 'on a platter of gold'.* Nigerians are generally passive.

In 1995 the sixth military regime went on a detention spree. It detained thousands of its opponents including Chief Abiola, General Obasanjo, Dr Beko Kuti, and Gani Fawwehemi, the foremost Human Rights lawyer in the country. Then it turned to the people of Ogoni, a tiny community in the Niger Delta with lots of oil wells on their land.

For several years they have agitated through their organisation, Movement For the Survival of Ogoni People, on account of damages to their land and environment due to oil and gas pollution through exploration. Since 1993 their agitation had been seen by the military as disturbing the flow of oil money into the treasury. Now the sixth military regime was determined for a showdown with them.

In 1994 there was a riot in Ogoni and four of the leading members of the Movement lost their lives. As the police were investigating the matter for possible prosecution of suspects, the military stopped the police and took the matter over. Then they appointed an ad hoc tribunal to try fourteen members of the Movement for murder. Within ten days of the tribunal's judgement of guilt on nine of the accused, they were all hanged in November 1995 and the tribunal was later dissolved.

The incident provoked the anger of the international community more intensely than any before it in Nigeria. The Commonwealth at its Prime Ministers Conference in Auckland, New Zealand at the time, immediately suspended Nigeria, as the first country to be ever so punished. The European Community

* Declared jubilant Dr Azikiwe (Zik) at the Enugu stadium in 1958 as he addressed a crows of supporters after the London constitutional conference.

countries and the United States of America promptly threatened to impose sanctions on Nigeria. All these countries and several others withdrew their ambassadors from Nigeria for a while, and they reduced their contacts, making Nigeria one of the few pariah countries in the post colonial world.

Only thirty six years earlier, in the nineteen-sixties, several world leaders had lavishly praised Nigeria as 'A budding democracy'. Now, the country has disappointed millions around the world that had complemented her with the inspiring epithet 'Giant of Africa'. And people everywhere are asking the question 'What went wrong?'

What went wrong seems to be the lack of understanding by millions in the world that more than two hundred heterogeneous communities or tribes each with its own distinct language, aspiration, religion and borders, cannot develop peacefully into a modern nation, thirty short years after they have been merged together – it's impossible. A much longer period of gestation of three to four centuries might have been adequate.

Admittedly, despite the inter-ethnic strifes in the country, which began in 1945, the colonial government embarked on material developments in a way that was quite fast, and was not attempted in other parts of Africa. For example, more than four universities were established in Nigeria between 1948 and 1958. There was none before 1948. These universities were thought to be good enough right from the beginning that they were recognised and even supported world-wide. Also, during that period, the general civil administrations, including the public services, the judiciary and the legal system, were comparable to those in developed countries. These gave confidence to foreign businesses, and they rushed to Nigeria in droves. It also made the people proud of their country.

Most of the opinions and observations expressed or made

about Nigeria at the time, stemmed from the point or considerations of these developments. Now, on hindsight, they were only skin deep. They were built on the background of the social evils of ethnic distrust, jealousy and North versus South wild struggle for supremacy. As soon as the colonial authority terminated, all the developments began to fall apart. The military only came in as a consequence and finished off the country.

Then foreign business began to withdraw and Nigerians themselves fled the country as if it were a house on fire.

Again, many Nigerians are asking the question 'What's the solution?' Some intellectuals in both Nigerias want the country to revert to its pre-amalgamation position; that is Northern Nigeria and Southern Nigeria to be different countries. They believe that "Will at least reduce the number of different tribes in each country. It will also eliminate the crises and conflicts that spring from religion."

They remind other Nigerians of India. It was administered as one country for more than two hundred years. At independence in 1947, it was realised that, on account of religious conflicts in their communities, the partition of the country into India and Pakistan was the only possible solution. Although the partition cost both India and Pakistan more than one million lives, each of them has developed without bitter internal religious crises.

In Nigeria, it is difficult to see any other solution than splitting the country to the position before the amalgamation. It is likely that there may be further splitting as in Pakistan splitting again to Bangladesh. But it makes for peaceful development which the people of the two Nigerias need after fifty-two years of continuous crises and conflicts that are likely to continue through the next century.

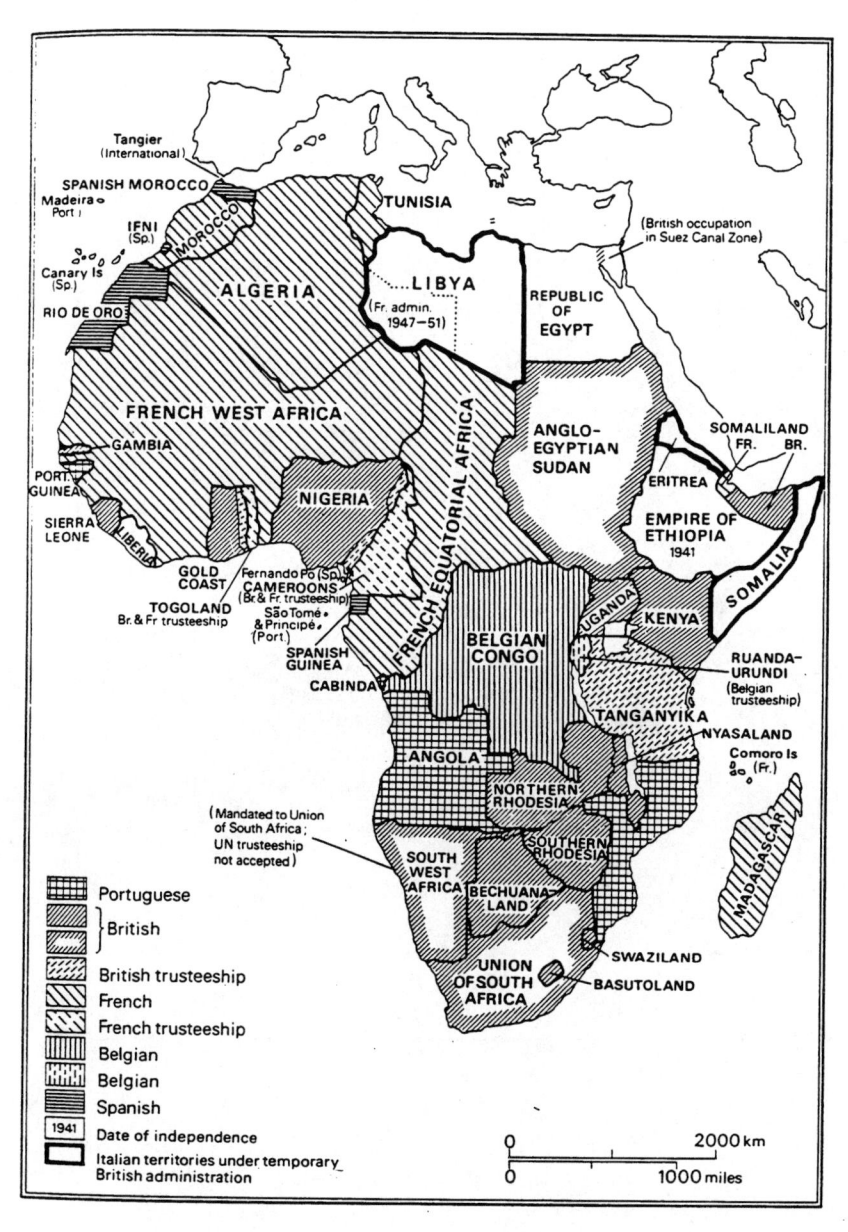

Map of Africa at the end of Hitler's war in 1945, and before the scramble for de-colonisation.

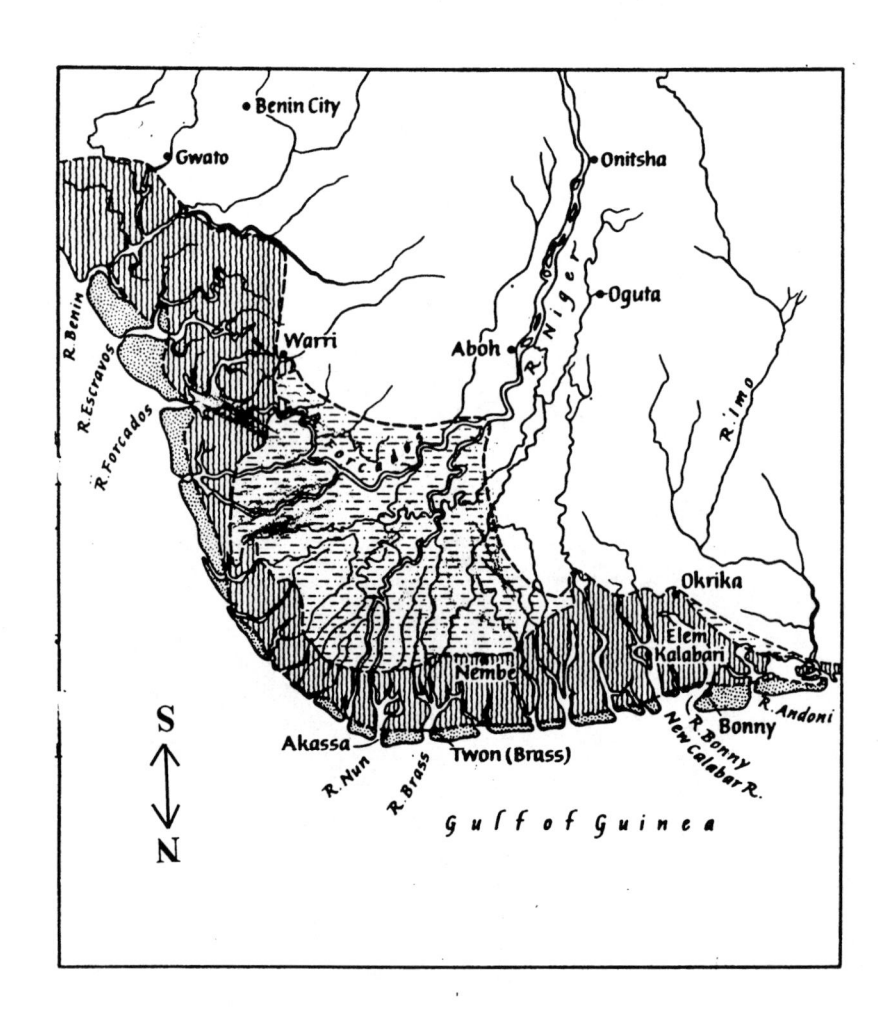

The Niger Delta before 1900
The labyrinthine creeks, rivers and swamps of the Niger
Delta terraine presented difficulty before maps were
introduced in the area in the 19th century

# CHAPTER 1

# How Colonization Began (outline)

**A. Southern Nigeria**

Nigeria was the last territory in West Africa to be turned into a colony. Before that, it was one of the largest slave markets in Africa. In 1807 Great Britain abolished the slave trade by an act of parliament. When they later resolved to end it in all places under their influence, it was on the territories that later became Southern Nigeria that they focused their attention.*

These territories included the Niger Delta on the bight of Biafra, and Lagos on the Bight of Benin. In the Niger Delta, at that time, a more honourable trade in palm oil was beginning to replace the slave trade, and it attracted several European traders, particularly from Liverpool and Glasgow. In Lagos, Great Britain had encouraged a large settlement of freed slaves and Christian missionaries, as was done in Freetown, Sierra Leone.

For effective surveillance of the area, the British authorities took over Fernando Po, a tiny island off the coast of West Africa close to the Niger Delta. Among the British officers in Fernando Po was one John Beecroft who had known the coast of West Africa fairly well. When the British later left the Island and the Spanish resumed occupation, they appointed Beecroft as governor of the Island in 1843. But he was not to retire in the service of Spain. In 1849, the British appointed him consul for the Niger Delta with jurisdiction extending to Lagos.

Before long, Beecroft was deeply involved in the politics of succession to the throne of Lagos. His presence in the area

---

*At that time much of the West African coast was known as the Slave Coast.

did not have much effect on the slave trade. It went underground. In the Niger Delta the people's excuse was that they needed slaves to supplement their small population. In the Lagos area, the inter-tribal wars of the hinterland Yorubas were providing slaves to traders in Lagos and Badagry, twenty miles away on the creeks. This was the time when the French too were combing the forests of Africa in search of spheres of influence and colonies. Beecroft concerned himself in warding off the French from the area. He was determined to secure British interest firmly in the area before the French went any deeper.

At that time Kosoko was the king of Lagos. But a bitter struggle was raging between him and his uncle Akitoye for the crown. Kosoko was accused of supporting the slave trade. Beecroft warned him to stop and the influential missionaries supported Beecroft in this respect. But Kosoko did not heed the warning. Beecroft got Akitoye to undertake that if he became king of Lagos, he would fight to suppress the slave trade and would co-operate with the consul in other respects. To assist Beecroft two gun-boats were stationed in the entrance to the Lagos lagoon, only a few miles away from the mud hut that was Kosoko's palace.

In a disturbance between the two contenders, Beecroft backed Akitoye's side and Kosoko was beaten. Akitoye became the king of Lagos. He made treaties of friendship and co-operation with the consul. This pleased the missionaries. By the time Beecroft returned to his post in the Niger Delta, after he had secured Lagos firmly under British sphere of influence, Akitoye was still in power. But in 1854, an attempted move by Kosoko to revert the situation in his favour was subdued by Benjamin Campbell who succeeded Beecroft as the new consul, now exclusively for the Lagos area.

When Akitoye died a few years later, his successor

Docemu could not adhere to the terms of the treaty with the consul. With a little twisting of arms, he easily ceded his whole territory of Lagos to the British crown in 1861; this time to the disgust of the missionaries, and even the freed slaves, most of whom had now been highly educated. However, Lagos thereby became the first British colony in what later became Nigeria.

Later slaves freed by the British on the West African coasts were domiciled in Lagos. Assisted by the Church Missionary Society, the Methodist Church and other Christian movements, educationists flooded the new territory and opened many more schools and hospitals. Soon Jesuit Catholic priests from Ireland followed in great numbers, as the British Government provided assistance and continued civil administration with all its paraphernalia. And the new territory began its evolution into the modern age.

While Beecroft was away in Lagos, trade in the Oil Rivers* got into serious problems. He found that the Niger Delta chiefs had whipped up their objections to European merchants getting to the hinterland where lay the merchandise. The area was an El Dorado of palm oil and its products. Since the 15th century the chiefs had traded with Portuguese sailors on their South-bound voyages, providing them goods from the hinterland. Also during the slave trade they continued as middle men, particularly as they did not have agricultural lands. They believed that the hinterland was their preserve, and that they could continue to be middle men, even in the expanding trade in palm oil and palm products.

The terrain of the delta made it difficult for foreigners to sail upstream to the main river without guides. There were no maps and charts of the area. The delta at that point comprised more than one hundred islands, sometimes described as 'floating islands', on the labyrinth of creeks and rivers welded to gigantic

---

* The Niger Delta and its immediate hinterland were called the Oil Rivers. Later it was declared a Protectorate.

mangrove forests. More islands continue to form from the debris of the slow running meandering rivers and creeks that terminate in the Atlantic. Mosquitoes, crocodiles and alligators abound. Even in their motor-powered crafts, European traders needed escorts to the main river Niger. It was quite simple for local adversaries to stymie their movements at that period of the 19th century.

The most recalcitrant of the Delta merchants against foreign traders was King Jaja of Opobo. He was a manumitted slave of the royal House of Bonny. In 1868, the British consul had encouraged him to rebel and break away from the King of Bonny and found his kingdom nearby at the mouth of the Imo river. To the dismay of Bonny, the consul recognised Jaja as king of the nearby tiny new territory which he called after the king of Bonny who manumitted him. The territory held at the time less than four thousand people; but the consul helped it to become more powerful than any other in the region. The consul was alarmed that Jaja later became as powerful as to want to challenge him with weapons he imported from England on his official visit there. As there were also in the area German and French colonists and traders, the consul refrained from a showdown with Jaja.

Then came the Berlin Conference of 1884-85,* initiated by the then German Chancellor, Otto Von Bismarck, and attended by the European powers in search of colonies in Africa. They agreed that the river Niger should be an international water way like the Danube. But more importantly, by agreement among themselves, each of them would recognise the claims of each of the others in respect of territories held as being under the one's 'sphere of Influence'.

In the Oil Rivers† which was the Niger Delta and its hinterland, its immediate effect was to strengthen the hands of

* Congress of Berlin 1885.
† Oil Rivers Protectorate is proclaimed in 1891.

the consul against contumacious chiefs and local merchants such as King Jaja. Jaja could not imagine the almighty power behind the consul whom he continued to cross. In 1888, the consul invited him for a conference on board the HMS Goshawk which was stationed on the creeks of Opobo. Jaja was suspicious of the intentions of the consul, and his European friends warned him that he might be walking into a death trap. But the consul assured him of his safety in convincing manner. Nevertheless, Jaja was not allowed to leave the boat. He was shipped to the West Indies for banishment. In 1891 on being returned home, he died.

The banishment of King Jaja frightened every clan and tribal leader and merchant. They queued up to sign treaties of co-operation and protection with the consul and other agents of the British Government.

Earlier some British merchants had formed the United Africa Company which was later, in 1886, granted royal charter as the Royal Niger Company. Its charter gave it jurisdiction to administer territories outside the Oil Rivers Protectorate controlled by the British Government through the Foreign Office.

By 1893, almost all the territories south of the confluence of the rivers Niger and the Benue had been brought under British sphere of influence. This included the Yorubaland in the hinterland of Lagos, which is also Yoruba speaking. Included in this area was the powerful kingdom of Benin. It was also the most fetish-ridden and superstitious part of the region. It had earlier made a treaty with the consul to refrain from human sacrifices.

Despite the treaty, the king of Benin, Oba Ovanramwen, lapsed into the practice. In 1897 an attempt by the deputy consul from Calaba requiring the Oba to end the practice, ended in a fight in which the deputy consul, General Phillips, was killed.

Benin also lost several lives. News of the death of General J.R. Phillips and his men was received with 'shock and horror' in London. Like the wind, a battalion of eight hundred men and officers was dispatched to Benin on a bloody punitive expedition. They bombarded the palace to submission and banished the Oba to Calabar. According to the Benis, several of the Oba's men were tried and executed in public and thousands of their valuable bronze treasures and magnificent carvings and other works of art, were looted by members of the expeditionary force.

After the more powerful Benis had been subdued, all others in the region rushed to submit themselves to the colonial authorities. Great Britain continued to be recognised by the signatories of the Berlin Treaty to have sovereignty over all the territories South of the confluence of the rivers Niger and Benue. Calabar remained the capital of the territory now called Niger Coast Protectorate.* Eastwards it bordered with German Cameroons and Westwards it bordered with the French Dahomey.

On January 1st 1900 the Royal Niger Company's charter was revoked. The charter was granted to it in 1886 and it empowered it to administer the territories it acquired outside the jurisdiction of the Consul appointed by the Foreign Office. By the time the charter was revoked the company had acquired lots of bits and pieces of territories by treaties with local chiefs and Islamic Emires North of the river Niger. But much of these were disputed by the French colonialists backed by their own government.

When the company lost its charter, part of its territory to the South of the river Niger was merged with the Niger Coast Protectorate. Finally in 1906, in a grand merger, the colony of

---

* The name Oil Rivers Protectorate was changed to Niger Coast Protectorate in 1893. Its first governor was Sir Claude MacDonald, an officer more understanding than Lugard after him in 1914.

Lagos was added to the Niger Coast Protectorate, This new territory later became Colony And Protectorate of Southern Nigeria.

It was a brand new country with more than one hundred different tribes that did not know one another at all before the advent of the colonial system and the consul fifty years earlier. English became the official language though less then ten per cent could read and write it in 1906. However, all through the period and to 1997 there have never been any tribal riots or other clashes among them; except among the clans of the Niger Delta within themselves. Instead, they all live in tolerance. This is sometimes attributed to Christian missionary efforts that impel common moral values and discipline even among those who did not go to their schools. They sponsored education with vigour and established hospitals and clinics where there had never been any; while the colonial administration established every branch of a modern government. Roads and bridges were constructed and genuine business developed fast in place of the slave raiding industry.

**B. Northern Nigeria**

By 1890 the territories North and South of the river Niger and its main tributary, the Benue, had all been under British sphere of influence. But they consisted of three distinct sections – 1. The Colony of Lagos, with Lagos as its headquarters, was under the colonial office. 2. The Niger Coast Protectorate with its headquarters at Calabar, was administered from the Foreign Office. 3. The Niger Territories with headquarters at Lokoja was administered by the Royal Niger Company. Its area extended far into the Islamic North to the semi desert districts. But, as has been said earlier, the company was always in territorial clashes with French colonists who, supported by their own government, were also searching for territories in the area.

In view of the French threats, to the company's jurisdiction, Sir George Taubman Goldie, a former Royal Marine Engineer had urged the company to employ the services of Captain Frederick Lugard, an Infantry Officer in the British Army in East Africa, to come to the company's aid and consolidate its territories, and establish a military presence for it.

Lugard promptly arrived at the scene and did his job perfectly well. But the French continued their territorial claims against the company. As a result, the British government intervened and settled the dispute in the Anglo French Convention of 1889. That ended the French threat. It also caused the revocation of the company's charter in 1899-1900 as earlier discussed. Earlier in 1893 Great Britain had concluded the Anglo German Agreement that settled territorial claims between the two countries.

However, notwithstanding the settlement with the French, Lugard, assisted by Colonel Morland, had to fight wars of conquest to subdue each of the several Islamic rulers or Emirs in his own small territory. The most powerful of the Emirs was the Fulani Sultan of Sokoto, who was also the spiritual leader of the whole Islamic region.

The Fulanis were a numerous pastoral people who lived on the fringes of the Sahara Desert in the region of Mali and the river Senegal. During the period of the slave trade and the Islamic Jihad or Holy War, they had conquered most of their neighbours including the Hausas. But they easily absorbed themselves as to language and the Islamic culture with the native Hausas and others. Before the beginning of the colonial era, which in this work include the period of the consuls, the influence of the Fulani stretched to the borders of Yorubaland in the South-West of the Niger. Apart from their spiritual leadership, and slave raiding occupation, at the time, they did not have effective central administration, though they were better organised than any community in the South.

When the British government took over the territories of the Royal Niger Company, they also took over the responsibilities of the company in providing stipends and other renumerations to the chiefs and Emirs whom the company used as prefects to keep the peace in their various communities. In consideration of their continuation of these services and for collecting tax from their communities, the colonial authorities maintained each of the Emirs with trained troops and paid them handsomely. The system worked so satisfactorily that in those areas where there were no Chiefs and Emirs by tradition, the colonial authorities set them up and maintained them as prefects over their own people. The system was later developed to what was to be Indirect Rule. But it created a feudal structure that got so entrenched that forty years later it became an impossibility to introduce democracy in the area which is more than three times the size of Southern Nigeria in territory.

Lugard* later became the High Commissioner for the vast area. As in the South, roads and bridges were constructed; and a modern administration was introduced with the assistance of clerical workers from the South. But Christian missionaries were not encouraged to penetrate into the North to open schools and hospitals.

In 1887 Miss Flora Shaw, later Mrs Lugard, and Lady Lugard, as the London Times Correspondent on colonial matters, suggested that the former territories of the Royal Niger Company be called Nigeria instead of Niger Territories, as the company called it. After considering other names such as Niger Sudan and Niger Protectorate, the name Nigeria was accepted, not only for the former Niger Territories, but also for the Niger

* Later Lord Lugard (1858-1945). In 1922 he published the Dual Mandate in Tropical Africa, which set out the thesis that Europeans were in Africa for the reciprocal benefit of Europe's Industrial classes and for the benefit of Africans.

Coast Protectorate. Consequently, the one became Northern Nigeria and the other Southern Nigeria; but they remained separate countries or separate Dependencies of Great Britain.

## C. The Amalgamation of the Two Nigerias

During his term of office as The High Commissioner for Northern Nigeria, Lugard enjoyed his power and authority. The position kindled his ambition as an Empire builder in the footsteps of Clive of India. And he often compared the Niger Territories with India. Even when he became the Governor of Hong Kong, he continued his ambition for the Niger. He mounted a desperate campaign for merging the two Nigerias. In this regard he had lots of support in Great Britain. The South was yielding lots of revenue from the coastal areas. The North was not viable, and its administration was subsidised by the British tax payer.* The merging of the two territories would end the burden on the British tax payer. There were also the arguments about the absurdity of maintaining two adjacent Dependencies and administering them separately; particularly as the one provided an easement for the better enjoyment of the other. There was no access to Northern Nigeria except from the Southern Nigeria's coast. Construction of a railway to convey goods from Northern Nigeria for export needed the use of Southern Nigeria ports. In other words, to ensure economic development and continued colonial administration, it was sensible to merge the North and the South.

Typically of the colonial system, only territories and profit were considered; never the people that inhabit the territories or will inhabit it for eternity.

By 1912 the Imperial Government had fallen to the argument. They appointed Lugard Governor of Northern Nigeria, and also Governor of Southern Nigeria. As some put

---

* The British tax payer had already paid the Royal Niger Company compensation for the revocation of their charter.

it, "Lugard was crowned the king of both Nigerias." Then he was commissioned to go to the territories and unify them. In official parlance to Amalgamate Northern Nigeria and Southern Nigeria.

At that time in 1912, Lugard hardly knew Southern Nigeria yet he had no stomach for Southerners. Sometime in comparing them with Northerners he said "After the 'civilised' trousered-Negro of the coast, who takes no stock of the white man and seldom raises his hat to a white man, not even to the Governor, it was refreshing to see this far finer race of men with their respective salutations prostrating themselves on their faces before the Governor."*

Hardly did he know that it is not the custom in most of the South to greet or salute by prostrating to humans. Thousands of colonial officers like Lugard, because they did not understand the language and custom of the peoples they ruled, often did the wrong thing even with the best of intentions.

It has been difficult to find where Lugard has ever given credit or value for the work of Christian missionaries in Southern Nigeria. These missionaries include the Anglican with their imprint, the Church Missionaries Society, together with Jesuit Catholics, Presbyterians, Methodists, Baptists and several others. They established schools, colleges, hospitals and other organs of mental development with the support and encouragement of the colonial administration headed by Sir Claude MacDonald, Governor of the Niger Coast Protectorate. Above all, they eradicated witchcraft and superstition almost completely. But Lugard had only spite and contumely for their achievements.

Anyway, two years after his commission, Lugard completed his assignment. By Order in Council of the Imperial Government, dated First of January 1914, Northern Nigeria and Southern Nigeria were joined or amalgamated to be one

* Elizabeth Isichei: A History of Nigeria; Longman London 1983.

country, Nigeria. But their respective distinction continued. In both countries very few knew what had happened or its significance. Of course no one could have understood its implications correctly.

In later years in Southern Nigeria, people refer to the Order in Council as 'the marriage certificate' of the two Nigerias, but they always argued about who is the wife and who is the husband in the marriage. Others speak of the Order In Council as 'The Iron structure that cages us together'.

The Amalgamation was not without some benefit to Southerners at the time. Every one in the South with some education could quite easily pick up a job in the Public Service or the Commercial undertaking in the North that was opening up. Lugard disallowed Christian missionaries efforts to open in the North. This was why the public services and the commercial undertakings in the North recruited Southerners to assist the British in the administration. Also, in those days, the civil service required the simple formal dress of trousers and tie. The North viewed this as too much bearing on Christianity. Unfortunately, in the colonial setting of the period, public servants were the aristocrats as the ordinary folks in the North saw them. Very few could foresee that it could not be so all the time.

The total area of the amalgamated territory was 332,400 square miles. Of this, the North was 255,700. This was later increased to 296,000 square miles by the inclusion of Northern Cameroon to the North. The area of the South remains at about 78,000 square miles.

The geographical features of the territory vary considerably from dense mangrove forests on the Niger Delta and the Bight of Benin to evergreen jungles, immediately South of the Niger. Then the vegetation thins upwards to savannah stretching further North to semi deserts on the fringes of the Sahara.

In ethnic composition, and number of languages, the territory surpasses the number that was engaged in building the legendary Tower of Babel. Culturally, the North generally adopt Arabic-Islam way of life, including morals, manner of dressing and even in name- bearing. The South generally adopt European Christian way of life in many aspects including manner of dressing and name-bearing.

The administration took off peacefully throughout the huge new territory. For the first time peace was restored in the North as they continued under deep Arabic-Islamic culture which the British administration did not disturb. Southerners and other Africans were kept out of bounds of Northern towns and cities. Under Native Administration, British Officers supervised the Emirs to rule the people in what Lugard devised as 'Indirect Rule'. The central government was administered by British Officers assisted entirely by Southerners. The administration included the management of the Railways, electricity, water construction and every other essential amenity and utility for the country.

Some older people who saw the last days of the slave trade, and were fortunate to witness the beginning of the colonial system in Nigeria, took pleasure in comparing the two periods. They thought that the colonial system was miles better than the slave trade 'which it replaced'. But they 'Wonder how some good could have come out of such an evil system that took over other people's countries and mix them like rubbish.' Unlike the slave trade, the colonial system does not remove people from their motherland and fling them away to distant lands in eternity. Parents did not have to watch their children like hens watch their chicks for fear that slave raiders might kidnap them into slavery. No one needed to give his child tribal marks to identify its birthplace. In Southern Nigeria, Christian missionaries brought education and introduced the Feast of

Christmas which replaced numerous idolatrous festivals celebrated sometimes with human sacrifice and all tribal wars ended.

These were some of the innumerable blessings of the colonial system. It has accounted for the rapid development of the peoples of Nigeria, as it has done in other countries in Africa. Yet, it is also thought that, if the European colonialists had been humane in Africa as the Romans were in Europe dozens of centuries ago, Nigeria as well as other parts of Africa, might have progressed in a more orderly way at their exit in the aftermath of Hitler's war. It cannot be to the credit of the colonial powers that in almost every territory in Africa and elsewhere chaos has followed their exit.

Anyway, some scholars have held the view that such humane administration might not have been possible.

> "African tribes backward, disunited and weak were helpless before Europe, especially since the perfection of the machine gun ... Abyssinia (now Ethiopia) could have been civilised by the help of international advice and money without losing her independence. But even for that Europe was not sufficiently humane. For the rest of Africa it is difficult to imagine, even if wholly unselfish European nations were willing to serve without return that they could have civilised Africa without taking over its government. The differences in civilisation and race between ruler and ruled, was so great as to invite oppression and unnecessary bloodshed. But in British territories, Africans should realise that the liberal and humane traditions in Britain have struggled with more selfish and short-sighted desires." *

* Dame Margery Perham: Africa and British Rule. Oxford University Press 1941, and reproduced with their kind permission.

## CHAPTER 2

# Thirty Years of Peace 1914-1944

Some Juju priests in the Niger Delta often insist that the dreadful First World War which began in 1914, after Southern and Northern Nigeria were amalgamated, was a sad omen for the new country. Though the assertion is utterly superstitious, a good many in the country believe whatever the juju man says, it is as if the juju man were as infallible as His Holiness the Pope. They attribute the fluctuation of the unhappy events in the country to be the fulfilment of an omen.

However, the poor nascent country was just trying to begin to crawl out from the stone age, when powerful European nations with interests around her, declared war on one another. On the immediate East of Nigeria were the Germans in the Cameroons, South of the Cameroons the Belgians were in the Congo. West of Nigeria, the French colony of Dahomey and next to it, but only forty miles away, was again the German colony of Togoland. No one person in Nigeria knew what the war was about, but thousands died fighting in it on the side of Great Britain. At the end of the war in 1918, the country was visited by the most deadly epidemic of influenza, said to be caused by poisonous gas used in the war. With only a few hospitals or medical facilities, the epidemic was more devastating than the Great Plague of London in 1664-5.

Before the war began, the French in West Africa were experimenting with democracy in their colonies. In Senegal they returned elected deputies to the French Assembly in Paris. But only Creoles were returned. It was in 1914 that the first indigenous Senagalese was returned, Baise Diagne.

The war did not stop the regular sailing of ships along the West coast to Europe. This helped the spread of news all through the towns along the coast including Dakar, Monrovia, Freetown, Accra, Bonny, Takoradi, Lagos, Calabar, Abonnema and Sapele.

Along the coastal towns of Nigeria, Sierra Leone and the Gold Coast, news of Diagne's return to Paris was received with much envy and jealousy among the educated elite, all of whom qualified in British institutions. After the war, in 1920, they were urged by a Gold Coast lawyer, Caseley Hayford, who was an activist in the Pan African Movement headed by Marcus Garvey, to organise themselves and demand some form of democracy from Great Britain.

Thereupon a group of them formed the National Congress of British West Africa. Their first conference was held in Accra, in the Gold Coast, which later became Ghana. The conference was held on March 29th, 1920. Delegates from all over the coastal towns attended, although it was disfavoured by the British colonial authorities.

The purpose of the conference, among other things, was to discuss: "matters concerning the advancement of the people of the respective territories of the delegates within the British Empire". In later periods, that subject could have been quite in order. But in 1920 the idea touched the British colonial authorities on the raw. Nevertheless the conference bravely went on as members spoke of the British Empire with more approbation than their later generations, and they resolved to be always within the Empire and: "to maintain the manifold blessings of Pax Britannica".

They finally declared that: "the policy of the Congress shall be to maintain strictly and inviolate the connection of the British West African Dependencies with the British Empire and to maintain unreservedly all and every right of free citizenship of the Empire and of the fundamental principles that taxation goes with representation ... to aid in the development of political institutions of British West Africa under the Union Jack ... and to preserve the lands of the people for the people".

Before the end of that year, the Congress followed up its intentions and sailed to London for a meeting with the Secretary of State Lord Milner. The delegation was demanding a Legislative Council consisting of some elected members for each colony. They wanted a say on the taxation and the use of the money within the colonial status of the territory. They wanted to abolish discrimination in the senior section of the Public Service which was exclusively reserved for natives of the United Kingdom. Their other demands included a university for each colony and government assistance in education.

In London the delegation waited more than four weeks, trying to have a meeting with the Colonial Secretary, Lord Milner. When they finally met him, it was for ten minutes. They reported that he treated them: "like dirt", and they returned to their respective territories empty handed and bitter. However, there were no demonstrations and no seditious speeches.

In Nigeria the Governor, Sir Hughes Clifford, who succeeded Sir Frederick Lugard, convened a special meeting of the Nigerian Council, a mini parliament consisting exclusively of top British colonial officials, for the purpose of discussing the Congress and its mission to London. Opening the debate, Sir Hughes raved with 'Imperial anger' as he condemned the Congress saying:

> "The Congress is represented by a handful of gentlemen drawn from half a dozen towns, men born and bred in British-administered towns situated on the sea coast, who in the safety of British protection have peacefully pursued studies under

British teachers, in British schools, in order to enable them to become ministers of the Christian religion or learned in the law of England, whose eyes are fixed not upon African native history or tradition or policy, or upon their tribal obligations and duties to their natural rulers which immemorial custom should impose on them ... that there is or can ever be in the visible future such a thing as West African Unity or nation is as manifest an absurdity as that there is or can ever be an European Union or Nation".*

Battered about with such tirades in Lagos, Accra and Freetown, the Congress faded away with no other conference to follow. But the delegation had, before then, made the point which touched the hearts of many humane British people. These implored politicians to urge the authorities to consider the demands of the Congress.

Notwithstanding his own tirades against the delegation, some months later Sir Hughes Clifford himself announced that the British government was pleased to announce the introduction of a constitution for Nigeria. Under it there would be some elected members and that, henceforth, throughout the country land could never be owned in fee simple or freehold by any person who was not a native-born Nigerian. Only short leases could be granted to companies of whom the members were not Nigerian and with the written consent of the Governor. The move gladdened the members of the Congress and all who understood its meanings.

Sir Hughes Clifford's constitution worked quite well and appeared satisfactory for nearly thirty years. Under it, the British Colonial Governor was the President. It had 26 British officials many of whom represented a department of government. There

*See Legco Reports 1922-23 Lagos Nigeria Government Press.

were three elected members representing the capital city of Lagos. One elected member represented the city of Calabar which was the capital of the Niger Coast Protectorate. Eleven appointed members represented one each of the eleven provinces that made up the administrative divisions of the South. Each province was headed by a British officer entitled Resident. He was accountable to the Governor in Lagos. Four members were nominated to represent business and commerce. The main business of the Council was to approve the budget of the government each year, beginning at the end of March. Its jurisdiction was limited to the powers conferred upon it by the Imperial Government: BY ORDER IN COUNCIL

The situation in Northern Nigeria was quite different. There, the Clifford constitution did not apply. The Governor in Lagos ruled personally through British administrative officers who supervised the traditional rulers in the system of 'Indirect Rule' introduced by Sir Frederick Lugard.

At a lecture which he delivered at Birkbeck College, University of London, in 1928, Lord Lugard, as he later became, explained the concept of Indirect Rule when he said: "the system of employing native rulers as agent of an alien government, or as in India and Malaysia, of recognizing their independence and attempting this device to guide them, has been employed in various parts of the Empire. The African system of Indirect Rule differs from those systems however, in that the rulers are not employed as government agents and they are not recognised as being independent. It is assumed that they will need the guidance and control of a higher civilization and will not be fitted for independence within any period now visible on the horizon".

The native rulers he referred to were the Emirs who ruled their respective 'city states' and collected taxes. Within their jurisdictions they established Koranic judicial systems and built hospitals and Islamic study centres where passages from the Holy Koran were recited continuously. Unlike the central administration which used the English language as its official language, in most 'Native Administration' centres the Hausa language was in use. The system enabled the Hausa language to be widely used through Northern Nigeria.

Southern Nigerians always condemned indirect rule as being very feudal and regressive. But many British apologists for the colonial system held it dear. "Most educated Africans, especially in West Africa and the Sudan, criticize or even strongly condemn indirect rule", wrote Margery Perham. "They say that indirect rule gives power to uneducated Chiefs and elders instead of to the educated; that it strengthens tribal feelings and so continues the disunity of the country. It is, they say, part of the old policy of 'divide and rule' by which an imperial power keeps its subjects weak and prevents their advance towards self government. In answering this I must remind you of what I said about the mixed character of men and ideas on the British side. I expect some of the less liberal of the British in Africa and at home may have this idea, sometimes unconsciously, but, I do not think it plays a large part today in Africa. The tribal divisions there are so great that they cannot be overlooked. The new unity is something built above them from outside by foreigners. These drew lines on a map and called the areas with the great collection of independent tribes which happened to be inside those lines, by a convenient new name like Nigeria or Kenya. They then set up a single twentieth century foreign government over all these tribes".*

As has been said earlier, Lugard prevented Christian missionaries from settling in the North and establishing schools and hospitals as they did in the South. Consequently the North did not enjoy the education 'renaissance' which surged through

---

* Margery Perham: Africans and British Rule, Oxford University Press, Oxford, England, 1941

the South in the advent of the colonial system. Secular education was almost totally absent through the North. As the North steered a totally different course, the central public services headed by British colonial officers were manned entirely by Southerners even in the North. The fact that the country had a unified administration made Northerners even more excluded from the stream of administration. For example, it would be quite abnormal to see a Northerner as a clerk in a government office. In later years the situation caused extreme bitterness against Southerners.

As Trevor Clark put it in his biography of Sir Abubakar Tafawa Balewa:

> "Northern leaders looked at the post office, railway stations and workshops, the clerical services, public works, yards and commercial stores, hospitals and professional men's offices, garages, airports, even in Kano, all full of Southern workers, and many of them using no Northern employees at all ... and it caused boiling frustration to Northerners."*

The 'Boiling frustration to Northerners' must be blamed on Lord Lugard. It was he who founded Northern Nigeria and gave it its form. Unfortunately he had a frightening understanding of the effect of education on the African and he demonstrated this energetically in Northern Nigeria during his time and beyond. 'Frederick Lugard even claimed that Western education made the African less fertile, more susceptible to lung-trouble and other diseases, and to defective dentition.'†

As he kept the North unspoilt, he disallowed Christian Missionaries from getting in and establishing schools there, as

---
* Trevor Clark: A Right Honourable Gentleman-Abubakar from the Black Rock; A Biography. Published by Edward Arnold. London 1991.
† Elizabeth Isichei; A History of Nigeria. Longman, London, 1983.

they freely did in the South and gave their best to Southerners. 'The attitude of the European colonial administrator towards the people of Nigeria is riddled with paradoxes. He reserved his most venomous ridicule and hostility for those who resembled him most closely, and had taken his own culture as a model. Perhaps it was because, subconsciously, he feared the rivalry of the Western educated.'

Above all, Lugard and his successors in the colonial administration, created divisions between Northerners and Southerners. In the North, they made the people believe that Southerners slavishly fell prey to European culture in religion and education, because they had no civilisation of their own and they mimic like monkeys. In the South, they spoke of Northerners as backward illiterates who spend all day reciting verses from the Koran and praying to the sun, instead of going to school and getting themselves educated like the advanced people of the South. The public services did not employ Northerners at all because they did not go to school; also because they looked at the services as anti-Islamic European orientated organisation to which only aping Southerners could be attracted. The fact that the two groups lived separately everywhere in the country, made contact and understanding impossible; and there was no leader wise enough to remedy the situation with understanding. Instead Nigerians themselves fanned the divisions in later years. However, Northerners were recruited into the very lower ranks of the Army.

# Chapter 3

## Emergence of Tribalism

In the years between the two World Wars, the British Empire was at its apogee. There was no world opinion capable of animadverting its course. At that time Nigeria had been enlarged by the inclusion of part of the former German colony of Cameroon, following the League of Nations' Mandate. But the authority of the League was weakened by Mussolini's contempt of it and his conquest of Abyssinia (Ethiopia). In Nigeria and other parts of West Africa, many feared that European ambitions in Africa were still alive and that Germany might return after Hitler had finished taking his pick in Central Europe for his dream of a Greater German Fatherland.

The fear was borne out when, in January 1938, the British Prime Minister, Neville Chamberlain said that: "No satisfactory settlement with Germany was possible without the settlement of colonial territories in Africa with Germany". This view was supported by the Foreign Secretary, Lord Halifax. Many in Nigeria thought that Chamberlain might appease Hitler to the extent of returning the Cameroons plus Nigeria to which it was attached. It was not enough that British colonial officers in Nigeria tried to allay these fears. They were too remote from the cut and thrust scenes of diplomacy in Europe at the time. The saving grace was that Hitler's continued successes in Europe temporarily satisfied him, and he did not turn to Africa while he was capable of so doing.

Nigeria was still shivering from the supposed ambitions of Hitler, when Dr Nnamdi Azikiwe, later popularly known as 'Zik', slipped in from the neighbouring Gold Coast, having been indoctrinated heavily in the political philosophy of Thomas Paine, Jefferson and others in the United States of America.

Born long before the amalgamation, he grew up as a Nigerian but had six years earlier ventured to the United States without money or sponsorship, yet with the burning ambition for high excellence in education. At that time a great many in Southern Nigeria believed that the lack of education was the only cause of the under-development of Africa. Probably many among African-Americans thought so too, because Zik succeeded due to the patronage of these sympathisers. They enabled him to share in the largely menial jobs they were limited to at that time. He thus educated himself in universities such as Lincoln's Storer College, Columbia and other institutions. He later became a professor, having obtained a long string of American degrees, which was quite unique in those days in Nigeria. But the colonial administration did not consider American education to be of much value.

Within three months of Zik's arrival in the Gold Coast he was appointed editor of the *Accra Morning Post*, an African-owned newspaper with a large circulation throughout the West Coast, including Sierra Leone. He had not quite settled at his desk when one Wallace Johnson, a highly respected trade union leader in Freetown, submitted an article to the newspaper. Its title was: "Has the African a God?" The article discussed that: "If there was a God, then no African in his right sense should worship Him because he unjustly enabled European powers to terrorize and plunder Africans in their own homes and snatch their lands and make colonials of them".

This type of expression was thought by the colonial authorities as likely to cause disaffection against them and therefore, seditious punishable by imprisonment. Zik and the author, Wallace Johnson were charged with the offence and convicted. Neither of them pleaded for mercy.

As they stood in the dock waiting for their punishment, Zik made a speech and said:

> "The fight for liberty in Africa has only just begun. It is only people like us who are prepared to face all odds with a will that knows no defeat – having right as their armour, and the sword of truth as their weapon – must follow the thorny road which was trodden by Socrates, Jesus of Nazareth, Paul of Tarsus, St. Peter, Thomas More and a host of other immortals of history".

However, he was acquitted on appeal. After that episode he decided to return to Nigeria. His prosecution had made him more popular; but he avoided pious invectives against the establishment during the rest of his political life.

In 1938 Zik began to publish his newspaper, the *West African Pilot* with enrapturing slogans such as: "Show the Light and the People will find the way ..." And the paper was: "independent in all things, but neutral in nothing that affects the destiny of Africa". To a community of second-generation school leavers, these slogans were uplifting. His editorials and other stories aroused nationalism. Yet, he did not try to introduce any particular political ideology, not even when he made his debut during a general strike by government workers.

He was a powerful speaker and he quoted Jefferson, Lincoln, John Locke, Tocqueville and Thomas Paine; but never Karl Marx, Lenin or Engels. Through his newspaper he urged the youths to follow his footsteps and adventure to America and Europe in pursuit of the 'Golden Fleece' by which he meant higher education. He likened the pursuit of higher education to Jason in Greek legend venturing to find the fleece of gold from the ram.

In response to Zik's persuasion, thousands of youths from Southern Nigeria ventured out of the country in various daring ways, even stowing away in ocean liners and boats during the thick of the war. Some resigned from work and used their little savings to travel to Europe or America in order to work and study as Zik himself did. Others sold their properties and went abroad with their families for further studies. This was the time when Chief Obafemi Awolowo and Chief Samuel Akintola former school teachers, and many others left the country for higher education. There was no age limit and many left the country even at sixty. A great many of them such as Awolowo, Akintola and Osadebay later became Regional Prime Ministers and leaders of large political parties. It was Zik who showed them the light. Zik exploited the belief that the underdevelopment was due to lack of education. Hence everyone was determined to obtain a higher education abroad as there was none at home at that time.

While individuals ventured abroad on their own, some clans and communities soon began to get together to fund members of the clan or community to enable them to travel abroad for a higher education – in pursuit of the 'golden fleece'. These were the days when scholarships were totally unheard of. Even when scholarships began to be awarded towards the end of the war, they were usually very few each year. A great majority had to depend on themselves or on the communities and clans. Soon, besides giving financial help for studies, the various ethnic groups were organising unions in order to give social assistance to those outside their homeland.

The unions helped newly-arrived members of the communities to get jobs or to find accommodation or even assistance in the way of capital to start a business. This was so, particularly among Southern tribes resident in the North where the two groups had no meeting points at all; not even in the markets. However many Northerners were the carriers and labourers in the Sabon-gari markets. Sabon-gari is the name they called the areas in the North where Southerners and other Africans lived. In the years up to the end of the war, there were not many Europeans in the North who were not British; most of them colonial officials. There were many Arabs and a few Europeans not in the service. They too lived in Sabon-garis.

Soon tribal unions, particularly the Ibo State Union, became very powerful. In the North the Ibo State Union established schools and churches. They assisted the unemployed and sick members of the tribe, and they even made funeral arrangements for their members. When politics became country-wide in the late forties, tribal unions lent their weight to politicians of their choice who of course would be members of their tribe. Zik himself at some point became the leader of the Ibo State Union to the disappointment of his admirers from other tribes.

The Ibo State Union organised the Ibo National Day on the 6th November each year throughout the North. It did not do much of that in the South. In the Northern town of Zaria, that is, in the Sabon-gari, Zaria, for example, the celebration of Ibo National Day usually began with a demonstration of loyalty to the tribe. Then followed feasting and merriment. Every member of the tribe was bound to attend these celebrations. There were sanctions for failing to attend or to fund the celebrations. Sanctions were by way of exemplary fines. If a member of the clan or the tribe neglected to attend the celebrations, he would be fined; and if he refused to pay, no member of the tribe would socialize with him or his family. No member of the tribe would visit him if he were sick and no one would attend the funeral of a member of his family. If he were a professional man, no member of the tribe would patronize him. No one would buy or sell from him, if he were a trader. In a community with no recreational facilities or cinemas, it would not be long before a recalcitrant member of the tribe pleaded for the lifting of the sanction.

Almost every tribe in the South tried in vain to copy the example of the Ibo State Union, but many lacked the determination and the skill to impose effective sanctions. It was quite late in the forties when Chief Awolowo got the Yorubas to organize themselves in a similar tribal movement. The Hausa-Fulani were never known to attempt any formation of tribal organisation. Though 'the large Moslem North' contains more than one hundred different tribes, they did not practise tribalism among themselves, and they had no tribal unions during this period. It seems that to them kinship in the religion of Islam can be stronger than tribe or race.

# CHAPTER 4

# Dreams of Self-Government in Southern Nigeria

Sadly, several of the elders and rulers who saw the beginning of the colonial era were killed, banished or subdued. But the generation that succeeded them began to live in peace and relative prosperity. By 1930 many of the killer diseases such as yaws, cholera, elephantiasis and malaria had been fairly well controlled. The power of jujumen and their shrines, including the most fiendish of them, the Aro Chukwu Long Juju, had been destroyed or, at least greatly reduced. Millions of children in the South were attending fee-paying Christian mission schools with future employment in the junior sections of the public service almost guaranteed. That was the only sector that employed people, as there was little commerce in the country. Millions of others eked out some sort of subsistence in a situation that was largely free from strife.

There was little dissent at this time against the colonial system. In 1935 the silver jubilee of King George V was celebrated most gloriously in every town and village throughout the country. Every year, the 24th May, Empire Day marked the day on which the Empire was celebrated. A day when every mother adorned her child in his or her school uniform for the march past and parade as the Union Jack was hoisted in towns and cities. The colonial official in the uniform of a naval officer usually took the salute of the school children and the representatives of the different branches of government.

With that degree of admiration for the Empire, not many spoke of self-rule, let alone independence. However, when the war began in 1939, Southern Nigerian school leavers joined the British Army which offered more pay and better prospects than even the public service, yet the qualification required was lower than that required by the public service. Some of the Nigerian recruits were shipped to North Africa, India and Burma.

In North Africa, the Nigerians fought under Field Marshal Montgomery in the Eighth Army against the German General Rommel. By late 1941 some of them had returned to Nigeria wounded or on leave or even as deserters. They told fantastic stories of their bravery and how they captured Italians and Germans. But even the captured prisoners of war taunted them as being soldiers of fortune, fighting as slaves for their slavemasters. Terribly humiliated by these remarks, they returned to Nigeria and joined "the fight for self-government".

The voices of the Southern troops from North Africa were soon joined by those from India and Burma. Some of these claimed that they attended rallies of the Indian Congress and met with Mahatma Ghandi. They had been converted to nationalism by Ghandi and were determined to introduce it into Nigeria. Zik, through his newspapers gave them every support. They called the movement the Gospel for National Self Determinism.

Though there were several times more Northern troops, mostly in combat divisions, fighting abroad than Southerners, Northerners did not involve themselves in politics. The few Northerners who spoke on the matter, like Alhaji Ribadu, accused Southerners of 'morbid nationalism' and they generally refused to have anything to do with the movement.

It was during this period in 1941 that a sudden news flash was received. President Roosevelt of the United States and Prime Minister Winston Churchill, following a meeting on board the USS *Augusta*, made a firm declaration to the effect that they would fight to restore: "the rights of all peoples to choose the form of government under which they would live". This was the Atlantic Charter.

Although the declaration was obviously intended to reassure those countries in Europe under Nazi occupation, Zik and his group for 'National Self Determinism' did not let it slip off. "What's sauce for the Goose, is sauce for the Gander", the politicians chanted. Every day Zik's newspapers published stories of messages from far and near on the issue. Later they decided that a Nigerian delegation must travel to London: "to fight that the Atlantic Charter should apply to Nigeria". In London the delegation received little attention from the British government.

However, on their return, the delegation realised for the first time that a large section of the British public were against oppression and the colonial system. Men like Fenner Brockway, D.N. Pritt, KC and several in the Fabian Society gave them much encouragement. Of course, that was the most active anti-colonial period in Britain. Arthur Creech-Jones, who later became the Colonial Secretary in the first post-war Labour government, was part of the trade union movement. Together with Ernest Bevin of the Transport & General Workers' Union, they were part of the anti-colonial movement in Britain. The Colonial Office itself was dominated by liberal scholars like Andrew Cohen, a Cambridge don. It was Cohen who insisted that: "Self-government in any form is better than colonial government". A hundred years earlier, in the early nineteenth century, Sir Thomas Fowell Buxton, then a member of parliament after William Wilberforce, had championed the anti-slavery movement. Their manifesto titled: "The African Slave Trade and Its Remedy" had led the movement for abolishment of the slave trade. They also contributed to the founding of Sierra Leone. Great Britain in the 1940s was also full of similar liberal thinkers. Among them was Dame Margery Perham who wrote:

"I wonder if Africans realise how closely their educational advancement is followed in England by many people".*

However, in Nigeria itself many of its people were not ready to benefit from this kind of liberalism. They opposed Zik's delegation in the demand for self-government. They thought that the colonial system in Nigeria had not been too oppressive and the numerous tribes could not live peacefully together: "once the cage which enclosed them together was broken". Some argued that: "We're not ripe for independence". Their opponents responded: "Are we mangoes?"

Those who advocated independence claimed that all that was necessary was to replace British officers with Nigerians. No one considered at that time that the North too, was entitled to participate. Some argued that even if Nigerians were able to replace British officers, one must take into account the very tribal outlook of most Nigerians and their close ties with the extended family, clans and so forth. These ties, they argued, would breed nepotism, jealousy, greed and could not stand the tolerance that independence required. "No, a good constitution would solve all these problems", some believed.

In 1945, the then colonial governor Sir Arthur Richards suddenly announced that a new constitution would be introduced that would involve Nigerians in the government of the country. It was this constitution that began the process that eventually led to independence.

---

* See Margery Perham's book: *African and British Rule*, Oxford University Press, 1941. Dame Margery was a member of the Advisory Committee on Colonial Education, 1938-46. She died in 1982.

CHAPTER 5

# 1945/1947 and the Crises Began

"When Lugard amalgamated Northern Nigeria and Southern Nigeria in 1914, it might have seemed to him that he was lumping together under the same administration groups of mutually-incompatible peoples" *

As the world was in 1914 there was not much evidence to suggest that unspoilt and heterogeneous communities could not be merged successfully to develop into one nation. There were the examples of Germany and Italy to point to the fact that separate, independent communities could be brought together and become single nations that could be great. In these cases however, the different independent communities spoke the same basic languages. More importantly, their cultures and ways of life were similar, evolving from the same source – the Roman Empire and the Roman Church. It was likely that the British authorities in Nigeria, like other colonial powers in Africa, did not quite understand the depth of differences among the peoples whose territories they merged for their own conveniences or the conveniences of settlers.

Shortly after the end of the Second World War, Sir Roy Welensky † got the British Government to amalgamate three Dependencies in Southern Africa. They were Nyasaland, Northern Rhodesia and Southern Rhodesia. But the Africans in these territories in 1953 were less ignorant, less primitive and less timid than Nigerians were in 1914. They fought against

---

* See Michael Crowder: *The Story of Nigeria*, Faber & Faber London 1966.
† A former local heavyweight boxer whose father, a Luthuanian, settled in Southern Rhodesia before his own country was annexed by the Soviet Union under Joseph Stalin.

the amalgamation which was in their case called Federation. It lasted only ten years. Each of the three later became independent as Malawi, Zambia and Zimbabwe respectively. Today, their peoples are by far more settled and their countries more peaceful and prosperous than Nigeria. This notwithstanding that they were more repressively colonised than Nigerians were.

Some cynics have suggested that 'Lugard was probably acting like a prison warder; he locked up ten or more prisoners in the same cell. He did not need to consider their backgrounds particularly, as he hoped that his authority and those of his successors in the system would be present at all times to guard them and 'they will not be fit for independence within a period of time now visible on the horizon.'

Nigerians of later generations have never spoken kindly of 'the ill-starred amalgamation.' In April 1996 Doctor Alex Ekueme, a former civilian vice President 1979-1983, speaking at a seminar on Reconciliation and Democracy at Pope John-Paul Centre, Wuse, said 'Only a courageous determination to remedy ourselves of the wretched Amalgamation of Northern Nigeria and Southern Nigeria in 1914 can make the people in these territories progress meaningfully.' Chief Awolowo, the first Premier of Western Nigeria, until he died in 1991, had insisted that 'Nigeria is only a geographical expression to which life is given by the diabolical Amalgamation of 1914 ... that Amalgamation will ever remain as the most painful injury a British Government inflicted on Southern Nigerians.'

Also, as discussed elsewhere in this work, Sir Ahmadu Bello, The Sadauna of Sokoto, thought very little of the Amalgamation in the same manner as his Deputy in the Northern Peoples Congress, Sir Abubakar Tafawa Balewa, the country's Prime Minister at independence. Speaking in the Northern House of Assembly, Kaduna in 1952, Malam Abubakar Tafawa Balewa, as he then was, said 'The Southern people who are swamping into this Region daily in such large numbers are really intruders; we don't want them; and they are not welcome here in the North. Since the Amalgamation in 1914, the British Government has been trying to make Nigeria into one country. But the Nigerian peoples are different in every way, including religion, custom, language and aspiration. The fact that we're all Africans might have misguided the British Government. We here in the North, take it that 'Nigerian Unity' is only a British intention for the country they have created; IT IS NOT FOR US.'

Unfortunately, none of these leaders fought to terminate the Amalgamation. Instead, each of them fought to dominate the Amalgamated entity.

Lord Lugard died in 1945. That was the year when, in pursuance of the 'British intention', one of his successors, Sir Arthur Richards, introduced in the country a constitution which opened the way to: "independence within a period of time then visible on the horizon". In his constitution Sir Arthur did not let the sleeping North lie. He woke it up with a mighty bang that caused panic in the South.

It will be remembered that, since the Amalgamation and until the introduction of the Richards' constitution, the whole country, both North and South, was centrally administered, although the North was not represented in the Clifford constitutional arrangement. The country consisted of 22 provinces similar to counties in the United Kingdom. Each province was headed by a Provincial Administrative Officer who was a British national. In the North his main duty was to supervise or give advice to the Native Administrative Authorities and the Emirs. In the North, the Native Administrations were more powerful than their counterparts in the South.

In both the North and the South the provinces were so arranged that many of them contained people of the same ethnic group split into smaller units. Some provinces contained many smaller ethnic groups who spoke different languages. These were grouped in such a way that no one ethnic group was larger than any two put together. Probably it was on this account that there were never any accusations of domination by any one tribe over another.

For example, in the South, both Oyo and Ondo Provinces were entirely Yoruba-speaking. Onitsha and Owerri Provinces were both Ibo-speaking. Benin, Calabar and Rivers Provinces each contained more than ten ethnic/language groups, none of which was large enough to dominate the others. A similar arrangement was adopted in the North, though on a much larger scale.

Sir Arthur's constitution ignored the arrangement and suddenly converted the country into a federation of three units or regions. The huge North he left as one region. The smaller South he divided into two regions, West and East of the Niger respectively. Each of the three regions, North, West and East, consisted of one large ethnic group and several minority groups. In the West the Yoruba predominated, in the East the Ibo and in the North the Hausa-Fulani. The Northern leaders were pleased but many of the smaller ethnic groups were bitter that: "by his constitution, Sir Arthur has bequeathed to each of the major ethnic (language) groups, a colony of smaller ones". The Ibos and Yorubas criticized the new divisions as it afforded the North a much greater representation in the Central Legislature.

Sir Arthur did not say he consulted any local community in advance but it was alleged that he consulted Lord Lugard before he died. Some opponents of the constitution pleaded for the retention of the 'Provincial System' or a federation based on the provinces as the unit with any amendment that might be necessary.

Some other minor laws were promulgated at the same

time as the constitution was announced. They included a law to enable the authorities to appoint and depose traditional rulers, and another which vested all minerals in the 'Crown'. Although the term 'Crown' in the context, was known to be the country, opponents of the constitution argued that it meant the British crown. Wherefore they lumped all together as an 'obnoxious Legislature' to be fought.

Just about that time the workers were agitating for more pay and better conditions of service. They consisted of government workers in the railways, electricity, Ports Authority, civil service and several others numbering more than one hundred thousand. As there was hardly any industry beside government-owned concerns, a strike would affect the government very directly.

On the instigation of some Nigerian-owned newspapers and of political leaders, including Zik and some of his lieutenants, the workers staged an effective general strike. It ranked as the most effective country-wide strike that had ever been staged in Nigeria. Its determined leader Michael Imoudu, together with some other leaders were arrested and detained. The strikers wanted all the 'obnoxious laws' to be abrogated. Zik's newspaper was involved and was punished by censorship.

Later, the government acceded to the demands of the workers only in respect of conditions of service and pay; but not on the constitution and the other legislation. The step by the government dented Zik's influence. Suddenly he fled to the East and hid himself in a village, claiming that a signal to assassinate him was intercepted by his wireless operator, Mark Paul West of Abonema in the Rivers Province. Later, Zik himself probably thought that many did not believe him; for he wrote an account of the matter and explained how the news got to him. He headed his account: 'Assassination Story – True or

False'. Thereafter, the agitation against the constitution became weaker, but it continued.

Initially the British government intended that the constitution would go on for nine years. But in 1947, a new Governor, Sir John MacPherson arrived. He sensed the tensed-up feeling of the people, that is Southerners, and probably convinced the British government that it was necessary to review the constitution. Accordingly, within three months of his appointment, Sir John announced that the constitution would be revised, and this time entirely by Nigerians themselves.

It was during this time that the most distinctive and one of the three giants who dominated politics in Nigeria, arrived from the United Kingdom; Obafemi Awolowo, aged about 46. Like most politicians in Nigeria, he came from a humble background. Before sailing to England he had, through studying at home, obtained a BA in Commerce at London University. Living with his family in London, he studied law and was called to the English Bar. While in England he published one of his most popular works, entitled: *Path to Nigerian Freedom*. It advocated a federal form of constitution with units based on linguistic considerations as much as possible. He was unquestionably one of the most capable and hard-working of politicians who could have become the national leaders, to the country's advantage, if it had not been afflicted with tribalism. Awolowo found that he had to begin as a tribal leader, but later it became difficult to wriggle out of the stigma of tribalism. Even as a student in London he had founded the Egbe Omo Oduduwa as a Yoruba political movement disguised as a cultural organisation. It returned to Nigeria with him as the harbinger of the Action Group, the name of the Political Party he founded.

In 1948, while discussions on the MacPherson constitution were in progress, the Egbe Omo Oduduwa was inaugurated in Nigeria under the chairmanship of Sir Adeyemo

Alakija, a barrister of long standing, and a one-time member of the Legislative Council introduced by Governor Clifford. In his address at the inaugural meeting, the chairman declared that: "Henceforth Yoruba people will never be relegated to the background in the future". The object of the Egbe was: "To create and actively foster the idea of a single nationalism throughout Yorubaland and to co-operate with existing ethnic and religious associations in matters of common interest to all Nigerians, so as thereby to attain a unitary Nigeria". A motion praying that the Egbe should fight to have the name of the country changed to: "United Tribes of Nigeria" brought by more detribalised members was defeated. The following year the Action Group Party was formed with almost the same executive as the Egbe. Awolowo was the leader of both organisations. Henceforth he was called: "The Leader".

At the discussions for the revision of the constitution, Awolowo and his party were more concerned with the inclusion of Lagos and all Yoruba-speaking areas of the North into the Western Region. They easily succeeded in Lagos becoming part of the Western Region but the North would not agree to the idea of Ilorin which is Yoruba speaking being incorporated into the Western Region.

Instead, the North's proposal was for a stronger federation with complete regional autonomy, except for defence, external affairs, customs and the West African Research Institutions. They also wanted all revenues to be regional, except customs and even this to be collected and paid to the region from which it was collected. They wanted each region to have its own public service independently; and public utilities like the railways and electricity to be controlled by a common agency. None of the regions demanded any substantial changes in the federal structure. The East demanded the creation of another region or state in the North and the West, but not the

East. The North wanted another region or state to be created in the East or the West but not in the North and the West had similar demands. In the end they all agreed to postpone the issue to a later round of revision of the constitution, while the smaller tribes in each of the three regions continued the struggle for their: "freedom from domination".

The MacPherson constitution did not provide for direct election to any of the Legislative Houses. By a cumbersome electoral system, those elected to the House of Assembly in each of the three regions met in their respective legislatures and elected members out of their number to represent the region. Lagos now formed part of the Western Region. Zik had lived there since his return from Accra in the Gold Coast (Ghana). His NCNC Party won all the four seats in Lagos, and also surprisingly won several seats in other parts of the Western Region. Before the date of selection of members to represent the Region in the Federal Legislature, Zik and his colleagues in the NCNC had met and decided on the members that would be selected to represent the Western Region.

When the House of Assembly at Ibadan met on the first day, the first business was the selection of the members that would represent the Region in the Federal Legislature in Lagos where the House was situated. As the Speaker welcomed the members to the House, many of the NCNC members were crossing the floor to sit with the Action Group Members. The NCNC members had 'sold their passes' and had become the Action Group. Zik could not believe his own eyes as he saw his members deserting him for his opponent. He was not selected as he had expected. Also, his party had now become the minority party in the House of Assembly in Ibadan.

As he nearly lost his temper, some of the deserters added insult to injury when they shouted at him saying: "Why don't you go to Enugu where you belong?" Enugu is the headquarters of the Eastern Region where his own tribe the Ibos were the main ethnic group. He did not go to Enugu that day, but waited and accused the Action Group of tribalism. Eventually he left the Western Region and found a seat in Enugu. There, his lieutenant Dr Michael Opara took another seat and Zik became the Premier of the Eastern Region.

Even before this incident there were no Ibo in the Action Group. The Easterners in the Action Group were the non-Ibos. Many of the Yorubas in the NCNC left the party for the Action Group. None in the North joined any of the Southern parties. But dissidents in the North formed their parties and affiliated with either the Action Group or NCNC.

In Nigeria the main topic of discussion when more than two people were gathered together was politics, particularly the ongoing constitutional discussion. Tribal unions were also growing in number. During an argument in one of Lagos's premier social clubs, a young Ibo lawyer * was reported to have said that the: "domination of Nigeria by Ibos is only a matter of time". People could not believe that they had heard him correctly; for it was the type of statement with which they could buttress the argument for strengthening their own tribal unions. "Say it again", some goaded him to repeat the statement. And he did: "Write it down if you mean it". So he wrote it down. Soon the table had been surrounded by curious listeners and others expounding the argument. It was a near riot. The man was eventually escorted out of the club premises before the police arrived. For more than two decades the incident remained the classical manifestation in support of the claim that the Ibos had the ambition to dominate Nigeria. People quoted it like a verse from the Holy Bible.

By 1953, the MacPherson constitution had been in operation for two years. In many regional headquarters it had

* Charles Onyeama, later a Judge of the High Court of Lagos. And later a Judge of the International Court of Justice in The Hague.

created a new class of elite, the ministers. In some regions, to support their new status they imported large American limousines and inscribed 'Regional Minister' above the number plate at the back. "This is the type of car that befits us", many of them would say as they sank down on the back seat behind the chauffeur. To many of them, money became central to their lives, needing more and more to support their positions and their potential supporters in the next elections. In addition to this, the ministers had to meet the expectations of their extended families and clans. There was no social security or free services such as in education and health. Added to this, money was needed for party organisation.

Very few political parties in Nigeria can be supported by subscription or donation only. The party must therefore expect its financial support from those politicians in government. These funds far exceed the income of ministers in government. Before long, many of the politicians found themselves being led into corrupt activities in order to survive.

Although the Republic of Dahomey (Benin) and the Cameroons lie so close to Nigeria on either side, many Nigerians feel greater affection for the Gold Coast or Ghana. In 1953, the news that the Gold Coast had progressed far towards independence made Nigerians green-eyed. Chief Anthony Enahoro, who had been a staunch disciple of Zik's for several years and had later joined the Action Group, initiated a motion in the House of Representatives praying that Great Britain should grant independence to Nigeria in 1956. The motion was defeated by the Northerners.

Many of them argued that unless the motion was intended for propaganda value, it was not called for. In their view, the country had gone so far without any struggle on the part of anyone in the country. All the progress so far had been initiated by Great Britain herself. They had implicit confidence that the

British would guide the country to independence in peace. It was therefore, they argued, not necessary to try and pretend that politicians got independence for the country.

But the action of the Northerners in this regard provoked widespread anger among Southerners. They accused Northerners of being 'Imperialist Stooges'. Throughout that period, Northern leaders were jeered and abused publicly in the South, and even by Southerners in the North. This small insult enraged the Northerners passionately. They were not used to being heckled at all. Soon the more intolerant of them were instigating their thugs to unleash bloody assaults on Southerners in the North. In Kano, Kaduna, Jos, Bauchi and other places hordes of fanatical Northern thugs pounced upon Southerners, killing them and burning down their houses and belongings. Within three days, more than two thousand Southerners were reported butchered in different cities in the North.

Sir Ahmadu Bello, the Sardauna of Sokoto, later narrated some of the incidents and said: "This journey (from Lagos) just about finished us. We were all not only angry at the treatment, but indignant that people who were so full of fine phrases about the unity of Nigeria should have set their people against the chosen representatives of another region while passing through their territory and even our own. What kind of trouble have we let ourselves in for, by associating with such people?" He continued: "Lord Lugard and the amalgamation were far from popular among us at the time. There were agitations in favour of secession; we should set up on our own; we should cease to have anything more to do with the Southern people; we should take our own way... Two days before this meeting – that is Saturday – trouble broke out between Kano City and Sabon-gari, the area outside the walls, occupied by native foreigners, mostly Southerners This was the culmination of a series of incidents in the past few weeks which had had their origin in the troubles in Lagos. While the Action Group in Lagos had been the prime mover, they had been supported by the NCNC. Here in Kano, as things fell out, the fighting took place between the Hausas, especially from the tough suburb of Fagge, and the Ibos; the Yorubas, of the Action Group persuasion were, oddly enough, out of it. Very large numbers were involved in both sides and the casualties were severe in number though not in proportion to the crowd involved ..."

An inquiry instituted on the incident by the Federal government blamed it on widespread tribal sentiments, inflamed by reckless politicians. They warned that it could happen again in a more terrifying dimension, if tribal politics continued.

CHAPTER 6

# In Search of a Constitution for Peace

By 1953, it was only forty years since the amalgamation. In the summer of that year scores of Nigerian politicians arrived in London to continue the discussion on the type of constitution which would enable the different tribes to live in peace so that the country could progress.

They were all happy to be in London, because they all knew that the glue which still held the country together was Great Britain. They had nothing else in common. If their chief host, the Colonial Secretary, Oliver Lyttelton had known them better, he could have helped them to arrive at a better result by insisting on the reconstruction of the federation, even if that had meant prolonging colonial rule, so as to stabilise democracy and tolerance. He could have easily broken up the country and recreated it into any reasonable number of smaller countries, each with fewer different tribes. Of course there were viability questions to consider, but peace very often helps an otherwise poor country to develop viably.

The other hosts of the Nigerians were the staff of their hotels. They hadn't seen before so many Africans adorned in glorious costumes that were very different from one another in style, design and elegance. But their motley dresses only portrayed their tribal differences.

When later Mallam Abubakar Tafawa Balewa spoke at the conference and said: "I represent seventeen and a half million Northerners who must be entitled to more than fifty percent of the seats in the Federal Legislature", his less-informed audience thought he was speaking of a different country that wanted to join the Nigerian Federation. In 1950 the population of Nigeria was estimated to be 35.4 million, of which The Northern Region was 18 million.

He was in fact speaking of the North as one of the three regions of the federation and which contained a number of tribes he represented. The party he led was the Northern People's Congress (NPC) which, by its constitution, was not open to Southerners. Because the North was entitled to more seats than the other two regions put together, it was its leader that became the Prime Minister of the whole country. Abubakar Tafawa Balewa later became Sir Abubakar.

This was the kind of fault in the constitution which many others sought to change. One did not need to be a fortune teller to see that it could not work towards a peaceful co-existence of the numerous ethnic groups.* The North also insisted that it would not grant suffrage to women and that people from other regions should not canvass for votes in the North. It wanted every region to be autonomous except as to currency, defence and external affairs. It also demanded a separate judicial system whereby it could practise Islamic jurisprudence and set up a Sharia Court system with no secular courts.

The political party that ruled the Eastern region was the National Council of Nigeria and the Cameroons in which there were no Cameroon members. The party consisted of Ibos in the majority, but many Yorubas opposed to Chief Awolowo's party joined the NCNC and were quite vocal.

At the conference the NCNC said they supported: "the territorial structure of the present constitution", but did not support the advantages enjoyed by the Northern Region. "The advantages enabled the North to dominate the whole country and still they are looking for more advantages", they argued. It

* The Colonial Governor in Nigeria was unanswerable to the Imperial government through the Colonial Office in Whitehall.

condemned the North's refusal to give women the vote and its attitude towards restricting the free access to people from other regions to engage in political activities in the North. The NCNC also condemned the North's demand for complete autonomy because they: "will use it to exclude others from the North while they use their majority to rule the whole country."

Eastern Cameroons was at that time still a British Mandated Territory, as a result of the Treaty of Versailles in 1919, but was administered as part of Nigeria. At the beginning of the Richards constitution in 1946, South Eastern Cameroon was made part of the Eastern region because it is situated East of the Niger. It did not accept inclusion in the NCNC and it formed its own party, the Cameroon People's Congress. North-Eastern Cameroons formed part of the Northern Region and was controlled by the NPC. At the conference, South-Eastern Cameroons was led by Dr Endeley who had lived in Nigeria all his adult life. Later, at Nigeria's independence, the Cameroons in the Eastern Region voted to join the French Kamerun while those in the North voted to remain in the Northern Region.

One of the few political parties formed by the smaller ethnic groups, found it difficult for its faint voice to be heard, even by the Colonial Secretary who was the chairman of the conference. The faint voice was that of Professor Eyo Ita, who like Zik went to the United States and studied with the benevolent help of African-Americans. His party, the Nigerian Independence Party, demanded the creation of a region to be called Calabar-Ogoja Rivers (COR) which were not Ibo-speaking but were lumped with the Ibos by the Richards constitution in 1945. Ita did not get the support of the Eastern Regional leaders. Like Eyo Ita, Joseph Tarka, a member of one of the smaller tribes in the North, made a similar demand for the creation of a Middle-Belt Region to include the Tivs and other non-Muslim areas in the North. The conference, however, gave little attention to these minority demands. This led to the view by many that Britain was never interested in the protection of minorities in Nigeria.

The British government also did not support the creation of any more regions. They, like the Nigerian regional leaders thought the agitation would die down when time had healed the wounds. Others thought they could use force after independence to snuff out any agitation.

Unfortunately, every group in the country was agitating for something and accusing the others of domination of some sort. Zik, speaking for the Eastern Region said: "The North is so large that it will perpetually dominate the rest of the country". For the Western region, Chief Awolowo wrote in his book entitled: *The People's Republic of Nigeria*,* that: "The British are aware of the monstrosity and abnormality of Nigeria's federal structure. They know that whichever political party ruled the North as an undivided unit, was sure to have electoral advantages over any other political party". But the North too had much to fear from domination by the South. In 1956, Abubakar Tafawa Balewa said in the Federal legislature that: "There are 46,000 employees in the public services. Out of this number less than one percent are Northerners." This put the North in perpetual fear of Southern domination. Thus both the North and South feared domination by each other, causing considerable distrust amongst their respective communities.

At the London conference Chief Awolowo was the most steadfast of the Southern leaders. Unable to convince Zik and the NCNC that the South should 'Stick together and fight for Secession Clause in the constitution', he fought alone to enlarge the Western Region by including all the Yoruba speaking areas of Ilorin, Kabba and Lagos. Here he was defeated by Zik and the NCNC joining up with the Northern leadership and the Colonial Secretary.

* Oxford University Press 1961.

Angered by his defeat, Awolowo threatened that "The City of Lagos will witness the worst blood-bath that any part of Africa has ever seen."* Everyone was baffled that the language was 'too intemperate' for the occasion.

"What did I hear you say, Chief Awolowo?" riposted the Colonial Secretary.

"I mean we will adopt constitutional means to make the constitution unworkable." Said Chief Awolowo.

"In that case we might as well end the conference and Her Majesty's Government will rule directly as we've been doing."

But Chief Awolowo walked out of the conference that day.

Outside the conference in a home in Kilburn, North London, Awolowo accused Zik and the NCN for being 'DEAD BLIND TO REASON. They cannot see the subterfuge of the British Government. They're bent on handing over the country to the feudal North. But we shall continue the fight.' He assured his followers.

However, Chief Awolowo returned to the Conference the following day. After sitting for nearly a whole month, the conference ended when the Colonial Secretary announced that the British Government would be willing to offer self-government to any Region that wanted it; but only in certain matters of administration. And that the date of such self-government would begin in August 1956. The Eastern and Western regions both grabbed the offer and were henceforth free to replace the colonial service officers with indigenous officers. This included the Lieutenant-Governor, but jurisdiction in respect of security, policing, currency, defence and external matters remained with the Colonial Office.

The conference's final decisions included continuation of

* Awolowo's critics at the time accused him of speaking and threatening with little or no understanding of the mousey traits of his own people.

the territorial structure of the federation, removal of the Lagos area from the Western Region and placing it as federal territory to be administered by the federal government. The federal legislature would have representatives from all the three regions and Lagos as follows: ninety members for the North, forty two members for each of the Eastern and Western regions, six members for the Cameroons and two members for the capital Lagos. The leader of the government business in the Eastern and Western Regions would be styled as the Premier, but not for the North which did not want self-government. The conference was adjourned to continue in Lagos in January the following year.

When the Nigerian leaders returned home, it was Zik alone who expressed jubilation "for the successes of the conference." Addressing a large audience in Enugu he declared: "We have got self-government on a platter of gold", amidst a thunderous ovation. Nigeria was the first country in Africa to be offered independence without much effort on its part. In Nigeria itself many thought that she did not deserve it.

CHAPTER 7

# The Road to Independence

When the conference resumed in Lagos in January 1954, Awolowo had not fully recovered from his embittered feeling of defeat over Lagos, Ilorin and Kabba. His party had suffered financial losses for the thousands of tee-shirts, bubas (large jumpers worn by men as well as women) and other materials they had ordered in advance for the celebration of victory. However, many of his top followers had pleaded that the matter be put aside, at least for the time being. One of his friends, Dr Bankole Akpata, formerly a student at Charles University in Prague reminded him of the problems over the Sudetenland Germans in Europe and also in Africa where: "As a result of the colonial system there are several tribal spreads or overflows. Europeans saw Africans looking alike as we see Europeans looking similar to each other. So they lumped peoples together. You can always think of Ilorin as Yorubas in the North".

As it was in London, in Lagos the Colonial Secretary, Oliver Lyttelton presided. After they had confirmed the matters decided on in London, Chief Awolowo urged that a secession clause be inserted in the constitution. Both Azikwie and Abubakar objected to the clause. They were supported by the Colonial Secretary who said that a secession clause in a constitution would paralyse the government in future. So here again Chief Awolowo did not succeed. The conference lasted only a few days. The Colonial Secretary was pleased with its outcome; so too, were Zik and Abubakar Tafawa Balewa. Awolowo, however continued to nurse his frustrations. In this regard he was supported by a great many of the elite in the

South and they saw Zik as a weak, wet and ever-compromising politician.

After the January conference the party leaders went on to continue ruling their respective regions. Each of them had before the regionalisation sent his trusted lieutenant to the central legislature in Lagos. In the case of Awolowo, it was Chief Samuel Akintola, a former Baptist school teacher, who after a career in journalism had studied law in England about the same time as himself, that he sent to the central legislature in Lagos, while he remained in Ibadan.* Unlike Awolowo, Akintola spoke other Nigerian languages than his own Yoruba. He spoke Hausa fluently, and that soon put him in a special relationship with Abubakar and other NPC leaders, first in the central legislature in Lagos and later in the North as well. Azikiwe, who also spoke Hausa, also sent his deputy to the central legislature while he remained in Enugu. However, like any compromiser or middle-ground politician, he began to be uncontroversial.

In order to ensure a peaceful administration, the leaders of the main political parties agreed in 1954 to form a coalition government in the central legislature in Lagos. There being no special ideological persuasion in any of them, it was a coalition to reconcile tribal and personal special interests. Really, ideology has never formed part of the political consideration in Nigeria. Several Nigerian elite had belonged to Marxist-Leninist movements as students abroad, but they did not return to Nigeria with those views.

The reason for this was that, apart from the general struggle to establish themselves professionally, many of the elite later realised that the type of situation that existed in industrial Europe at the time of Marx and Lenin, did not exist in Nigeria at that time. There were, for instance, no wealthy and powerful

* Ibadan was the headquarters of the Western Region; Enugu was the headquarters of the Eastern Region, while Kabadan was the headquarters of the Northern Region.

royal houses, no capitalists, no large industries. No Nigerian employed more than 15 workers. The businessmen that succeeded Jaja of Opobo were mainly salesmen and factors to foreign merchants or companies which were not landowners. There were no rich landowners, as land was vested in trust for the benefit of the whole clan. All business concerns such as the railways, electricity, construction and mines, were entirely government-owned. It was a case where no one had anything. Also imperialism, which some other colonies in Africa applied Marxist methods to fight against, was in 1950s Nigeria under voluntary liquidation. It was tribalism that reared its head as the most dangerous phenomenon, and many of the elite exploited it to their benefit.

By 1950 Awolowo had returned to Nigeria from the UK highly impressed by the class system there. It was he who from 1952 introduced the craze for becoming chiefs to the educated elite. And in their thousands, particularly in the South, the elite scrambled to become chiefs in their respective villages, but with no national significance whatsoever. Those Nigerians to whom His Holiness, the Pope, bestows such honours as Knight of Saint Gregory, use the title 'Sir'. Others who make the pilgrimage to Mecca, use the title 'Alhaji' in pursuit of amour propre. Those Christians who visited Israel and saw Jerusalem used the title JP – meaning Jerusalem Pilgrim. The trend is that the elite is always craving to play the role of a king in the country of the blind.

The situation in 1954 was that, although Awolowo's party joined the coalition in the central legislature, he himself did not have confidence in its authority, nor did he wish it well, basically because it was led by the NPC. He accused the leaders of the NPC of: "resisting progressive and radical innovation" and that they were seeking to compel or promote their own political system in other parts of the country. "Because of their control of the country's revenue they are able to attract a large number of opportunists of Southern origin", he accused them.

The last of the constitutional conferences was held in London's Lancaster House in the summer of 1957. Despite the gloomy air over London caused by the Suez crisis, the British government was ready to continue the discussion for granting independence to Nigeria. The new Conservative Prime Minister, Harold Macmillan, gave his full support to the conference which was chaired by the new Colonial Secretary, Alan Lennox-Boyd.

As almost every matter had been agreed upon during previous conferences, the only difficult matter this time was the question of the minorities who continued to demand their own regions or states. To the utter frustration of the leaders of these groups, the conference did not decide to create new regions. It only referred the matter to a Commission to inquire into the demand of the minorities and to determine whether they were prompted by genuine fears of domination. The Commission, headed by Sir Henry Willink, was warned that in no circumstances should they recommend the creation of more than one region or state in any one existing region. At the end of the conference the British government offered independence to Nigeria with effect from the first day of October 1960.

In Nigeria the announcement of independence was not received with much excitement and rejoicing, as was the case in Ghana where the announcement of independence was seen as the culminating triumph of their struggle. Many in Nigeria thought that if there had been a plebiscite on independence, a good majority might have voted against it. People did not think that the right people were in power. Some of the politicians in power were openly arrogant in their confidence of winning. Slogans such as: "Whether you vote for us or not, we will win" and: "If you want to chop* with us, don't criticize us". Many in fact kept their own personal armies of thugs and minders. In

* Chop in pidgin English means to eat or acquire benefit or advantage.

addition, since the Richards constitution, regionalisation had been so rigidly applied that every Nigerian wanting a job other than in the federal government, had to return to: 'his region of origin'. State-sponsored schools did not admit children whose parents were not indigenous to the region, even if the parents had lived and paid their taxes there all their lives, they would be bound to send their children to schools in their 'region of origin'. On top of these discouraging factors, there had been blatant corruption and greed amongst many of the people involved in politics. Extremely disdainful, these panjandrums were not seen to be in politics to serve the people.

However, many more understanding young men and women supported independence: "Because there's nothing more dignifying than freedom; and it's simply human to value freedom and personal prestige, more than wealth in slavery". But in later years that reasoning was thought to be faulty as thousands of young men and women escaped from the country in the face of military regimes, political subjugation and economic misery. Many sojourn in foreign countries even as illegal immigrants and refugees.

Still, millions of Nigerians were jubilant as the 1st of October approached. It was beyond the dreams of everyone that the country could be absolutely independent with so little effort, as had hitherto been the case in other parts of the continent and in Asia. In Nigeria none of the leaders was ever in trouble with the colonial authorities. None was ever detained or imprisoned or faced prosecution. The very few followers of Zik who were prosecuted for sedition in 1949 were disowned by him. As for Awolowo, he had hardly settled down to his law practice after qualifying at an advanced age, when he entered politics; and he retired as a very wealthy man. It was two years after independence that he and twenty-four of his followers were detained without trial and later prosecuted and imprisoned for fifteen years. Alhaji Ahmadu Bello and his lieutenant in the NPC, Alhaji Abubakar, were both knighted immediately after the conference.

Compared to other countries, the colonial system in Nigeria had not been terribly ruthless after the initial conquests; in the case of Southern Nigeria before 1900 and before 1912 in the North. As Sir Alan Burns, a former colonial governor, put it: "Relations between Africans and Europeans in Nigeria have in the past been reasonably harmonious. There have been exceptions, due in most cases to bad manners rather than to malice, but many personal friendships have existed between individuals of the two countries and there is a general mutual respect. Let us hope this mutual respect will remain and that Nigerians will believe, as the British are justified in believing, that Britain has little to be ashamed of in her past dealing with the country.*

In the decade that followed the introduction of the Richards Constitution 1945-1947 the colonial administration launched its most ambitious development in the country. No such development was seen anywhere else in Africa at the time. Within the ten years from 1948 to 1958 more than four universities were established in the country where there had been none at all; and many more were in the pipeline. Several top academicians from British universities happily raced to give their services for the development of learning, to the extent that, right from the opening of these universities, they were recognised and assisted worldwide in the hope that Nigeria would progress rapidly and take a worthy place in the modern age.

During that period, the Colonial Development Corporation, later called Commonwealth Development Corporation, embarked on an agricultural scheme in Northern Nigeria where pyramids and mountains of sacks of groundnuts and cotton

*See Sir Alan Burns: History of Nigeria, Longmans, London 1965.

waited at Kano and Zaria for export. Elsewhere in the South, there were the cocoa boom (as they called it) and the timber boom and the rubber boom. From the proceeds of these crops, the colonial administration stored enormous wealth into the various regional and federal treasuries for an independent Nigeria.

And the country is not short of valuable minerals. Among the list of minerals are iron ore, coal, tin, gold and petroleum. There was also an abundant human resources and manpower 'Southern Nigeria alone produce more graduates and professional men and women than the rest of Africa put together' remarked Dr. T. Oruwariye in Ibadan in 1959. And the country had an efficient public services, an upright judiciary and a dependable legal system. All these facts impressed visitors to the country and they complemented Nigeria with the inspiring epithet 'Giant of Africa'. The situation also attracted foreign businesses to flock into the country. Albeit, later events generated by deep tribal divisions, distrust and jealousy, shattered all hopes as reckless military interventions hasten collapse.

Anyway, in order to usher in the sovereign nation, a brand new federal government was proposed. For this purpose there would be a general election to the Federal House of Representatives in 1959. There were to be 312 members in the House. Of this number there would be 184 members to represent the Northern Region. The Eastern Region would have 73 members and the Western Region 62. Lagos would have 3 members. Lagos was The Federal Capital and was administered by the Federal Government. The constitution was of the Westminster model, but also like Canada in view of the federal structure. Each of the three big political parties was heavily patronised by one of the three large tribes, but there were several alliances. The parties were also tribally led.

Yet, each of the two leaders of the big parties in the South, that is Zik and Awolowo, and the deputy leader of the big party in the North, Sir Abubakar Tafawa Balewa, swore that he would win the election and become the first Prime Minister. Each of them called it 'The Crucial Election' to be contested physically, if necessary. At least their supporters understood it that way.

In the case of Awolowo, in order to fight the crucial election he swapped position with his deputy, Akintola. Akintola therefore returned to the Western Region and became the Premier. This would enable Awolowo to try his luck and become the Prime Minister of the whole country, if his party won a majority throughout the country. But he did not make Akintola the leader of the party. "Chief Akintola was in contrast to Chief Awolowo in many ways, smooth, witty, politically slippery and cunning", wrote Jakande, an executive member of the party, in his work: *The Trial of Awolowo*. While fighting the crucial election Awolowo continued to be the leader of the party, the Action Group.

Of the political parties, Chief Awolowo's Action Group was considered to be the best organised and it was also the richest.* For campaigning at the election, the party bought hundreds of vehicles to ply the air, land and sea. In the air the party's numerous helicopters hovered daily from village to village trying to address audiences. The difficulty in the North was that none of the local population came out to listen to them because the village heads had warned everyone to keep away from Kafiris, meaning infidels as Southerners were called. Awolowo thought he could get over that hurdle by employing the services of lawyers. He flooded the North with lawyers from the South. But the Northern authorities refused to give them accommodation in the government-owned and managed rest houses which were the only hotels available in most parts

* The party controlled the Western Region, to which the Colonial government had left huge revenues from cocoa and timber, which had boomed just before 1960.

of the North. In 1959, nearly all the hotels in the country were government-owned and managed.

Despite his efficient organisation, Awolowo could not make any headway in the North. He complained that the village heads were in most cases members of the NPC and many of them were candidates in the election. He was nearly driven mad when it was announced on the eve of voting day in the North, that 36 NPC candidates had been returned unopposed. This despite the fact that the Action Group claimed that it fielded a candidate in every constituency in the North. But no one agreed to co-operate with its lawyers for the purpose of litigating on the matter.

As Awolowo's Action Group party fought audaciously to win votes in the North, NPC members were determined that they would not succeed even in predominately Southern areas of Sabon gari. In many places there were only free-for-all fights; these developed into murder and arson, that continued day and night. The police could not cope with the situation and in several towns and villages troops were called in to maintain order. Similar disturbances characterised the election throughout the country. By November the crucial election had been given the name: 'Do and Die election' as the murder and mayhem continued.

Abroad, the Cold War was threatening to hot up around events in Korea, the Belgian Congo (now Zaire) and Cuba. But these did not interest anyone in Nigeria. It was also the time when next door in Ghana, President Nkrumah was busy with his Preventive Detention Laws. Nigeria presented a facade of calm and jollity especially in its capital, Lagos. Many visitors were carried away by the seeming maturity compared with: "others in Africa". But the various regional leaders enjoyed the plaudits.

The commendations endeared the country to the world powers and they urged Nigeria to send troops to help the United

Nations' efforts to restore peace in the Congo. Earlier, on account of the approaching independence, Nigerian leaders requested Britain that the military should be Nigerianised. Britain agreed. An indigenous army needed a strong officer corps which it was thought ought to be young and university educated. Thereupon, for the first time Southerners became attracted to the military. Prior to 1950, there were hardly any Southerners in the Nigerian military. A few joined the army during the war but only as noncombatants. Only Northerners joined the military before the war, and they all served under British officers.

So it came to be that the Nigerian troops which went to the Congo were mostly commanded by young Southerners newly commissioned from British military colleges in Sandhurst and Aldershot. A good many of them were very political, with leanings towards Nkrumah and Abdul Nasser's foreign policy. In Nigeria some of them: "reluctantly agreed" to join other troops sent to quell disturbances in parts of the North during the 1959 election campaigns.

Voting in the 'Do and Die' election began on the 10th December 1959. By nightfall on the 12th, the results showed the NCNC and Action Group had scored a total of 152 seats while the NPC by itself had scored 118 seats declared. The two Southern parties then began negotiations to form a coalition, possibly also with some of the smaller parties joining in. The plan was then to present themselves to the Governor-General, Sir James Robertson, to form the government and Zik would take the position of Prime Minister, with Awolowo his deputy. After a period of six months the British Governor-General would retire and Zik would take his place and Awolowo would become Prime Minister. It was later seen by the North as: "a Southern conspiracy".

However, before this could be settled, the content of the negotiations was leaked. The North was furious. Sir Abubakar went straight to the Governor-General, warning him that if the Southern parties conspired to steal the office from him, the North would secede at once. He followed up his threat with a public announcement. Meanwhile more results had come in and they increased the NPC vote to 142 seats, NCNC to 89 and Action Group to 73.* Even before the final results arrived, the Governor-General had appointed Sir Abubakar as the Prime Minister. The NPC gave to the NCNC what the Action Group would have given to it. Zik became the President of the Senate whilst waiting to become the Governor-General after Sir Robertson had retired. The NCNC was given portfolios in the Federal Cabinet.

Now it was Awolowo who was bewildered. He raged, claiming the office of Prime Minister had been stolen from him. He was reminded of what he had done to Zik at Ibadan in 1950 when he urged members of his tribe who were in Zik's party to desert for the Action Group. At that time they had taunted Zik, telling him to return to his roots in the East.

While millions of Nigerians on the victorious side of the election were getting ready to celebrate the oncoming independence, Chief Awolowo and his supporters, now reduced in numbers, continued to be muddled. He had swapped his grand position as the Premier of the Western region with Chief Akintola. He had spent a fortune on helicopters and sky writing; bills were still coming in for the thousands of motorcycles, cars, jeeps, boats, canoes, flags, tee-shirts, etc that had been ordered for the celebration of the victory that was expected. For the first time Awolowo did not easily find someone to fight. But someone had to be blamed. He blamed the British for giving too much support to the North. He blamed the North for being too backward and he blamed Zik for his dirty tricks. He was not in a mood for celebrating anything, let alone independence. But he did not show his feelings to visitors.

* These figures included a few of their respective affiliated parties in the north.

## Chapter 8

# Independence

On the 30th September 1960, at an official ceremony in Lagos, the Union Jack glided down, for the last time, from the tall pole that had proudly displayed it. For one hundred years, in Lagos, it had symbolised the country's colonial status. In its place, for the first time, rose the green and white flag of the Federation of Nigeria, accompanied by the National Anthem. It began with the words: "Nigeria we hail thee ..." and it went on to remind us: "Though tribe and tongue we differ, we must stick together."

Unfortunately, far more than three quarters of the country's population did not understand the meaning of the Anthem and could not even sing it.* They did not know what independence was all about. If they were told that it was the end of the 'foreign rule', that would confuse them; because in Nigerian languages everyone who did not belong to your tribe was a foreigner. If you told them that Nigerians had taken over the government of the country from the British, that would mean very little because the Governor and many other top administrators were to remain for some time. Some people explained the significance of independence and said it was the end of white people dominating us. To the illiterate, white people included Lebanese, Moroccans, Iranians and even Libyans; many market women had these as their customers and their tenants. They got frightened to hear that white people would have to leave the country because of independence. At any rate very few in the country even knew the name of the country. You learnt it only at school, if your parents had money to send

---

* It was not translated into local languages.

you to school.

At mid morning on the 1st October 1960 amidst the crowd of well wishers from several parts of the world, Her Royal Highness, Princess Alexandra handed over the Constitutional Instrument to Sir Abubakar Tafawa Balewa, the Prime Minister of Nigeria. With him were all the members of the Federal House of Representatives and the regional politicians. The message from HRH Princess Alexandra was as follows:

> *"My husband and I retain the happiest memories of our visit to Nigeria and our thoughts are with you on this memorable occasion. As you assume the heavy responsibility of independence, I send my good wishes for a great and noble future. It is with special pleasure that I welcome you to our Commonwealth family of Nations. May God bless you and guide your country".*

Amidst jubilation and cheers the overflowing crowd at the Lagos stadium greeted the Prime Minister as he rose to respond to the speech read by the Princess. Several people especially women wept for joy and as she wiped tears from her eyes, one market woman said to her friend softly: "I'm wondering, can we make it?"

"God's there; He'll help us".

"Yes, but we need a real super Almighty God".

"That's true".

Then the Prime Minister began: "At last our great day has arrived and Nigeria is now indeed an independent sovereign nation. Words cannot adequately express my joy and pride as being the Nigerian citizen privileged to accept from HRH these constitutional Instruments which are the symbols of our

Nigeria's independence ... This great nation which has now emerged without bitterness or bloodshed ... successive British governments have gradually transferred the burden of responsibility to our shoulders. The assistance and unfailing encouragement which we have received from each Secretary of State for the Colonies, and their intense personal interest in our development has immeasurably lightened that burden".

He proceeded to express his gratitude to the British officers, past and present, many of whom were present at the ceremony.

"Do not mistake our pride for arrogance. It is tempered by the feelings of sincere gratitude to all who have shared in the task of developing Nigeria politically, economically and socially. I say thank you for your devoted services which helped to make Nigeria a nation".

The Sunday that followed was Thanksgiving Day on which the church offered prayers for peace and progress throughout the country. In Nyemoni, a former palm oil-exporting town on the Niger Delta, and which was part of the original Oil Rivers Protectorate from where the consuls crept deep inland and created Nigeria, it was a 'big Sunday'. The sermon was delivered by the retired Assistant Bishop of the Anglican Church of St Augustine, the very Reverend Franklin Opuwari who celebrated his eighty-ninth birthday the week before. The Bishop ended his long sermon with the following: "Nature put us Africans too far away from the civilisations of Greece, Egypt, Rome and the Christian Church ...We and the rest of Africa South of Egypt did not benefit from the civilisation which had flourished since more than two thousand years ago. Then fortunately, the British came; and within my own lifetime, they have catapulted us from the age of darkness into this wonderful modern age – the age of peace, the arts, of science, and technology. I saw part of the beginning; and now, I thank the Almighty God that He has allowed me to see the end. The difference is incomprehensible. Praise be the Lord."

To every African of the age of Bishop Franklin Opuwari, it was indeed an inconveivable phenomenon to witness European empires in Africa scrambling for collapse, faster than they were established. Some of these empires lasted less than some sixty years – from Bismarck to Hitler.

However, thirty five years later, in another church in the area, a young priest was praying for "The restoration of peace in the Niger Delta". And he said "During the colonial era, the country was not free; but we all know that the people were free; they could say their minds on any matter. Now the country is free, but the people are not free. I cannot preach to you and express my feelings about the military Government and its brutality. In this country today, only the sychophants are happy ... but God of Abraham will deliver us."

## Chapter 9

## First Two Years of Independence

Since 1946 the leaders of the Northern Region had ruled the country, but Northerners still represented less than ten percent of the public services of the federal administration. The situation made the Northern leadership uneasy and it was not quite to the delight of many in the South who foresaw that if the imbalance continued, the Northerners would carry on lowering the entrance qualifications to the public service and thereby reduce efficiency even in the educational system which the South held in great esteem.

Be that as it may, when the new federal parliament began, Chief Awolowo became the Leader of the Opposition. In Nigeria that office did not sound quite acceptable. Besides the fact that the parties are not motivated by ideological principles, Nigerians are never impressed by an office or position which does not have the power to dish out favours or jobs or award contracts to its fans. Leader of Opposition is an office just like that.

Chief Awolowo gambled in 1959, when he abandoned his position as Premier of the Western region and sought to be the Prime Minister of the whole country, as earlier discussed. It was the failure of that gamble that 'reduced' him to be 'Leader of the Opposition' in the Federal Parliament. Now it was the repercussions of that failure that would impel the course of events in the country during several decades that followed.

The gamble began when he installed Chief Akintola as Premier and he himself remained the leader of the party. When he lost the election for which he had abandoned the premiership, he also lost almost everything for which a great many followed him. He lost both political power and economic power. He was not now able to provide contracts and give jobs to his fans. It was not possible any more to use his name to frighten or intimidate adversaries. Thousands of his erstwhile henchmen discovered that he was of no use any more.

On the other hand in Ibadan, capital of the Western Region, Chief Akintola, who was a member of a larger clan in the Yoruba tribe than Chief Awolowo, was beginning to be the centre of gravity in the region. Soon he was pulling every needy party supporter to himself. Stooges and sycophants were hastily deserting Awolowo for Akintola, and singing his praises. Awolowo was amazed at how fast that could happen. It was not easy to retrieve the position. Soon, envy, jealousy and intrigue crept in and created open dissension between the two leaders. Before long their respective followers were taking sides and there were talks of a pro-Awolowo faction and a pro-Akintola faction. Akintola was ready: "to fight to finish". Hopelessly, Awolowo watched Akintola dishing out cozy jobs to professional men and women and graduates. Many businessmen were getting contracts and deals that brought in lots of money.

Within twelve months after the federal election, Chief Awolowo was commanding very little of the party. He was fast losing his political and personal clout and becoming simply an 'ordinary man'. A situation unbearable to most African leaders; and Chief Awolowo was very African.

Even in the Federal House of Representatives where he was the Opposition leader, no one took much notice of him or what he had to say. He decided to fight back, this time with Akintola as one of his main adversaries. Still the leader of the party, if in name only, Awolowo set up a Court of Inquiry in the party to try Akintola for subversive activities against the party.

On the 19th May, 1962, the Inquiry found Akintola guilty. The party, having found the Premier of the Western Region guilty of subverting his own party, did not readily know what punishment could be meted out. Three years earlier the trouble in the Congo began when the Prime Minister and the President sacked each other from office. Both refused to leave office, and the country went up in flames. In Western Nigeria, the same thing was about to be repeated. A region in Nigeria was equivalent to a province in Canada in that it has a Governor and a Premier, being a unit of a federal nation. By the Constitution, the Governor was appointed by the Head of Government of the region, that is the Premier.* In Nigeria, the person appointed Governor was usually someone who supported the party in the region.

Taking advantage of its relationship with the Governor, the party made him dismiss Akintola as Premier and appointed Adegbenro to succeed him as the new Premier. Akintola, however, ignored the Governor's action, and instead removed the Governor and appointed Chief Ola Odeleye in his place. Fortunately both sides took the matter to the Supreme Court for decision. That fact maintained peace, but only for a few days.

While the action in Court was pending, Adegbenro asked the Speaker to convene Parliament so that a vote of confidence could be passed in his favour. Akintola and his supporters were determined that that would not happen. So there had to be a clash. The scene of the clash was Ibadan, the capital of the region. In 1962 it was a sprawling city of more than three million

---

* The head of government in the region was styled by the Premier. The head of the government of the Federation, that is the whole country, was the Prime Minister. In the regions the head of state was Governor. In the Federation he was Governor-General and later President.

inhabitants. Although there were no industries, it had a twelve-year old university college which at the time was one of a few institutions of higher education in the country. The 25th May was the 'Battle Day'. The day was bright and sunny as was usual in Ibadan during that time of the year. A surprise shower washed off the dust of the previous days, leaving the late morning cool. By 11.30am both sides were still in their respective homes preparing for the fight ahead. It was to be the first of its kind in Africa; and as the parliamentary system had only just begun, fist-fighting inside parliament had never been witnessed.

By 11.45am both sides were driving their respective grand American limousines along Queen Elizabeth Way to the Houses of Parliament. Many of them were armed to the teeth. However, no one carried a machine gun. That was not common in the country before the civil war, a few years later; only machetes, broken bottles, crowbars, daggers, spears and horse whips. It was said that a few hid bicycle chains in their robes. Press reports that some carried bows and arrows were denied. Those weapons were too primitive for 1962.

By 12.30pm the House was already full of members who only a few months earlier were all members of the Action Group party. Now, they belonged to two warring factions. Some did not quite know who their adversaries were. Having no permanent loyalty to either of the two fighting leaders, many changed from Akintola to Adegbenro and vice versa, several times even in one day. The visitor's gallery was also full of changeable fair-weather supporters and some wives of members.

Inside the Chambers of Parliament, as the Speaker began to introduce a matter, someone in Akintola's group began to play a gong. "Tell them to stop that stupid noise", bawled a member. "Send the idiots out", another member shouted. And the shouts became more incessant and one group began to push the other out of the chamber as commotion took over. Then the pushing and the fighting became more fierce as they continued to box and beat one another. Soon everyone was beating someone. The wives and friends from the galleries could not stand by and watch their husbands and their friends being beaten mercilessly. They flew down from the galleries and joined the fighting. The battle continued for a good hour with many seriously injured, before police were called in. They had to use tear gas to disperse everyone from the Chambers. Then by order of the Prime Minister from Lagos, the Chamber was locked up.

The hostilities inside Parliament were followed by widespread riots throughout Ibadan as thousands went on the rampage, killing, looting and committing arson and other crimes. That went on for the whole day into the night until the morning when troops quelled the trouble.

In Lagos the Prime Minister convened Parliament immediately to debate the matter. Within an hour members had voted for the Declaration of Emergency throughout the Western region. In consequence, the Constitution of the region was suspended. Under the emergency regulations several politicians were detained. These included Chiefs Awolowo, Akintola and Adegbenro. An Administrator was appointed to administer the region for the six months' duration of the Emergency.

In June that year, the Administrator instituted an inquiry to look into the finances of six statutory corporations in the region. Four years earlier a similar inquiry was instituted to look into Zik's real connection with the African Continental Bank in which almost all the finances of the Eastern region were deposited. In consequence the Bank was nationalised. But Zik was not punished severely. This time it was the turn of Chief Awolowo to face an inquiry into his conduct about public money.

From his place of detention he was brought daily to defend his conduct. The inquiry had not ended, when on the 17th September it was announced that the police had discovered a plot by Chief Awolowo and several others to overthrow the Federal government by force. The offence amounted to treason, punishable by death. With the larger charge of treason hanging over his head, it was impossible to defend the inquiry about finances very effectively. Within four weeks of the charge against him, Chief Awolowo looked like a skeleton of himself. He looked so pathetic that people began to be sorry for him as the underdog of the NPC and NCNC coalition in the federal government.

The treason trial lasted nearly two years, with a good many of his followers involved as co-accused. One of his ablest lieutenants, Chief Anthony Enahoro, was also accused but managed to flee to Britain. The case for his extradition to face the charges in Nigeria lasted nearly a year; but in the end Chief Enahoro was returned. Chief Awolowo and twenty of his followers were found guilty and sentenced to long-term imprisonment. Chief Enahoro was given a ten-year jail sentence.

In December 1962 the state of Emergency in the Western Region ended. Chief Akintola returned to the Region as its Premier. There was no one now to challenge him, as his opponents were all facing treason trial in Lagos.

CHAPTER 10

# Three Stormy Years 1962-65

After the emergency in the Western Region had ended, but while the treason trial in Lagos was still in progress, the scene of unrest shifted to the 'Pagan Areas of the North'. This was the area in the North which was not conquered by Islamic Jihad warriors before the colonial era. Probably, for convenience they were administered along with the rest of the territory as One North. They too had the Indirect Rule system of administration. However, when independence came, they struggles for their own security in their own corner of the country.

Their leader, Joseph Tarkar, a former school teacher, had attended all the Constitutional Conferences in the hope of convincing the colonial government that the area could not be ruled peacefully within the Northern Region. For this purpose they formed alliance with the Awolowo led Action Group; and Tarkar was one of the accused in the treason trial. On account of his arrest and trial, his followers escalated their agitation. For this, the Balewa led Federal Government stationed troops in the area and there were reports of military repression daily.

As the NPC and Balewa struggled with the problems of the pagan area, they were also beset with political intrigue and issues in the administration of the federal government, where they were in coalition with the NCNC. More than ninety percent of the NCNC were Ibo.

At this time, with Akintola as the Premier again in the Western Region, which is nearly all Yoruba speaking, many of the elite and intellectual in the Region rushed to him for jobs and contracts. As there were not many jobs in the Region, Akintola tried to get federal jobs, such as ambassadors and membership of Federal statutory corporations for his followers. But his enterprise in this regard quickly put him into rivalry with the NCNC members. As their party was in coalition with the NPC, they felt that they were more entitled to Federal jobs and contracts. They therefore whined that the jobs and contracts meant for them were 'going astray'.

When they reminded the Prime Minister about the 'coalition agreement' with his party, he ignored them. They complained to Zik, now the ceremonial President of Nigeria, but to no avail. Zik had long abandoned his newspaper business and had to give up his interest in the African Continental Bank following the report of a tribunal of Inquiry.* He was not prepared now to put himself in a position of challenging the NPC on behalf of his former party, the NCNC. Akintola noticed that the NCNC was unhappy about his close relationship with Balewa and the NPC and vowed to elbow them out.

They too sought to embarrass him, and to create a division between him and the NPC. The Western Region contained a large area of non-Yoruba speaking people, that stretched eastwards from Benin to Asaba on the Niger and down to Sapele. The NCNC initiated a plebiscite according to the constitution, which resulted in that area being separated from the West. The new region was called the Mid-West;† and it was the only state ever created under a civilian government. Its creation was not a triumph for Chief Akintola. The new region had more than fifty linguistic groups with none too big to threaten the others. Before the Richards constitution it consisted of two provinces, Benin Province and Warri Province.

*Sir Foster Sutton Tribunal of Inquiry into the African Continental Bank Ltd. 1956.
†It was later called Bendel state 1972-1990. Then it was made into two states – Edo and Delta

While the Mid-West Region was getting settled, the federal government set up a board to organise a population census of the country. The allocation of seats in the Federal House of Representatives had depended on a population count or estimate which gave the North 54 percent of the population. In addition, revenue from the oil and corporate companies in the country was distributed to the regions according to the estimated population ratio. The census result was therefore crucial to every region and tribe. So everyone had reason to inflate their numbers.

Early in 1964 the unofficial result of the census was leaked. It put the North at only 46 percent of the total population. The news devastated the Northern leadership, who then rejected it and refused to publish it. The remnants of Awolowo's Action Group were furious, but there was little they could do due to their weak support. The Mid-West was still settling down and were grateful to the NPC for creating the region and therefore were not prepared to challenge the action of the NPC. The NCNC were the only party in a position to oppose the Northern leadership and NPC for rejecting the census result. However they too did nothing, due to the fear of losing partnership in the federal coalition with the NPC. Nevertheless, the NCNC instigated their followers, particularly those in the North, to demonstrate against the Northern leadership.

The result of these demonstrations, organised by the tribal unions, was rioting in several parts of the North with serious damage to property and loss of lives. Zik, in his comfortable office as Governor-General (President) was still not prepared to support the NCNC against the NPC. Akintola kept the Western region out of the situation but seized the advantage of the weakening relationship between the NCNC and NPC. In 1964, the NPC invited him to join the coalition. The NCNC objected, but were ignored. Earlier, in anticipation of the invitation from the NPC, Akintola formed a new political party called the United People's Party (UPP), which interestingly attracted a considerable number of NCNC supporters. In anger the NCNC left the coalition. It was the end of 1963 and nearing the end of the first term of the federal government. The election was to be held in December 1964.

Before the political parties began their respective election campaigns or 'battles', Issac Boro, a former university student, declared the secession of the Niger Delta from the country. He and his colleagues put up stiff resistance before federal troops dislodged them. Boro claimed he was taking the area out of the Eastern region, on the grounds that he was freeing it from Ibo domination. All the secessionists were sentenced to death and remained in prison until they were released by Yakubu Gowon in 1967.

The conviction of Issac Boro and his men embarrassed Chief Harold Biriye who was at that time in alliance with the NPC, hoping they would assist him to get a separate region for the area. His party, the Niger Delta Congress, was a staunch ally of the Northern leadership; so too was the Egbe Yoruba Parapo. In order to fight the election, all the parties proceeded to look for alliances. The simplest way to explain the complicated alliances may be to mention just a few, beginning with the West. There, Chief Akintola's new party, the UPP, joined up with a breakaway faction of the NCNC and a small Ibadan-based party, the Ibadan Parapo. The three, together with a number of even smaller parties, formed the Nigerian National Democratic Party (NNDP). The NNDP and the NPC, which had its own satellite parties such as the Niger Delta Congress and Egbe Yoruba Parapo, formed the Nigerian National Alliance (NNA). The leaders of this alliance were Sir Ahmadu Bello, the Sardauna of Sokoto, Sir Abubakar Tafawa Balewa and Chief Samuel Akintola.

In the Eastern region, the NCNC were still strong, despite the internal strife which Zik had controlled before he became Governor-General. Nevertheless it had lost considerable ground when many members left to join Chief Akintola. All that were left for the NCNC to align with were the remnants of the Action Group in the West and a number of small floating parties in the newly created Mid-West, the largest of which was the Mid-West Democratic Front (MDF).

In the North, there were a number of parties formed by non-Muslim as well as more 'radical Muslims' The people of the 'Pagan area' formed their own party. They detested remaining in the North where they complained of domination by Muslims. Their party was the United Middle-Belt Congress (UMBC). Also a group of more radical Muslims who resolved to change the Koranic teaching, formed the Northern Elements Progressive Union (NEPU). All of these parties, together with a number of smaller ones, formed the United People's Grand Alliance (UPGA). The total number of parties formed for the country's first election since independence was estimated at 128. Many of these through their alliances took part in that first election in December 1964. During the colonial period they were all dormant.

Throughout 1964, the agitation for the creation of more states or regions continued with greater intensity, more so, since the Mid-West had been carved out of the West. But the federal government was adamant in its resolve not to go any further on the matter, hoping that the issue might die down. "The longer the Hausa-Fulani rule continued, the more difficult it will be to dislodge it and establish a domination-fear-free nation", warned a group which called itself Citizen's Committee for Independence. They called on the leadership to learn from the crisis in the Congo.

The news of the crisis in the Congo came to Nigeria as a great surprise. Very few had ever visited that country; all any one knew about the Congo was the little one read from geography books. Now, Nigeria had to send troops there on behalf of the United Nations. It was the first outing for the Nigerian Army, small as it was.

It was still a highly-disciplined army fashioned on the British military. From the time of Lugard it had existed; albeit only with exclusively Northern troops. They were predominantly illiterate and no Southerner was ever attracted to the military. Southerners looked at the military with disdain and as a purely colonial establishment to perpetuate imperialism. Also, of course, the South did not have much of a military tradition as did the Northerners who had fought jihad wars for ages. During the Second World War, many Southerners joined the army, but not as combatant soldiers, only in the clerical, stores, ambulance and other such auxiliary sections.

At Independence Balewa's government decided to recruit young Southern graduates to the Nigerian Army as officers. The initial experiment was a disaster, as one of the graduate officers, Major Adewale Ademoyega wrote later. "After I was commissioned into the Nigerian Army ... my first impression which really distressed me was that it was not a Nationalist organisation, and it was far from being revolutionary ... the British looked upon the Nigerian soldiers as soldiers of fortune, who had no personal stake in the continuity of the British Empire ... this was the reason why they were encouraged to remain stark illiterates."*

By October 1964 the election campaign was warming up; members of the UPGA alliance moved to the North, determined to get as many votes as possible. However, Northern villages and towns were under the grip of the village heads who could punish them if they became too close to foreigners, and Southerners were foreigners. However, as the elections

* Major Adewale Ademoyega: *Why We Struck*, Evans Brothers (Nigeria) Ltd. 1981.

would be won or lost on tribal appeals, there were many ethnic Westerners who could vote and it was possible that by default a Southern party might do quite well.

In the 1948 constitutional conference, the Northern delegation had sought that there should be a proviso in the constitution whereby Southerners resident in the North could not vote there. But they failed. However, during that election, they were still determined that Southerners should not have the opportunity and facilities to campaign in the area.

On this account the early period of the campaign was marked by riots and murders of Southerners trying to get to Northerners. Later the village heads and the Alikalis or local magistrates sent Southerners to jail: "pending trials", which never came. And as in earlier elections they refused accommodation to Southerners and refused to patronise them in the markets.

Thereupon the Southerners asked Zik as the President to intervene.* In a broadcast in October 1964, Zik appealed to the nation and warned that the way the electioneering was going on, the politicians were likely to endanger the unity of the country; he said certain political parties were preventing their opponents from having the opportunity to conveniently explain their party policies and programmes and that he had received hundreds of letters and telegrams pleading that he should use his good offices to ensure a free and fair election. He then urged all concerned to refrain from victimisation of opponents. He warned: "If this embryo Republic of ours must disintegrate, then in the name of God, let the operation be a short and painless one".

In November 1964, about a week before the election date, it was announced that 67 candidates of the NPC in the North had been returned unopposed. A similar situation occurred

* In 1963 Nigeria became a Republic and so the Governor-General became the President.

in the earlier election. The news sparked off spontaneous riots in the North by Southerners and non-Muslim Northerners. In these areas in particular, the fighting was so fierce that troops had to be called in to quell the disturbances. In the Western region, Akintola's party supported the announcement but the riots still spread to Ibadan and Southern Yoruba areas. Akintola himself came from a large clan in Yorubaland and his own clans stood staunchly behind him.

In the Eastern region, the ruling party, the NCNC fought vehemently against the announcement and declared that it would boycott the election totally. There was therefore no election in the Eastern Regions as well as in some UPGA areas in the West. This meant that even those parties in the East that aligned themselves to the NPC, could not vote. During the week-long period of the election, rioting, killing, arson and looting continued throughout the country. Zik as President tried to intervene and again broadcast the following:

> *"Fellow countrymen and women, we have embarked on a dangerous road which if not stopped at once, will make the crisis in the Congo look like a child's play ... Whether our beloved Nigeria will continue to remain united as one country or will become disintegrated into minute principalities depends now upon two factors – whether our politicians would desist from inciting our communities to liquidate themselves and whether our politicians would co-operate so that the law abiding elements in this part of Africa will experience free and fair elections ... Should our political leaders, after bearing all the above factors in mind, prefer to crucify the unity of this country on the Golgotha of their inordinate ambitions for*

*naked power, then hundreds and thousands of Nigerian patriots, who sacrificed dearly for its unity and its freedom, must take note and pass this information to prosperity. In which case, it would be an irony of history that the liquidation of our national unity occurred after we had become free from political bondage that lasted almost a century".*

Following Zik's radio speech, Dr Michael Opkara, the Premier of the Eastern Region, warned that the East would secede if the Northern leaders continued to be intransigent. This was followed by Zik calling for a meeting of all the leaders to discuss the crisis. But, Sir Ahmadu Bello, the Premier of the North and leader of NPC, warned that the North and the West would not attend such a meeting. He then issued a statement saying that he thought that the purpose of the meeting was to declare the secession of the East, and that "If the East wanted to secede because of the oil discovered in the East, it should be allowed to do so in peace".

On the following day, 30th December 1964, Zik promptly denied that any secession was being contemplated, and that the meeting was convened: "to discuss matters of national interest calculated to promote the unity and solidarity of the Federation."

However, notwithstanding the deepening crisis, the UPGA announced that it would not recognise the federal government formed on the basis of the 'Fraudulent election'. After the parties had engaged in bitter recriminations against each other, a compromise solution was finally agreed upon.

It provided for an election in the Eastern region, after which there was to be a federal government in which all the alliances would participate but under the control of the NPC.

The type of grouping to form a national government was usually satisfactory to many of the politicians, because it created broader avenues in which a wider range of the people could have access to the national cake. That was what politics was about to a great many.

While they were busy sharing out the national cake, regional elections came up. In the Western region it was to be a straightforward fight between the remnants of the Action Group supported by the NCNC on the one hand, and Akintola's UPP, supported by the NPC on the other. To many observers that election would determine the fate of Akintola. It was also a matter that would take the lives of thousands in the region. The technique of making Molotov cocktails was not commonly known in Nigeria, but an easier method of causing death with petrol and fire was quickly devised early in 1965. At political meetings and campaign parties, petrol was sprayed on people and fire thrown at them. Motor cyclists soon found a new form of lucrative employment by riding past their victims, spraying them with petrol and then setting them alight. The practice spread from the streets, to offices, homes and common areas. Fire fighting equipment was in short supply and the result was the loss of businesses and homes for many. This practice was known as 'Operation Wettie', because victims were 'wetted' with petrol before being burned alive.

A dusk to dawn curfew and the deployment of troops failed to stop the destruction of people and property, which in fact intensified. The parties each accused one another of fraud and election malpractice. Akintola presented to the outside world that his position was secure, but he ordered bullet-proof suits from America and began some military training. But his wife preferred a bullet-proof outfit from the Soviet Union "Because the American bullet-proof was not successful for President John Kennedy".

# Chapter 11

## 1966: The Coups Begin

By the end of the rainy season in 1965 the riots and other disturbances had been country-wide except in the heartlands of the NPC leadership; that is north of Kaduna and Jos. Even in these areas, spasmodic clashes between Northerners and Southerners were frequent.

However, the most seriously troubled area was the Western region. Akintola began to lose some of his support as soon as people realised that he was not able to provide them with the lucrative contracts and jobs he promised. Adegbenro, who succeeded Awolowo in the Action Group was also determined to work against Akintola's administration. In November 1965 he called a press conference in which he blamed the riots in the region on Akintola's unpopularity. "More than 615 people have been killed and you can go to the sheds we call hospitals and see the bodies for yourselves ... the few mortuaries cannot cope with the situation", he said.

Some days later, an Action Group member of the Federal Legislature, Shitta Bey, tabled a motion urging the federal government to declare a state of emergency in the West as it did in 1962. However, the motion failed. At that time, Akintola, having elbowed the NCNC out of its earlier coalition with the NPC, had replaced them. That heightened the acrimony between the two parties.

While the politicians continued their fighting and rioting, young graduates who were newly commissioned as officers in the Army were organizing themselves for action. As has been discussed earlier, on the insistence of the politicians on the eve of independence, the British government had agreed to recruit graduates into the newly created Nigerian Army. This enabled many Southerners to join. Some of them were fans of Fidel Castro of Cuba. Later they formed themselves into a secret 'Revolutionary Group'. One of them, Major Adewale Ademoyega, twenty-seven at the time, later wrote:

> "The political trend in most parts of the world in the late 1950s and early 1960s was towards a military take-over of government, in which the soldier-statesmen emerge from their barracks during a political tension to restore their country to social and political peace ... Nigeria was by no means different".*

Though members of the Revolutionary Group were all trained in British military colleges, they did not cherish their connection with the British military tradition as discussed earlier. The group consisted of seven young men of the average age of twenty-six. They thought of themselves as completely de-tribalised. Of the seven only on, Major Ademoyega, was Yoruba; the rest were all Ibo. In Nigeria that combination presented a terrible imbalance under normal circumstances. Many would look at it with suspicion as in Nigeria even a first eleven football team for the country which does not juggle with tribal balance, may not be forwarded; and very many may not wish it luck. This would apply even more to a group of military officers that proposes a political action.

Led by a twenty-six year old Major, Chukuma Kaduna Nzeogwu, the group had as their hero President Kwame Nkrumah of Ghana and Fidel Castro of Cuba. Nzeogwu, like many of them, was trained in Sandhurst, a first class military

* Adewale Ademoyega: Why We Struck, The Story of the First Nigerian Coup, Evans Brothers (Nigeria) Ltd. 1981.

institution in Great Britain. He was the first Nigerian to be trained in military intelligence and in 1958 he was appointed Senior Instructor in the newly-established Nigerian Military College near Kaduna. Rather flippant as a revolutionary he was outspoken about the intentions of his group. They all looked on their superior officers as stooges who tried to be in the good books of politicians for patronage. Most of them were Majors commissioned barely three years before 1960.

These conspirators watched all the events that were happening in the country. They: "were disgusted to the neck" and many of them were madly keen to act even as early as September 1965; but the group was not complete. Two of their members were out of the country. Ifeajuna, who was a co-ordinating member in Lagos, had just returned from Pakistan which he visited on a military mission. When the group met in Lagos in September 1965 to consider their respective positions for action, and the day on which to strike, they had already lost two undecided members whose manner of death the police were investigating. They thought it would be too dangerous to have another postponement of the D-Day. But, there was none yet to man the Ikeja Cantonment which had, the year before, been made into the Second Battalion. It was under the command of a Cameroonian whose loyalty they could not rely on.

The Armoury at Apapa was under the command of Unegbo, who, though a Nigerian and an Ibo, was 'not trustworthy', but they decided to deal with him adequately when 'the time comes'. Also, Ifeajuna had assured them that everything would be properly taken care of, as much as the Lagos area was concerned. Okafor was put in charge of the Federal Guard.

By far the most difficult nut to crack, as almost all the members of the group agreed, was Kaduna. More than half of the country's military installations were located in the area. It was the headquarters of the enormous Northern Region which frightened every Southerner. It was the residence of Sir Ahmadu Bello who was the most friendly of the Nigerian leaders with the British government. His home, Premier's Lodge, Kaduna, was built in 1959. Its two-feet thick, solid concrete walls, were comparable to the walls of a medieval European castle, like Dover Castle; except that the Premier's Lodge was on surroundings less elevated than Dover Castle, though it was constructed on land raised ten feet about ground level. This gave it a shorter focus to spot an on-coming danger early enough to ward it off. But its walls, thickly concreted as they were, had only nine narrow windows and two large gates, all grilled with thick iron bars. More than one hundred fully battle-armed troops guarded it day and night; and powerful electric bulbs and neon lights shone over it at night. Inside, according to the Islamic custom, was a large population of dependants including wives, adult issues, and other hangers-on. There was also a large mosque which held divine services daily and nightly.

Several times between September and the end of December 1965, Nzeogwu, with other members of the group, and sometimes by himself, drove around the Lodge, studying its design in relation to bomb throwers and artillery bombardment.

Outside the Premier's Lodge, the city of Kaduna was a very quiet place compared to its counterparts in the South. Here in Kaduna, there were only a few industries. Its Christian population, made up of mostly Southerners and people from other African countries, retired usually as early as ten o'clock at night. From then on the city was as quiet as a graveyard. All these points were fully studied by Nzeogwu, who had complete access to all sorts of military weapons and hardware, stored in different parts of Kaduna. He was also in charge of military training, and he trained artillery gunners.

The group decided to strike on 7th January; but the Commonwealth Conference on Rhodesia came as a nuisance. It was the first of such conferences ever to be held in Nigeria. Unable to settle his problems in Nigeria, Balewa: "dabbled into wider regions where many were praising Nkrumah as the leader of African opinion in the continent". Balewa had thought that the Commonwealth Conference held in Lagos, would help to improve his very poor image in West Africa. Due to the presence of many heads of state in the country, the group postponed the date on which they would strike.

On January 12th, the group held one more meeting. It lasted only twenty minutes; but it was enough for them to compare their respective notes about preparedness. The meeting of the Commonwealth Prime Ministers had ended and the members were flying off to their respective homes. However, Archbishop Makarios of Cyprus developed an idea which irritated the conspirators. He decided to visit the Eastern Region which Ifeajuna thought he could get to by helicopter after dealing with his Lagos assignment. This assignment included attacking the Prime Minister and Major-General J.T Aguiyi-Ironsi, the only general in the Nigerian Army and its highest-ranking officer at the time of Independence in 1960.

Zik had already left the country said to be for medical attention in London. It was the time of the Commonwealth Conference, the first to be held in Nigeria. As head of state, many thought that it was odd that he chose that particular time to leave the country. A member of his clan, Nwafor Oriju, was holding the seat in Lagos for him. Balewa, the Prime Minister, was warned of the on-coming coup, but he did not believe his informant. "You know I was a teacher in the North for a long time; these young men in the army are only enjoying themselves; when is Nigeria ever going to war? All around us are ants, and we're the elephant. It's only the remnants of the Action Group that we're bothered about; haven't you got anything about them?" He dismissed his top intelligence officer.

In Ibadan Chief Akintola was terribly unsettled. Some of his colleagues, who felt as unsettled as him, had consulted sorcerers who had advised them to offer sacrifices daily for fourteen days, in order to ward off the on-coming catastrophe. But Akintola and a few others, flew the following morning, that is the morning of 14th January, to Kaduna to discuss the: "strong rumour and intelligence report" with the Sarduana of Sokoto, Sir Ahmadu Bello, the Premier of the North.

Sir Ahmadu Bello had just the day before returned from one of his frequent pilgrimages to Mecca. He still had absolute faith in the power of God Almighty to protect him against evil. His disbelief in Chief Akintola's briefing made the chief feel like Jeremiah. Depressed, he arranged his return flight to Ibadan accompanied by three of his supporters.

Meanwhile, the Revolutionary Group, which also called itself 'progressive', reconsidered the date on which they would strike. An earlier decision had settled on the 21st January but on account of the movements of their intended victims this would not be appropriate. They suspected that too many at Ibadan and some top military officers now knew of their plans. But the top politicians, not knowing much about their own foes, did not believe a coup was possible in Nigeria. Almost all of them scoffed at the warnings of their own intelligence officers.

According to the account commonly reported immediately after the coup, since early January Nzeogwu had kept a close watch on the Kaduna Lodge, the home of Sir Ahmadu Bello. He had earlier taken advantage of his position as artillery instructor at the newly opened Defence Academy in Kaduna, to move soldiers to different parts of the city for artillery practice even during the night.

At their penultimate meeting in Kaduna, Major Okafor briefed the group and told them that the NPC leadership was planning to subdue the whole of the South with the assistance of Chiefs Akintola, Oko Tie Ebo and other Yoruba elite. He also alleged that the Sardauna had sworn to the Arabs that he would 'Islamatise' the whole of the South including the East within the space of five years. Everyone believed him and they were determined to act at once. Earlier they had fixed the date on which they would strike as the 21st of January when all the VIPs who had been attending the Commonwealth Conference on Rhodesia must have returned home. Later they changed that date.

The last meeting was said to have been conducted by signals and telephone from the home of one of them in the Apapa military barracks. There, a new date of 14th to 15th January was agreed upon. Ifeajuna, the group's co-ordinator then signalled Nzeogwu in Kaduna as follows: "Chief Oni Wahala arriving 28 depart 30 at 0200 definite." Nzewgwu understood the message to mean that the operation would be on the night of the 14th in full readiness to strike at 2.00am on the 15th January.

Meanwhile Chief Akintola, reputed to be a very courageous person, arrived at Ibadan accompanied by some of his colleagues and advisers. He was reminded that he should always wear his bullet-proof outfit like most other politicians did at the time. With only very few industries and night life, Ibadan was usually dead by nine o'clock at night. On the night of the 14th January it was more dead than usual as the miasma of rumours and gossip of: "military coup any day" kept thousands indoors from early evening.

Also, in Lagos most nightclub-goers had on the 14th January already exhausted most of their funds and energy on the Christmas and New Year celebrations that had just ended. Traffic on the roads leading to the fashionable district of Ikoyi, where all the victims of the conspirators lived, had eased off by ten o'clock. The Prime Minister's convoy of cars from Lagos airport had only just driven to Ikoyi at about eleven o'clock. They had gone to the airport to see off the last of the delegates who attended the Conference on Rhodesia.

At the airport the Prime Minister was again fully briefed about the impending military coup; still only half believing it, he nevertheless decided that he would clamp down on the conspirators after the last of the delegates had left. He did not want to be seen to be an undemocratic leader clamping down on dissidents. That night he confided in Dr Elias,* and some other ministers at the airport that he would have a meeting with his security advisers on the Sunday 16th: "to do something about this rumour". That night the conspirators watched the convoy of cars led by police outriders with flashing lights and sirens to Ikoyi, but by midnight only the vehicles of the conspirators were about as they had already placed road-blocks on most of the roads. They themselves drove with only parking lights.

At the stroke of 1.30am on the morning of 15th January in Lagos, Ibadan and Kaduna, the conspirators charged into the homes of their sleeping victims and slaughtered them mercilessly. Within forty minutes it was all over. But the operation was not perfect. Lt-Col Jack Pam, the Adjutant-General, was killed only after he had managed to warn Major-General Aguiyi-Ironsi that the revolutionary group were approaching his house. When the got to Ironsi, he was already prepared for them. He told them he too was with them. But as they turned their backs, he got his troops after them to begin a counter-coup.

In Kaduna, the Premier's Lodge was reduced to rubble after three hours of continuous artillery bombardment at four points around it.

Sir Ahmadu Bello and his two senior wives were killed. Others killed in the building included several troops, two of his

* The Federal Attorney Justice at the time. Later a Judge of the International Court of The Hague

sons and many hangers-on. For several hours the building discharged balls of fire and thick black smoke like a volcano. Brigadier Ademulegun, a Southerner and second-in-command in the Nigerian Army, was killed together with his wife in their home. The revolutionary group led troops to the houses of several politicians and they were picked up and detained. At 4.45am Major Nzeogwu went to the radio station and made his first announcement "Good morning, fellow countrymen and women; today is a great day for our beloved country, Nigeria. We have successfully dealt a blow to feudalism, tribalism, corruption and all the evils that have plagued this country for more than fifteen years. From now on the Revolutionary Council has taken over the government of the country; and I warn everyone that looting, arson, homosexuality, tribalism, rape, embezzlement, corruption and false alarm will be severely dealt with by execution. Let everyone go about his or her business and be grateful to God Almighty". At that time of the morning on a Saturday, only very few Nigerians heard Nzeogwu.

In Ibadan, Chief Akintola saw troops approaching at about 2.15am. He made for his rifle with which he had, during the past six months, been practising shooting. He fired a few shots, but missed. Thereupon, he was shot dead at his home. A few of his guards who tried to shoot were wounded.

In Enugu, capital of the Eastern region, the troops that were to deal with the Premier, Dr Okpara, got to the residence of the Premier and thought that Bishop Makarios was still in his company. Their leader, scared about what to do, particularly as he was himself not a member of the group, removed his troops without any killing or arrest. The Mid-West region had not quite settled at the time of the coup in January 1966; its leadership, like that of the East, was not thought of as being violently opposed to 'progress'.

In Lagos, very few knew the details of the coup. But by 9am news that Balewa, Akintola and Ahmadu Bello had died had reached the masses. There was spontaneous jubilation throughout the city as thousands of market women, students, workers and others, filled the streets, dancing merrily and congratulating one another that there had been a coup, though none expected that there could be one in Nigeria. But soon, many began to fear that it had not quite succeeded, particularly as Ironsi, having bounced back, had set the country's troops scouring for the perpetrators of the coup. Now, all the adversaries of the men in government and their favourites, became highly-strung, as they prayed fervently that the adherents of the slain politicians might not regain control of the country. At 11am in Lagos, the Prime Minister, Sir Abubakar Tafawa Balewa, was still being driven about in the Land Rover of Major Ifeajuna who had kidnapped him. As Ifeajuna was audaciously trying to track down Ironsi, he kept Balewa alive and seated on the floor of the vehicle among twenty-eight dead officers.

But as the cargo of the dead officers and the living Prime Minister was becoming a great burden on him, because he was himself being hunted by Ironsi's own troops, he took Balewa to a nearby clump of banana bushes, and shot him. All the bodies were then dumped on the ground with instructions to his troops to bury them, while he continued his search for General Ironsi. A few miles from the grave of the Prime Minister, his Minister of Finance, Chief Festus Okotie-Eboh, was similarly shot and buried in the bush. As the day progressed, Ifeajuna's hopes and enthusiasm for capturing Ironsi faded. He gave up the hunt, thought of his own escape, then commandeered a private car at a petrol station and drove to Accra, the capital of Ghana. There he became the guest of Prime Minister Nkrumah.

Nkrumah was pleased to see Ifeajuna and he said: "I see the coup was perfect".

"Not quite Sir, we missed Ironsi, the only General in our Army".

"Why, is he not a Southerner?"

"He is, and an Ibo like me; but he's a fool".

"He must be; does he not realise that in Nigeria those Northern feudal Muslims were favoured by the British Imperialists, because they think they can control them more easily. They will forever want to rule the country, however badly. You people have stone heads. I'm sorry, but you must try again. We in Ghana can only wish you good luck. I'll put you up with other Nigerians".

However, not all the members of the group were as lucky to escape as Ifeajuna. In Nigeria, many of those troops who supported them had been picked up. A few of them were still on the run, as the resistance against Ironsi got weaker by the hour; particularly in the South. In the North, Nzeogwu was still in full control. However, a clash between him and Ironsi seemed imminent. Ironsi appreciated the situation. But he also knew that Nzeogwu would not like the army to be divided. He knew too that Nzeogwu respected him and that he could use these facts to lure Nzeogwu to co-operate with him. But before that, he had to settle his own position *vis-a-vis* those politicians in government that were not in hiding. He invited them to his office and demanded that, in order to enable him to deal adequately with the situation, they should transfer power temporarily to him. Some readily agreed; others hesitated, despite the fear of God he put in to them. Later, when they all agreed, his lawyer friend whispered to him that it would look more convincing if power was transferred in writing and in the presence of a respectable third person. The British High Commissioner, Sir Cumming-Bruce, was readily accepted by both sides.

On the 16th January, the politicians signed away power

to the military headed by Major-General Aguiyi-Ironsi. Everyone concerned knew that the act was not legal or constitutional; but they all convinced themselves that it was the best thing to do in the circumstances.

Ironsi's next move was to convert his de facto position to de jure authority, as head of state. To do this, he needed to defeat the coup leaders. He went on the radio and announced that he was in full control of the situation, and that many of the rebels who mutinied in the Army had been caught and that all the others would be caught and punished. On hearing his message, those troops who took part in the coup without conviction, sold their passes. Others continued to look for their own escape. Within the next twenty four fours, Nzeogwu's support had thinned out considerably.

With a brave face, Nzeogwu himself responded to Ironsi's broadcast and declared that he was in full control of the Northern Region. Speaking on the radio he proclaimed "In the Name of the Supreme Council of the Revolution of the Nigerian Armed Forces, I declare martial law over the Northern Province of Nigeria. The Constitution is suspended and the regional government and elected assemblies are hereby dissolved. All political, cultural, tribal and trade union activities, together with all demonstrations and unauthorized gatherings excluding religious worship, are banned until further notice ... As an interim measure all permanent secretaries, corporation chairmen and senior heads of departments are allowed to make decisions until the new organs of government begin to    function ... We promise that you will no more be ashamed to say that you are Nigerians".

Nzeogwu had the full support of the small Nigerian Air Force, established in 1963. Earlier in 1965, it had been sent to frighten political agitators in Tivland,* who were demanding

---

* The Tivs are a non-Muslim community in the Northern Region, near the River Benue. Alarge percentage of the Infantry is made up of Tivs.

their own region or state apart from the Northern region. Now it was ready to back Nzeogwu for the showdown against Ironsi. The showdown would mean Nzeogwu would march his troops from the North to conquer the South. But it was the South more than the North, which openly supported his revolution and the coup. Also his position in the North itself was becoming shaky. Ironsi, still requiring Nzeogwu's co-operation, dispatched two emissaries to plead with Nzeogwu not to cause a division in the army, to which the politicians had now transferred power, and that, that fact could make peace possible without upsetting the purpose of the revolution and the coup. The two emissaries were fellow Ibos, Lt. Colonels Nwanwo and Modibo.

Nzeogwu became convinced and gave some conditions which included the following – a guarantee of safety for him and his men who staged the coup and the other troops involved; compensation for the families of all who died during the coup; release of those already detained and an assurance to re-absorb all those who took part in the coup. It was alleged that the two discussed this on the telephone and that Ironsi readily agreed. But when Nzeogwu landed at Lagos Airport, there were thousands of troops in full battle outfit and readiness. Some of them were equipped with anti-tank recoilless rifles and cannons, the type he used to destroy the Sardauna's castle. From there he was escorted by a convoy of armoured vehicles with rifle-carrying troops to KiriKir prison outside Lagos, where other members of his revolutionary group were being detained.

Now Ironsi, fully in the saddle, began to acknowledge the congratulations and plaudits from all those concerned, especially those whose adversaries had been put out of circulation. The NCNC congratulated the new regime and declared that: "The Army as the bulwark and the sanction of any civil government have come to safeguard the principles of parliamentary democracy and the rule of law". Some of their leaders were highly qualified lawyers of more than twenty-years standing, who were aware of the unconstitutional and illegal nature of the military regime. Nevertheless they were still willing to make statements supporting the regime to the millions of Nigerians who did not at that time fully understand what democracy and the rule of law were about.

Not to be outdone, the Action Group declared:

"Our party believes that this military take-over is only a continuation of the people's struggle to preserve parliamentary democracy and the unity of the Federation".

In its editorial on January 18th, headed: "The New Regime", *The Daily Times*, which was at that period the most popular daily newspaper, wrote:

*"With the transfer of authority of the Federal Government to the Armed Forces, we reach a turning point in our national life. The old order changeth, yielding place to the new. For sometime now, almost right from the beginning when we came to our own, this country has been as if it were at sick bay. We have been groping along, rudderless, hesitant, unsure which foot to put forward first ... For sometime now – almost right from the day in October 1960 when we put out the flag and the bunting in celebration of the dawn of a new era – our experiment in parliamentary democracy, Westminster-fashion, which we watched our old masters practice does not appear to have flourished. Opposition was virtually*

*reduced to nil. For a long time, instead of settling to minister unto the people's need the politicians were busy performing a series of seven day wonders as if the art of government was some circus show ... Today there is a new regime in the Federal Republic of Nigeria, a military regime. About time too. The new regime deserves praise for the calm manner in which it effected the change without causing public panic. Something just had to be done to save the nation. It is like a surgical operation which must be performed or the patient dies. The operation has been performed. It has proven successful. And we welcome it".*

Three months earlier that same newspaper, along with others in the South, viewed with satisfaction the performance of the ousted civilian regime. On the 1st October 1965, it wrote an editorial headed: "Another Milestone" and said:

*"After five years of independent statehood this nation, we believe, no longer looks on today as an occasion for delirious emotion. If the first five years must be our guide for the future, then* The Daily Times *believes that, on the balance we have every reason to be optimistic. First, this nation where tongues and tribes differ, is still one, in spite of the cheerless prognosis of foreigners and the pessimism of the easily discouraged among us. Thirdly, we have begun to grapple with the urgent and immediate problems of providing a better life for our people, and any anxiety we may entertain on this half-way stage of our six year development*

*plan, should only serve to spur us on to greater endeavours ... Our stand in the community of nations gives us cause for satisfaction ...* The Daily Times *joins in today's rejoicing ..."*

It is not quite easy for many in Nigeria to have an independent outlook and express themselves on matters unfavourable to those in power even in civilian rule. The newspapers can be vulnerable. Like other businesses they depend on government patronage for many things, particularly advertising. As the government owns most businesses, advertising for the newspaper is generally more than 80 percent from government sources. Land allocation and interests in lands are all matters in which the government is fully in control. All these factors make the government in Nigeria more powerful than the average government in other countries. It is much worse when that government is a military one.

## Chapter 12

## The First Military Regime – General J.T. Aguiyi-Ironsi

Before the end of the first week of the coup, it became publicly known that the politicians who were killed included Sir Ahmadu Bello, the Sarduana of Sokoto, Premier of the Northern region. He was also leader of his political party, the Northern People's Congress (NPC) that was in power in the federal government. Also killed was his deputy in the NPC, Sir Abubakar Tafawa Balewa, who was the Prime Minister of the country, and Chief Samuel Akintola, a Yoruba, Premier of the Western region and leader of his political party, the NNDP, which was in alliance with the NPC in the federal government.

No political leader or member of the other parties were killed, as the Action Group and NCNC were in alliance. Neither of the two premiers in the Mid-West and Eastern Regions were killed, they were both Ibo. The country had four Brigadier-Generals at the time, two were Northerners and the other two Yorubas from the Western region. Three of the Brigadiers were killed, one of them Yoruba and the other two Northerners. The number of other ranks and troops killed in the coup was said to be more than one hundred. Of this number, only one, Major Unegbu, who was in charge of the Apapa Armoury near Lagos was Ibo. But their votaries insisted that they were detribalised youths and followers of Abdel Nasser, Fidel Castro and Kwame Nkrumah.

By the 20th January Ironsi was out of harm's way. He had defeated the revolutionary group, many of whom were now detained in Kirikiri Prison near Lagos His position was absolute, particularly as he had forced the politicians to transfer power to him.

Probably, after the storm had died down and some calmness had returned to everyone, Ironsi too, like many others in the country saw that the unexplained motive of the coup plotters appear t be tribal. In Nigeria, every political conflict or encounter had been tribal or sectional, particularly since 1945, and it was not easy to ignore the tribal slant in the perpetration of the coup. Ironsi did not say it in so many words, but his actions showed that he realised the position as he set up his administration.

He arrested and detained the top members of the political parties that were excepted by the coup, while he did not detain any member of the political parties whose leaders were killed in the coup. He also did not detain or arrest any Northerner or Northern troops, though many Northern troops were used to storm the Premier's Lodge and kill the inmates.

In a radio broadcast, he promised that all the perpetrators of the coup would be punished severely. The statement gladdened the Northern leadership and they looked to him to keep his promise. He could see their anger; but he thought he could redirect their expectations of the fulfilment of his promise, by appeasing them in some other way. He set out to reward them with lavish trips to Arab countries: "to brief their fellow Islamic Brothers that the coup had not been motivated by religious factors and there was no movement by Christians to subdue the Muslim North".

While trying to propitiate Northerners with soft words and lavish foreign travel Ironsi made two key appointments which undermined the loyalty of many in the South. The beneficiaries of the appointments were members of his own Ibo tribe. In the firs place he appointed Francis Nwokedi to the post of Chief Secretary to the government. Nwokedi was an extremely capable civil servant, who under normal circumstances was in line to succeed the outgoing British officer, Peter Stallard. However, because he was an Ibo, others in the South condemned the appointment as not being in the spirit of what many at the time termed: 'The Revolution'. The office was a powerful one because in the totalitarian setting of the military regime, the officer was next in control after the head of state, Ironsi.

In the second place, Ironsi appointed a capable barrister of long standing, and respect in the Nigerian Bar, as the country's new Attorney-General in place of the Yoruba, Dr T.S. Ellias. He was G.C. Onyuke a member of Ironsi's own clan in the Ibo tribe. Shortly after these appointment were made, an old friend of Ironsi's, Chief Bakare, a Yoruba, visited him and warned him of the gossip regarding the appointments. But Ironsi threw a tantrum. "Only you Yorubas can talk nonsense like that. Didn't the American President Kennedy appoint his brother as Attorney-General? What will you people say about that? If that happened in Nigeria, everyone would shout 'nepotism'. You Yoruba people, you're always tribalists. I'll stop tribalism in this country", he said.

But the Northern leadership also began to challenge Ironsi on these appointments and also the motivation behind the coup. They later wrote of Ironsi in a government publication as follows:

> *"In assessing the motives as well as the consequences of the incidents of 15th January 1966, attention should be drawn to the various interpretations and excuses offered. First, some people saw it as an end to Northern domination. Secondly, some regarded it as an attempt to remove corruption from government. Thirdly, others hoped that it would introduce an honest and just*

*programme to correct the structural imbalance in the federation. No one quarrels with these aims. Most regrettably, however, the actual events showed clear evidence of tribal bias ... the coup was a clumsily-camouflaged attempt to secure Ibo domination of the country. This impression was later reinforced by certain appointments and actions of Ironsi and his regime".* \*

Ten days after Ironsi had accused Chief Bakare of being tribalist, he went on the radio and vehemently condemned tribalism as: "the bane of the Nigerian society". He was again reminded of his appointment of Lt. Col. Odumegbu Ojukwu as Governor of the Eastern region instead of Col. Bassey, the most senior Easterner, a veteran of World War II who was an Effik. Many non-Ibo Easterners then also began to lose confidence in Ironsi. In April 166, Ironsi abolished the federal structure by decree and the country reverted to the unitary system of pre-1947. In his broadcast he explained the importance of the decree and said:

*"It is now three months since the government of the federation was handed over to the Armed Forces. Now that peace has been restored in the troubled areas of the country, it is time that the military indicates clearly what it proposes to accomplish before relinquishing power. The removal of one of the greatest obstacles to peace and settled government, is provided for in the Constitutional Suspension Decree which was promulgated by me today. The decree is intended to remove the last vestiges of the intense regional-*

---

\* A Government publication entitled: A Panacea for Peace, 1996, after the overthrow of the Ironsi regime.

*isations of the recent past, and to produce that cohesion in the governmental structure which is so necessary in achieving, and maintaining the primary objective of the Federal Military Government, and indeed of every true Nigerian, namely unity. By the decree the name of the country ceases to be the Federal Republic of Nigeria. It now becomes simply the Republic of Nigeria. The former regions are abolished and the country continues as Provinces as before the Richards constitution in 1947."*

To the Northern leadership, the change from federalism to a unitary form of government was the last straw. It was the federation with the huge North as one unit that gave them the advantage to rule the rest of the country even in a civilian regime. They did not think that they could compete with the rest of the country on equal considerations and without inbuilt advantages. They decided to fight against Ironsi. And now their politicians intensified their denigration of him.

Unfortunately for the country, at this time also, some Ibos were feeling arrogant because of Ironsi's position as head of state; and, of Nzeogwu in blasting the Premier's Lodge, Kaduna. In Kano, Zaria, Kaduna and other Northern cities, they taunted Northerners with passport-size photos of Nzeogwu, saying to them: "Look, this is the photograph of your new master, buy it and decorate your mud huts until you learn sense". They hardly cared about the pain they were causing their hosts.

Unfortunately, too, these were some of the places where the Ibo State Union established schools, colleges and even churches for their members. Those who said this did not fully understand the feelings of Northerners for the Sardauna of

Sokoto, Sir Ahmadu Bello, whom the Islamic North revered intensely; but whom, unfortunately, the South hated so bitterly. For exactly the very reason that the North exalted him, the South disliked him. Traditionally, he was more powerful in his domain of Sokoto and the Islamic North, than any other traditional ruler in the country and he tried to extend his influence to the whole country through his role as leader of the NPC. It was the Sardauna who had introduced politics to the North in 1945 when Sir Arthur Richards first promulgated his constitution which many in the South did not like. He aggressively fought the imbalance in education between the North and the South by obtaining dispensation for Northerners in the fields of education and so pushed the North towards 'catching up' with the South. He established the first university in the North, for Northerners to obtain admission without first qualifying in general educational levels. The university prepared them for 'basic qualifications' for the particular university. His demise angered the North intensely; but the South was generally pleased with the coup.

When Ironsi heard about the offensive pictures and songs that Ibos were using to taunt Northerners, he promulgated the Defamatory and Offensive Publications Decree 1966 (Decree No. 44). This made the publication: "in any form whatsoever or the display of any matter that is likely to provoke any section of the community an offence". The offence carried terms of imprisonment as punishment. He also banned all political parties and tribal organisations and confiscated their assets. More than 120 tribal organisations, including the Ibo State Union, the Egbe Omo-Oduduwa, Yoruba State Union, Ijaw Progressive Union, Egbe Omo Yoruba, Bornu State Union, Lagos Aborigine's Society and Ibibio State Union were banned. In his radio announcement concerning the banning of tribal unions Ironsi said:

> *"These organisations have been dissolved and will be buried along with the tribal, sectional and regional bitterness which they engendered ... every individual should be pre-occupied with the task of national reconstruction, not as ex-politician or politicians, but simply as a Nigerian with faith in his country's destiny ... from henceforth no reference to tribe will appear on any official document."*

None of Ironsi's decrees was favoured by the Northern leadership. Instead they continued to whine about the fact that the: 'rebels who murdered hundreds of people' had not been punished. But Ironsi knew that to punish the perpetrators of the coup would set the whole of the South against him and even the Ibos would strive to destroy him.

On the 26th May the North sent a delegation of Emirs to him to express these grievances and ask for the restoration of the regional system in the federal structure. His explanation that the decrees were merely temporary or transitional, pending the reports of the study groups he had set up, did not satisfy their desires.

Even before the delegation of Northern Emirs set off to meet Ironsi on 26th May, the bitterness against Ironsi in most of the North had spread generally to include Easterners living in the North. Easterners became the victims of intense hatred and hostility, first by the Northern leadership and later by almost everyone except in the pagan areas. And the Northern leaders discussed secession openly as they did eight years earlier when Sir Ahmadu Bello led the discussion to consider the matter in all its ramifications.

While Ironsi was still pacifying the Northern Chiefs, many of the Northern politicians, displaced by the January coup and becoming stoney broke, were burning for revenge on Easterners in the North. Like the wind, they successfully spread their false rumour, that another Ibo massacre was about to be unleashed against Northern troops and civilians. By 'bush telegraph', the news or rumour spread like wild fire all through the North.

On the evening of the 27th May 1966 hundreds of Northern troops from the barracks in several cities collected their civilian supporters for both defence and a revenge attack on Southerners in their areas, known as Sabon-gari or new towns, where Southerners lived in every city of the North. The two groups did not live together in any part of the North. They had lived apart since the time of Lugard; but not as strictly as black and white did in South Africa before 1990.

Armed with machine guns, Northern troops in uniform with civilian thugs, stormed Sabon-gari in Kano, Kaduna, Zaria, Sokoto, Jos, Bauchi, Bukuru and many other cities and towns in the North. Unprepared for the attack, Southerners fell like lame ducks as their properties and homes were set on fire. All through the night the killings continued undisturbed as troops returned for more slaughter after reloading their guns.

The following day the killing continued, even right into workplaces and offices. In these places, troops in uniform would enter and demand that all Southerners be brought out. When that was done, the lot were gunned down. By the afternoon of the 28th May, the killings became confined to Easterners, as many Northerners by that time had begun to distinguish Easterners from Westerners. Later still, many of the murdering soldiers began to differentiate between Ibos and others from the East; and so the killings continued with the Ibos. Every Southerner had to be prepared to show that he was not Ibo. They slew without allowing any escape, for they were everywhere, hunting Ibos in offices, railway stations, lorry parks and other places. The more morbid and savage ones would cut off a woman's breasts and send her away dying. And they cut off the genitals of many men and left them dying too. There was no Auschwitz in the North; Northern soldiers killed Easterners on the spot.

The Ironsi government was too frightened to give a full report of the incidents. But many foreign journalists gave a fairly accurate account of the events including the killings. David Loshal of the British *Daily Telegraph* gave the number killed in one city as 600.

Ironsi thought the report could frighten several people out of the country; for that reason David Loshal was deported immediately. Many others were similarly deported for telling the truth. They included Walter Schwarz, who reported for the BBC and the *Guardian* newspaper. The government itself put the number of people killed at 92.

Yet, Ironsi could do nothing; nor even did he try to discipline the perpetrators of these massacres. He could not, because, by this time the Army had become completely divided on tribal lines; but all were living on tenterhooks in the same barracks in several parts of the country. Earlier, he had locked up for five days the Governor of the Northern region, Lt. Col. Usman Katsina, a Northerner, for disobeying his authority. And soon the disloyalty by Northern troops against Ironsi became general.

Since the massacre in May, it had been common talk throughout the country that another coup was likely. Some thought that such a coup would be staged by some supporters of the revolutionary group whose leaders Ironsi had locked up in KiriKiri prison, near Lagos. Because of this rumour the detainees were removed from Kirikiri in Lagos to prisons in the Eastern Region, far away from Ironsi. However, some also thought that the coup would come from the Northern troops this time. It would be a revenge for the January coup. It was believed that Ironsi himself knew the situation quite well, because previously he had converted a few tiny cabins in one of Nigeria's few naval frigates for his bedroom. Every night he was taken from the State House on the Marina to the ship in the lagoon. This made it very obvious to many that he was really afraid of a likely coup, and that he trusted none of his own troops.

The rumour also had some effect on the troops. Among the Ibo soldiers and officers, several were unsettled and nervous, but alert. Northern troops were also for the same reason always suspicious of the movements of Ibo troops, especially when they spoke in threes and fours in corners. There was also the rumour that Ironsi had: "promoted eighteen junior officers, all of whom were Ibos like him; whereas, he promoted only three Northerners and no Yoruba or Westerners. In the South, the rumour of these promotions alienated many Yorubas and they lost confidence in Ironsi. They thought he condemned tribalism and nepotism, but practised them himself. Without a free press, the people were fed on rumours.

Someone might have told Ironsi that forty years ago, Lugard usually called the Northern Emirs together and briefed them on his policy. Now in 1966, Ironsi decided he would do that. He invited the country's 'traditional rulers' for a meeting with him at Ibadan on 29th July. Ibadan was the capital of the Western region which by Ironsi's new arrangement was then capital of the Western group of Provinces. He had five months earlier appointed one of the country's bravest soldiers, Adekunle Fajuyi, who was decorated with a United Nations Medal for bravery in the Congo in 1963, as Governor of the region. For the meeting at Ibadan Ironsi resided with Fajuyi, at the Government Lodge, Ibadan. The day was 29th July 1966.

While the meeting at Ibadan was in progress, some Northern troops in Abeokuta, thought that they saw some Ibo troops moving in a suspicious manner. They then put themselves on alert. That evening at Abeokuta, there was an electricity failure, which was quite usual. But that particular failure was put down to the Ibos wanting to resume their killing tricks. The Northerners did not wait for any more evidence to convince themselves. Some jumped into Land Rovers, armed to the teeth, and drove about in Lagos hunting Ibo troops. Some others arrested Ibo troops in the barracks and shot them. A few top officers in three Land Rovers, raced to Ironsi in Ibadan only fifty two miles away. There, in the Governor's Lodge were Ironsi and Fajuyi. They demanded to arrest Ironsi alone. "You can't do that; he's my guest", Fajuyi told the hostile officers. "Very well then, we'll take both of you", said the rebel troops; and they 'kidnapped' both Ironsi and Fajuyi. Two weeks later the news that they had been killed, came in trickles from foreign sources in Dahomey, next door. The killing of General Ironsi on the 29th of July was the second coup, though some take it as the third.*

    Notwithstanding the rumour of a likely coup, when it did happen, it shocked everyone. But it did not end the killings in the military barracks all over the country and in the Northern streets and Sabon-garis. From the North refugee Easterners flocked daily to Enugu. By the middle of August the East had received more than a million dead and dying people from the North. Added to this number were the bodies of troops killed in several barracks and brought in by their distraught families. The East became a huge camp of weeping and wailing people totally disheartened about their future in the country. All branches of the public service and schools were geared to trying to bury the bodies, healing the wounded and resettling the displaced.

    Some blamed it all on Ironsi. These thought that having wrested power from the revolutionary group, he hadn't a clue

\* Ironsi's snatching of power is considered a coup by him.

what to do next. "Instead, he spent most of his time apologising, appeasing and fumbling." He was not ambitious for wealth as many others after him had been known to have been. Neither he nor his friend Adekunle Fajuyi had any house or property anywhere when they were 'kidnapped'. Very good soldiers, they forced themselves into Nigerian politics which were characterised by lack of principles, tribalism, corruption, greed and a struggle for big money.

But the masses in the East, particularly from Ironsi's own clan, could not accept the fact that he had been killed; especially as they saw him on recorded television programmes. At that time in 1966, television was only quite new in the country. However, for more than two whole days after Ironsi had been 'kidnapped', no one claimed responsibility for the coup, and no one said anything about a new government taking over. It was all blank. It was the type of situation that fed rumour-mongering. It was worse in Nigeria under the military where freedom of speech and press freedom did not exist. All stories began with rumours. In July 1966 everyone hunted for rumour.

This time the rumour spread that Northerners were meeting to discuss secession of their area from the country. Millions of Southerners were glad about this and prayed that it would happen. Then another rumour came that they had decided to secede but were waiting to receive advice from British diplomats. In fact many believed that they sent a delegation to Britain for advice. While many in the South still kept their fingers crossed, in the hope that the North would secede, though it was not in their best interest to do so, having regard to the depressed economy in tin and groundnuts, and as they had regained control of the country which now could be rich from oil.

No one considered the danger that might have followed if the North had declared secession at that time. To say the least, in the process of settling boundaries and assets, the country could have witnessed a mini Armageddon.

That Armageddon could have started right from Lagos. There, even the officer next to Ironsi, Brigadier Ogundipe, a Southerner, though Yoruba, could not approach the military headquarters. His own orderlies, who happened to be Northerners, had detained him right inside his house. They did not allow him even to step out into the gardens. Ogundipe had been Ironsi's right-hand man in that military regime. Next to Ogundipe, who was the only one of the survivors of the four Brigadiers in the Nigerian Army at the time, was Lt.Col. Yakubu Gowon who was the Army Chief of Staff during Ironsi's command. Gowon was aged thirty-six and came from a small tribe called Panchin near Jos in the North. Earlier in the century, after Lugard, a band of Christian evangelists had converted them, and they remained a pocket of Christians, like an oasis, in the Islamic North.

For a good part of three days there was dead silence all over the country; only rumour and gossips flourished. But there were movements of troops; otherwise the country was cut off from the rest of the world and within itself; for all the country's borders were closed and so too were the airports. Travel by road within the country was also greatly reduced because of check-points almost every ten miles. Everyone was tensely unsettled and wondered how it would end. On 2nd August, it was the gruff voice of Yakubu Gowon that proclaimed the new regime. When his calm-looking face appeared on television, it restored some confidence to millions of Nigerians.

CHAPTER 13

## The Military Regime the East Refused to Recognise

As previously discussed, on the 29th July, the military officer next to Ironsi was Brigadier Ogundipe, Chief of Staff, Supreme Headquarters. This entitled him to membership of the military council that ruled the country. In addition to his military job, Ogundipe was also responsible for the allocation of houses, vacated by politicians, to army personnel. He was not part of the conspiracy to kidnap Ironsi and as such he was seen as an enemy by Northern troops. He was later dismissed from the army but appointed High Commissioner to Britain. Everyone thought he should thank his lucky star for moving away from the turbulence of Nigeria.

Lt. Col. Gowon, Chief of Army Staff had in fact been quite 'close' to Ironsi. On the 2nd August it was his voice that broke the silence and proclaimed the new regime.

> *"Fellow countrymen and women, the year 1966 has certainly been a fateful year for our beloved country, Nigeria. I have been brought to the position today of having to shoulder the grave responsibilities of this country with the consent of the majority of the Armed Forces and the members of the Supreme Military Council as a result of the unfortunate incident which occurred in the early hours of July 29th.*
> *"As a result of recent events and other grievous similar ones, I have come to the strong belief that*

> *we cannot honestly and sincerely continue in this way, as the basis of trust and confidence in our unitary system of government has not been able to stand the test of time ... Suffice to say, putting all consideration to test political, economic as well as social, the basis for unity is not there, or it has been so badly shaken not once but several times ..."*

He concluded by promising to end the killings which had, up to then, continued unabated. He also promised to convene a conference to determine the future of the country and he announced the governors for each region. He left Lt.Col. Ojukwu to continue as governor in the East; Lt.Col. Usman Katsina also continued as governor in the North; and David Ejoor remained in the mid-West and Lt.Col. Adeyinka Adebayo replaced Fajuyi who was 'kidnapped' with Ironsi in Ibadan.

Three of these officers accepted Gowon and the new situation; but Lt.Col. Ojuwku, on behalf of the East, did not accept him at all. There was therefore immediately to be a most dangerous clash which was to determine the course of events in the country for the future.

For a long time since the January coup, Easterners, particularly Ibos, had suffered the full force of Northern anger. In May they let loose what they called their revenge and they massacred tens of thousands of Easterners in the North. At the end of that killing, by the middle of June, Ojukwu thought that it was possible to forget the past, however painful, and to continue with a new spirit of good neighbourliness. He urged Easterners who had not left the North to stay in the hope of a new friendly era. He even encouraged the able-bodied refugees to go back to the North and resume residence. As a gesture of reconciliation, he appointed the Emir of Kano as Chancellor of the only university in the East and delivered lavish rhetoric at the inauguration.

When, despite these considerations, Northern troops set out on a rampage of pogrom to wipe out Easterners from other parts of the country, it was difficult for him to recover from the shock. This was the line of argument by the Eastern elite. On top of this, the 'kidnap' of General Ironsi, Ojuwku's own sponsor and kinsman and the replacement of Ironsi by a "Northerner, of junior rank and less well educated" than himself, exacerbated his pain.* He was shattered beyond control. "If what has happened is a military coup, then, it shall not succeed here in the East" Ojukwu resolved. With this doggedness, he made an announcement on Enugu radio as follows:

> *"I have considered with my executive committee the very grave events in some parts of the country regarding the rebellion by some sections of the Nigerian Army against the National Military Government which resulted in the kidnapping of His Excellency the Head of the National Military Government and Supreme Commander Major-General Aguiyi-Ironsi and the cold premeditated murder of officers of Eastern origin.*
>
> *"In the course of this rebellion, I have discussed with the Chief of Staff, Supreme Headquarters, Brigadier Ogundipe, who, as the most senior officer in the absence of the Supreme Commander, should have assumed command; my colleagues the other military governors and the Chief of Staff, Army Headquarters, Lt.Col. Gowon. During these discussions it was understood that the only condition on which the rebels would agree to a ceasefire were:*

---

* This was the line of argument by the Eastern elite.

1. The Republic of Nigeria be split into its component parts.
2. That all Southerners resident in the North be repatriated to the South, and all Northerners resident in the South be repatriated to the North...
"I have further conveyed to the Chief of Staff, Supreme HQ, my fellow military governors and the Chief of Staff, Army HQ (i.e. Yakubu Gowon), that the only intention of the announcement today is to restore peace in the country, while immediate negotiations are being begun to allow people of Nigeria to determine the form of their future association".

Meanwhile, rumour and gossip were still spreading, that the North were contemplating secession, the leaders of the non-Ibo area of the Eastern region led by Chief E.O. Eyo and including Chief Wenike Briggs and J. Umorem, had audience with the Northern leaders to talk them out of contemplating secession; because it would cause a prolonged conflict in which the Delta coastal areas would witness fierce, bloody battles, and without settling 'the issue' as they saw it.

As the tense situation continued, Ojukwu on 3rd August 1966 claimed that there was a plan by Northerners, assisted by foreign troops, to invade the East; and that on that account he had no confidence in the Northern troops in the Enugu battalion. In fear of his life, he had secretly sought residence in an undisclosed part of the East. Gowon found the 'allegation preposterous'. He quickly went on air and denied it.

Despite Gowon's public denial, Ojukwu continued to urge that Northern troops be removed from the East. "In the present climate of distrust and hate, I fear for my life among Northern troops here in Enugu". He urged Gowon to remove them without delay. He also insisted to Gowon that before any discussions on the country's future could begin, the Army should be broken-up on a purely regional basis because: "Ibos and Northern soldiers could no longer live together in the same barracks".

Gowon also agreed to this, but assured Ojukwu that: "All is now quiet. I can assure the public that I shall do all in my power to stop any further bloodshed and restore law and order, and confidence in all parts of the country with your co-operation and goodwill."

In order to strengthen his position, Gowon released all the Action Group members imprisoned during Balewa's regime for 'treasonable felony'. They included J.S. Tarka for the Middle Belt region of the North; Chief Awolowo, leader of the Action Group; Chief Anthony Enahoro and others. Later he announced his cabinet of mostly civilians and including many former politicians.

Later, on 9th August, Gowon convened a meeting of the representatives of the Regional Governors in Lagos. Notwithstanding Ojukwu's stand against Gowon, the East was represented at the meeting which agreed that immediate steps should be taken: "to post troops to the barracks in their regions of origin". It was also agreed that over-centralisation of the administration should end immediately; and that a conference should be held to consider and recommend the type of political association which they should adopt.

A few days after the meeting of the regional representatives, Gowon began to implement their decisions. First was the repatriation of troops to their regions of origin. Here, with respect to the Northern troops that were to leave Enugu, Gowon ordered that they should return with their weapons and equipment. On the other hand, with respect to Eastern troops returning to Enugu, transport contractors in Lagos picked them up in several locations and they were repatriated without their weapons or equipment, not even their uniforms. They and their frumpish-looking wives and their hungry children were driven the four hundred miles from Lagos to Enugu.

Many of them wounded and tattered, the scene of their return to Enugu was 'most distressing'. Looking like troops that had surrendered from their trenches after a fierce battle, the Eastern soldiers were taken to the Enugu 1st Battalion barracks. The sight of these poor refugee soldiers strengthened Ojukwu's determination in his confrontational stance against Gowon. These were the only soldiers he had, if he had to fight Gowon. They were less than 700.

However, he sent a six-man delegation to Lagos to attend the conference on the type of administration that would be most suitable for the country. The conference opened on 9th August 1966 with an address by Lt. Col. Gowon as head of state; though this was disputed by the Eastern delegates. They would not accept Gowon as head of state and at that time the exact whereabouts or fate of Ironsi had not officially been announced.

In his address to the conference, Gowon asked them not to discuss the military regime or a complete break-up of the country. He said they were to consider four possible forms of government:
- a federal system with a strong central government;
- a federal system with a weak central government;
- a confederation and
- an entirely new arrangement peculiar to Nigeria.

He added that recent experience had shown that Nigeria could not be successfully administered in a unitary form of government unless this was enforced and maintained by some form of dictatorship.

Further, that if the country continued to be politically unstable, it would severely affect the economic growth. "The country needs trust and confidence and mutual love and respect from every citizen to the other and there must also be tolerance." He would favour a constitution that would provide an atmosphere for these virtues.

A few days later the Northern delegates submitted their memorandum in which they advocated: "the creation of more states in the country so that one citizen did not think of the other as dominating him". They, however, warned that states must be created generally, and not only in one region.

The Western delegation submitted their memorandum which also advocated the creation of eighteen states at the same time throughout the country and included a map of the proposed new boundaries. The mid-Western region also supported the creation of states taking the former provinces as the units of the states. This they argued would be quite easy because everyone knew the extent of the provinces as they existed before regionalisation.

The Eastern delegation advocated that the country should not think of creating states at this difficult time. Rather, the regions should be given greater powers *vis-a-vis* the central administration. They said the creation of states should be left to each region to determine and could not be done now because: "It will involve a long drawn-out process in inquiries, commissions and plebiscites taking up many months or even some years which we cannot afford under the present crisis."

The Eastern stand on the creation of more states immediately caused near riotous commotion as passionate arguments began between the official Eastern delegation which was led by Dr Eni Njoku and the non-Ibo of the East, who were not on the delegation but attended the conference in order to lobby members for the creation of states in the East. On behalf of the non-Ibos in the East, Chief Eyo had asked Nujoku whether the British government set up commissions and plebiscites: "before they lumped you and us together?" He also accused the official delegation of insincerity in the matter of states creation. Thereupon, the non-Ibos in the East realised that they had to hold on to the Northern leadership in order to have their dreams materialize.

An *ad hoc* committee of fourteen delegates prepared a report on the structure of the administration and recommended a federal form of government as before except that the Army and the police should be organised in regional units composed entirely of persons indigenous to each region and that their operational control should be vested in their regional head, except in certain emergencies.

With respect to the creation of states the report stated that: "there was substantial but not yet unanimous agreement, that more states should be created". The conference adjourned until 25th October 1966. Meanwhile Gowon's government had changed the country back from unitary to federal form as before Ironsi. The country reverted to the Federal Republic of Nigeria. The Military Government became the Federal Military Government. The change was made at a meeting of the Supreme Military Council attended by all the Governors of the regions except the Eastern Governor, Lt. Col. Ojukwu.

In the Eastern region, the Governor, Lt. Col. Ojukwu, on the 9th October 1966 declared that in an effort to keep the region intact he had promised greater autonomy to the non-Ibo areas which were Calabar, Ogoja and Rivers Provinces. He further stated that Lt. Col. Gowon was not his military superior and that the Supreme Commander was General Ironsi, who according to his information was not yet presumed dead.

Chief Eyo responded to Ojukwu's promise of autonomy for the non-Ibos and said what was required was: "not autonomy like in the Russian Republic within the Soviet Union, but a region or state equal in all respects to what the Ibos have".

A day before the conference resumed a terrible event occurred in the premises of the Federal Palace Hotel where many Northern delegates lodged. It was the day when Emman Agu an explosives technician from the Enugu Coal Mine checked in at the hotel for two nights. At about 7 o'clock in the morning when the delegates were having breakfast, Agu parked his car full of explosives near the glass windows of the restaurant, and set the explosives to go off at 7.30am. As he locked the car and was walking away, the bomb suddenly exploded, blowing him to smithereens.

Fortunately there was little damage to the hotel and no other loss of life or injury. However, thousands of Easterners rejoiced and celebrated Agu's supposed act of trying to kill the Northern delegation.

The news of the incident reached the North at almost the same time as a news report from Dahomey stating that the bodies of Ironsi and Fajuyi had been discovered in a bush near Ibadan. The report added that a number of Hausas had been killed in Enugu and other parts of the East. These stories inflamed the Northerners who did not bother to wait and find out the real reason for the 'bomb' attack. Apparently Agu had only intended to kill a co-worker who had been awarded an overseas scholarship in preference to him.

But while the East was jubilant on account of the incident, the North was driven to madness because of it. And they went berserk, killing Easterners. It was everyone's mission to kill Easterners. Soldiers went with machine guns, civilians with spears, bows and arrows – just anything with which to kill

Easterners. And it began in Kano and spread to Jos, Kaduna, Sokoto, Zaria, Katsina, Bauchi and even to the pagan areas including Makurdi and Gboko. Other towns with military barracks followed as civilians guided troops to where Easterners might be hiding. At railway stations, troops rushed to catch escaping Easterners to kill them. And as they gunned down their victims they whistled away looking for more to kill.

In Kano, a Lagos-bound plane from Europe had just arrived at 6am on the first day of the killings. Armed troops surrounded the plane and ordered all the passengers to line up outside the plane. As they did that, and despite the pleas of the plane's captain and the crew, all those who could not identify themselves as not being Easterners were gunned down instantly. These included eighty six men, women and children. It was estimated that in Jos alone, more than 2,000 people were killed on the first day. There was nothing to stop them, only fatigue and shortage of ammunition in the barracks. In several cases whole families were wiped out. As they jogged about the streets looking for Easterners, many of the killers thought it was a duty they owed to God to kill Easterners; and they sang the Jihad songs.

On the 2nd October Gowon, in an appeal to the North to stop the killing, said in his radio broadcast: "Since January this year, when some soldiers put our country into confusion, the country has not recovered fully from the confusion. The sadness caused in people's minds by the January events has led to trouble by civilians in the North in May; causing loss of lives. I received complaints daily that Easterners living in the North are being killed and molested and their property looted. I am very unhappy about this. We should put a stop to this. *It appears that it is going beyond reason and is now at the point of recklessness and irresponsibility.* We must remember that we must be answerable to God ... It is the duty of each and every one of us to give all assistance and devote all energy towards finding a peaceful solution to our present situation".

Many in the country were appalled at the insipid and weak tone of the radio address. Many had thought that Gowon would speak with force and warn the perpetrators of the killings. For him to say that the killing: "is going beyond reason and is now at the point of recklessness and irresponsibility" seemed to say that there was some support for some of the killing, if it were not too much.

Later, on 9th October, Gowon at a press conference said that:

> "In spite of what had happened in the recent past, I am still convinced and sincerely hope that a firm foundation will be laid for the future of this country ... everything is being done to maintain essential services and minimize the disruptive effects of recent events in Nigeria on business life ... I regret that I cannot in this statement ignore the unfortunate incidents which preceded both the opening and adjournment of the Lagos conference while efforts and resources are being harnessed to convene the conference. These were the incidents of the bombing of the Ore Bridge, a vital link between Lagos, the West and the East, followed by more serious incidents of the blasting of a section of the Federal Palace Hotel, and an official residence in Ikoyi. The events are so related that one cannot, particularly in this hour of reconstruction, wave it off as the design of a struggle for injustice."

On account of the dangerous situation in the country, many in the Eastern Region became frightened to travel to

Lagos or the West except by air. This created difficulties in resuming the conference on the constitution on 24th October as was planned. Ojukwu therefore urged Gowon to remove all Northern troops from Lagos and the West. Fortunately for the Mid-West, there had never been any military barracks or presence in the whole of that region even from colonial times.

During the early stages of the conference, the East was quite happy with its progress. They thought that they had convinced the Northern delegations to accept confederation as the system of government, and to drop their insistence on the creation of states, then the conference was adjourned to 24th October. Before that day, the killings started again, and the East warned that its delegation would not travel to Lagos unless Northern troops were removed from both Lagos and the Western regions. That did not happen. Yet they travelled to Lagos for the conference on the 24th October.

However, unknown to the Eastern delegates, during the adjournment the leaders of the non-Ibo speaking East had successfully lobbied the North and they had changed their minds on the two issues. The Western and Mid-Western delegates were not particularly strong on either of the issues although they supported the creation of more states and preferred federation rather than confederation.

Thus, when the conference resumed the official Easterners were dumbfounded to hear that the North were against a confederation and advocated the immediate creation of states to end the imbalance that had existed since 1945. The furious Eastern official delegates walked out of the conference. Up until this point, those who supported the creation of states expected that there would to be one in the North and one in the East as the mid-West had already been created out of the West.

The one in the East would include the old provinces of

Calabar, Ogoja and Rivers. Chief Eyo and Wenike Briggs would be satisfied with that. But Chief Harold Biriye had for long advocated the creation of a Rivers State by itself, in the area formerly known as the Rivers Province. Unlike the provinces of Calabar and Ogoja, the people of the Niger Delta, otherwise Rivers Province, had centuries of close affinity with Southern Ibos, particularly those from the Owerri and Oguta areas would have liked the closeness to continue, albeit, not by one dominating the other on account of its larger population' insisted their leaders. Chiefs Harold Biriye and Wenike Briggs

Earlier, on the 21st October, the Federal Military Government in which the East was not represented declared that Nigeria was an integral and indivisible unit, and that any attempt by any section to use force to split the country or to secede would be regarded as treasonable. It also warned that, unlike the Congo, Nigeria would not allow foreign elements to encourage any section to attempt secession.

With the East withdrawing from the conference, there were hardly any more matters common to the rest of the country. Easterners felt themselves like pariahs in the country. The situation frightened millions of them everywhere outside their own region, and so the exodus gathered speed. Fearing for their lives, even those that had never been to the East before were compelled to leave their homes for their unknown roots.

The rhetoric between Ojukwu and Gowon continued towards a bitter confrontation and showdown. Ojukwu contended that to recognise Gowon as the successor of General Ironsi would mean that he had accepted the authority of a rebellious army and he insisted that that would: "spell doom for discipline in the military". Also, that if, however, Gowon and his friends in the army had staged a coup which had removed Ironsi, then that coup would not succeed in the Eastern region. He was reminded that it was an already undisciplined and rebellious army that kept him as governor of the East. Very often political arguments do not follow the line of reason, and Ojukwu held firmly to that line of argument.

Despite the threat of a civil war which the East was at that time unprepared for, Ojukwu confronted Gowon. Everyone in the Eastern Region who suggested a peaceful approach was considered a traitor, not only by Ojukwu but also by the great majority whose reasoning capacities had been destroyed by bitterness. Like many other leaders in Africa, Ojukwu did not like to hear voices other than his own. The regime detained dissenting voices, particularly from the non-Ibo areas. They were presumed to be fifth columnists.

While still not co-operating with Gowon, and therefore, the federal government, Ojukwu, on 20th November at the third meeting of the Eastern Region Consultative Assembly, which he set up, said that his regime would resist an attempt to impose any constitution on it. Everyone of its 360 members cheered enthusiastically.

A few days later, he suggested that all the regions of the federation should: "Pull apart autonomously for five years" and at the end of the fifth year, they should meet and consider a workable system of government. No other regional leaders supported this view; not even Chief Awolowo who had been advocating: *"A confederation of sovereign states with common essential services"*.

To these statements Gowon responded by warning that: "If circumstances compel me to preserve the integrity of Nigeria by force, I shall do my duty to my country". He then spoke at length stating:

> *"My long-term aim is the preservation of one Nigerian Army and one country. For a start however, and because of the general distrust and*

*suspicion in the country, the bulk of the Army in each region must be drawn from indigenous people of that region. In furtherance of this aim, steps are being taken to recruit more Westerners into the Army ... Those who advocate the withdrawal of Northern troops from the Western region admit that any immediate wholesale withdrawal of Northern soldiers from Western regions is not practicable. Law and order and the entire national security arrangement would break down if the troops were withdrawn at once ...*

*"We must also discourage any attempt to revive tribal consciousness and regional animosity ... It is quite clear that our common need in Nigeria is that no one region or tribal group should be in a position to dominate the others... Given the present size and distribution of the Nigerian population and resources, the country could be divided into not less than eight and not more than fourteen states. The principle for the creation of new states will be:*

*1. No one state should be in a position to dominate or control the central government;*

*2. Each state should form one compact geographical area;*

*3. Administrative convenience, the fact of history and the wishes of the people;*

*4. It is essential that the new states should be created simultaneously ... "*

Gowon's view was more popular as it was more likely to reduce tribal friction or conflicts, than those advocated by Chief Awolowo, the Western region and Lagos, which declared on

17th December: "That states should be created on linguistic and ethnic basis". The country has more than 400 different linguistic and ethnic groups. Of these groups, three each have more than 10 million people. The rest have an average of 100,000 people each. It would be difficult to create states as proposed by the leaders of the Western region without creating dominant tribal states in a community which is deeply tribally conscious.

The solution that many suggested was to create three or four states out of each of the larger tribes and to combine a number of the smaller tribes into other states. That was the position during most of the colonial era. Then, the Ibos were in two provinces while the Rivers Province, like the Calabar Province, consisted of more than ten linguistic or ethnic groups. These boundaries reduced the possibility of domination considerably.

By December 1966, the determination of Ojukwu for a showdown with Yakubu Gowon was becoming extremely dangerous by the week and it was getting clear to many that it would end in a bloody clash in which many more people would be killed than in all the coups, counter-coups and pogroms earlier in the year. It is the sad trait of leaders in Africa that they fight and fight each other on issues which may seem to others as unimportant. The often catastrophic consequences on their people is of little consequence to them.

Ojukwu's anger against Gowon seemed at first to be based on the leadership of the Army following the absence of Ironsi. But later the anger was enlarged to include the problems of North versus South and the massacre of Easterners. His tongue lashing of Gowon quickly inflamed the East particularly against Gowon, the North and the Federal Government. A successful revenge for the massacres could have given the Ibos some satisfaction. But revenge was impossible. That fact was frustrating and painful. An acceptance of confederation would have given the Eastern leadership some excuse with which to appease their followers. When all else failed, it was secession that was left for consideration. The region has everything that encourages secession. It had more than two hundred miles of coastline on the Atlantic as well as the Niger River providing access to the interior. Extensive oil wells had just begun to be exploited. There was also considerable sympathy for the Easterners on account of the massacres, from members of the international community. However, the East consisted of many other ethnic groups besides Ibos. They dominated the northern areas with about forty-five percent of the population. The other ethnic groups include Ijaw, Eches, Ogonis, Effiks and Ibibios who occupied the coastal delta regions where the oil wells were located. These people were not on the whole attracted to the idea of secession to the same degree as the Ibos. They generally supported a united Nigeria in a truly federal structure. 'It seems safer to belong to a minor tribe where there are many other minor and major tribes' they argued.

# Chapter 14

## Search for Reconciliation

In the days before 1966 there was little rapport between the leaders of Ghana and Nigeria. Both countries were drawn into the Cold War between the Warsaw Pact and Nato powers. In Africa, Nkrumah of Ghana was in the Casablanca group which had a greater sympathy with the East, while Balewa of Nigeria was in the Monrovia group with sympathy for the West. Balewa persistently accused Nkrumah of subverting his government. In 1963 the leaders of the Action Group, Chief Awolowo and almost all the members of the party's executive were convicted for treasonable felony in that they undertook military training in Ghana in order to return to Nigeria and overthrow the elected Federal Government headed by Balewa.

However, as it later happened, Nkrumah's government was toppled within ten weeks of the military coup that killed Balewa. The military regimes that succeeded both leaders did not inherit their aversions.

In December 1966 Ghana's military government was headed by General Akran who knew Nigeria fairly well. He realised that the differences between Gowon and Ojukwu would need the assistance of a third party, and he offered to help. Ojukwu had refused to meet Gowon anywhere in Nigeria and Akran suggested the two meet in Accra. A meeting was scheduled for January 4th 1967 in Aburi near Accra.

Akran did not attempt to chair the meeting but merely reminded them that: "the whole world is now watching you ... and you owe the fifty-six million Nigerians a duty to resolve your differences and forget the past in order to move forward."

One of Ojukwu's main concerns was the whereabouts of General Ironsi. He thought that that ought to be settled before any other matter was discussed. He felt that the continued silence about what had happened was unacceptable. Gowon, however, avoided the issue but the meeting nevertheless progressed. On Ojukwu's insistence the meeting agreed that force should not be used to settle the crisis; that there should be no more importations of weapons into the country; that there should be accurate information provided to all the regions about the weapons stored and where they were stored; and that the military should be re-organised to reflect equal admission in respect of the regions.

These matters were later stated in a communiqué at the end of the meeting, with the addition that a committee should be set up immediately to settle the problems of rehabilitation and the recovery of the properties of displaced persons. It was also agreed that the committee on the new constitution should continue to work.

The delegates returned home on the 6th January and expressed satisfaction with the meeting and its result. On the 15th January, the anniversary of Nzeogwu's coup, the Federal Government in a broadcast announced the death of General Ironsi and Colonel Fajuyi, a matter which everyone had known through rumour eleven months earlier. The broadcast also stated that there would be a period of official mourning for all those who had died since January 15th 1966. The Eastern region officially ignored the announcement.

A week later, Ojukwu warned on the radio and television that the Federal government was not implementing the agreement reached in Aburi, particularly in respect to the purchase of more weapons. He gave an example of the Federal government entering into contracts with the Italian government for the purchase of aircraft and arms. He also complained that there had been no move to get Northern troops out of the whole of the South, particularly Lagos and the Western Region. "The North still wishes to keep open a route to the South and to do so it must maintain its domination over the West", he said.

In order to enact legislation on the matters agreed in Aburi, the legal officers of the four regions and the Federal government met in Benin City late in January 1967. Within a few hours of the start of the meeting, those present realised that they had in fact differing views on the: "matters discussed and agreement reached" and that a clarification would be necessary. In particular, it was not clear whether a member of the proposed Supreme Military Council, the highest law-making body, who did not attend a particular meeting, could exercise the right of veto on decisions taken in their absence. The Eastern delegation thought that that would be the position but others did not agree. As another Aburi meeting could not be convened to resolve the matter, the meeting ended with the matter undecided.

On the 2nd March the Federal government released what it said was discussed in Aburi. According to the Federal government no firm decision was taken on any matter, and that the discussions could not become the constitution of the country. To this Ojukwu vehemently disagreed, and warned that if by the 31st March 1967, the decision at Aburi had not been implemented, he would have no alternative but to apply the decisions in the Eastern region. Then he went on the radio and spoke: "Today all high hopes and confidence born out of Aburi seem to be waning. There is evidence that those in authority in Lagos are determined to repudiate or evade the agreement reached by the country's military rulers ... the present unsettled state of affairs makes it difficult to complete plans and estimates for the coming year... and that the survival of this country, its normality and peace hinge on the implementation of Aburi".

Colonel Ojukwu also accused the Federal government of intending to blockade the Eastern region.

"These Northern-controlled governments are prepared to sink their tribal and political differences in order to achieve the objective nearer to their hearts, namely to dominate and rule Southern Nigeria. It is this policy that is today driving this country to the verge of disintegration".

Moving closer to the point of no return, Ojukwu released many of the officers detained after the January 15th coup, including Major Nzeogwu, Major Ifeajuna, who having escaped to Ghana, had been deported by General Akran after he overthrew Nkrumah.

As the military juntas continued to inveigh against each other, business throughout the country was declining fast. In the Eastern region the number of refugees now exceeded two million. In the North, with so many Easterners leaving, the Civil Service and commercial workforce had been reduced by some fifty percent. There were hardly any electricians or mechanics left in the North since it was Easterners who did this type of work.

Events continued to move fast during the month of March, with the Federal government enacting a decree which it said was a follow up of the matter discussed at Aburi. In essence, the decree established the Supreme Military Council as the highest law making body for the country. It consisted of all the four Regional Military Governors, each of whom would have absolute authority in his domain. But it did not accept secession of any region. And it provided that if any region defied the authority of the Supreme Military Council the Council could decide to take over the administration of such a region. This was an adoption of the Declaration of Emergency contained in the 1960 Constitution which enabled the Federal Parliament by a majority resolution to take over the administration of the Western Region in 1962.

The Decree, usually referred to as Gowon's Decree in the East, received different types of feelings among non-Ibos in the Eastern Region. Those at home favoured it and felt they could use it favourably, and, they tried to convince their Ibo fellow Easterners. In the Niger Delta, a delegation headed by Kalabo Onyeka met Sir Francis Ibiam, Ojukwu's right-hand man and former civilian governor of the Region, to discuss the decree.

The delegation pleaded with Sir Francis that if the Eastern Government agreed to the creation of states in the Eastern Region, all the non-Ibos in the Region would support secession with determination. They also pressed on him that the Gowon's Decree made secession much easier. "We do not think that the Yorubas in the West and the Edos and others in the mid-West will ever support a Supreme Military Council resolution to take over the administration of the Eastern Region; and it will be impossible for the North alone to undertake such a takeover." They also pleaded that the capital of an independent Eastern Nigeria must be located outside the Ibo area; and they suggested Calabar which was the capital of the former Niger Coast Protectorate that later became Southern Nigeria after 1906.

Sir Francis sympathised with the delegation but said "Time is too short to think of matters like these. Go home and support one Biafra. We're all in the same boat; we don't want Northern domination."

The non-Ibos of Eastern Nigeria who lived outside the Region, felt thwarted by Gowon's Decree. They thought it was a 'sell-out' in view of the promise to them that their interest would be protected. Their fear was that the Decree prepared the country for a confederation of the Regions "in which the East as it is will be a unit under one tribal rulership." To their most pleasant surprise, Ojukwu spurned the Decree out of hand. He wanted each Region to be autonomous at once and he did not wish to be subordinate to Gowon. A few days after the Decree was published, he went on the radio and made a long speech that he ended with a resolve statement: "We are ready to match Gowon force with force." By this time the fear of an inevitable catastrophe had begun to grip everyone in the country.

## CHAPTER 15

## The Drift to Civil War

Ojukwu did not only threaten to "Match Gowon force with force". He began to mobilise the Eastern Region. With an adequate sea coast available to him, he immediately embarked on the importation of weapons and other military hardware. He followed this up by setting up a battalion in every major town. Then he enacted laws that empowered him to declare any part of the region a 'Disturbed Area'.

The military administrator of any district declared a Disturbed Area was empowered to suspend civil administration in the area and imprison people without trial if he suspected them of subversion. In 'more serious cases' the suspect was liable to death by firing squad following the judgement of a Military Tribunal that observed no rules of evidence or of natural justice.

In order to promote a mass resolve 'To fight the North' Ojukwu published his Declaration said to be the second most famous 'Manifesto' in Biafra; the first being the Declaration of Secession. The declaration was titled ON ABURI WE STAND. It inflamed Eastern Nationalism and got the people ready for war as well as interpreting the agreement arrived at Aburi in January 1967. Ojuwku's interpretation was that at Aburi it was decided that Nigeria should become a confederate Republic in which the Eastern Region, as it was at that time, would be an autonomous state. In the preamble to the Declaration, he narrated some of the main squabbles between him and Gowon.

"Soon after our return from Aburi, Lt. Col. Gowon got in touch with me and informed me that the Government in Lagos had prepared a publication called: *Nigeria Today, 1966*. He wanted my view as to whether the publication of the booklet would be contrary to the spirit of Aburi. I personally saw in this approach an encouraging sign for the future co-operation and confidence. We discussed and agreed that since the publication had not been put out to the public it would be wise to withhold it. On the 15th January that publication was released. Its sole objective was to degrade Eastern Nigerians, dead and living."

Determined to control their own revenues, in March the East enacted The Revenue Collection Edict. This provided that the Eastern Region would from the first of April 1967 not pay any money to the Federal revenue. All revenue collection agents in the region were directed to pay all customs and other revenue including that from oil exploration and production direct to the region's exchequer. By the enactment the Federal government was immediately deprived of more than 60 percent of its revenue.

Gowon declared the enactment unconstitutional and warned all oil companies to ignore it. The companies now had to decide whether to obey the Federal government or the Eastern government where their offices and oil-producing equipment were located. While Gowon was still perplexed about the revenue edict, the East enacted another edict which transferred all the statutory bodies that carried out business in the East to the East. This included the railways and all its equipment and properties, the Nigerian Airways and all other corporations.

These acts were confirmation that there was now little hope for compromise. The Federal Supreme Military Council met on the 20th April and stated that it would disband the regions created in 1945 to 1947 by Sir Arthur Richards and in their place create states as the units of the federation. It also announced that it would convene a constitutional conference in order to conclude a new constitution and thereafter organise an election in order to prepare for a new civilian regime in 1968.

In an effort presumably to bid for time, Ojukwu announced on 23rd April that he had spoken to Gowon on the telephone and that both of them had agreed that they would not use force: "to settle the dispute". He also indicated that they had proposed to meet again outside the country in search of a solution to the crisis. However, the Federal government did not approve these assertions.

Gowon did not enjoy full support for the steps he took against Ojukwu. In particular, both the Western and Mid-West Regions were not in support of any drastic action against Ojukwu. Chief Awolowo, the first Premier of the Western region, who was imprisoned in 1963 for treasonable felony and released by Gowon, resigned from the Constitutional Committee to which Gowon had appointed him. His resignation was announced on 25th April. A week later he declared that if Eastern Nigeria were allowed to secede from the federation, then both the West and Lagos should not become involved. Earlier, he had persistently advocated confederation and the removal of Northern troops from Lagos and the West. In addition, the Governor of the Western Region, Lt. Col. Adebayo, had been absent from some meetings of the Supreme Military Council. Later he declared that a strong federation of the type: "which Lagos* and the North" wanted could not work under existing conditions. At the same time the Governor of the Mid-West, Lt. Col. Ejoor, said his region would not support one region against another. Many observers concluded that these actions and statements showed a dangerous lack of agreement

---

* Lagos here means the Federal Military Government controlled by Northern troops

with the Federal Military government.

In the East, Awolowo's statement regarding secession was interpreted to mean that the West would also secede. In fact, later, many who had 'misunderstood' Awolowo condemned him for not urging the West to secede at the same time as the East. Nevertheless, when the time came to act jointly, both Lagos and the West stood firmly behind the Federal government, particularly because of the concern for the non-Ibo population of the Eastern region.

Many influential people in Nigeria and outside had been pressing Gowon to look for conciliation. Early in May he set up a conciliation body including the Chief Justice and other influential people in the community. 'The body of peacemakers' visited Ojukwu and although the content of their meeting was not released, Gowon later relaxed some of the measures he had taken in response to the seizure of the properties of the Federal Military government. The first response was to allow Nigerian Airways to resume its flights to the East. But the plane which flew to Enugu in the East on 25th May was seized by Ojukwu, bringing the total of planes confiscated by him to three.

The day after the seizure of the third Nigerian Airways' plane, Ojukwu convened members of his 360-strong Consultative Assembly and asked them to give him the mandate to declare the secession of Eastern Nigeria as the Republic of Biafra. "It is for you as the representatives of 14 million Eastern Nigerian people to choose from: a) accepting the terms of the North and Gowon and thereby submitting to domination by the North; or b) continuing the present stalemate and drift; or c) ensuring the survival of our people by asserting our autonomy ..." He then warned them that independence might bring temporary hardship and might entail war, but after independence, there could be arrangements for association with other countries including Nigeria, and that Biafrans could still travel to Nigeria without having to carry passports and other documents. The essential thing was that the new country would look after itself. The Assembly gave overwhelming support to the mandate: "to proclaim Eastern Nigeria as the Republic of Biafra as soon as possible."

Alarmed by the finality of Ojukwu's action, and ignoring his 'wet' advisors and prophets of doom, Gowon took the bold step of creating the states he had earlier promised. Twelve states were created as the units of the Nigerian Federation, and each of them to a large extent reflected linguistic and ethnic factors. The Yorubas were placed in the Western State, whilst the Ibos were in the East Central State. The rest of the East was grouped into the South-Eastern and Rivers States. The creation of the S-E was a combination of the former provinces of Calabar and Ogoja; whilst the Rivers State remained as the former Rivers Province as it had been before 1945. It gave infinite satisfaction to all the non-Ibos in the East and weakened Ojukwu's strategy, because these two states contain the oil wells in the former Eastern region and they also contained all the seaports of the region. The next move was the fight to survive the assault of neighbouring Biafra which taunted the two states, saying they were: "paper states devised by Gowon to con the poor non-Ibos in the East to support his designs against Biafra". And they accused Gowon of treason.

The name Biafra had no relevance whatsoever to historical experiences in the area. Centuries earlier, the Portuguese had given the name Biafra to the large bay in the tropical Atlantic in the area about where the delta of the then unknown River Niger, emptied into the Atlantic Ocean. But in 1967, when the name was adopted by Ojukwu, many believed that some ancient kingdom of that name had existed and that it was now re-born. This earned considerable sympathy for the secession.

On 30th May, Ojukwu proclaimed Eastern Nigeria as the Independent Republic of Biafra, after reciting the events which began the crisis. In the proclamation he declared that:

*"All political ties between us and the Federal Republic of Nigeria are hereby dissolved ... All subsisting international obligations and treaties made on behalf of Eastern Nigeria by the Federal Republic of Nigeria shall be honoured. Eastern Nigeria's due share of all subsisting international debts and obligations shall be honoured. Steps will be taken to open discussions on the question of Eastern Nigeria's due shares of the Federation of Nigeria and personal properties of the citizens of Biafra throughout the Federation. We shall protect the lives and property of all foreigners residing in Biafra. We shall extend friendship to those who respect our sovereignty and shall repel any interference in our internal affairs. We shall faithfully adhere to the Charter of the African Organization of Unity. It is our intention to remain a member of the British Commonwealth of Nations. Long live the Republic of Biafra and may God protect all who live in her".*

The new Biafran anthem was played amidst the hoisting of the Biafran flag. The people congratulated one another, shouting: "Happy New Country; Nigeria is Dead; Long Live Biafra; Ignore the Paper States; Gowon has gone insane".

In Lagos, Gowon denounced the secession of Eastern Nigeria and said it was an act of rebellion which would be crushed. He re-stated his determination to use force to keep Nigeria as one unit. He warned all ships to keep away from the

Eastern ports and he ordered a general mobilization of all able-bodied servicemen. He closed all the principal ports of the East including Bonny, Calabar, Degema and Port Harcourt, and ordered the Navy to enforce the closure. In order to protect the Nigerian currency, which then was in the denomination of pounds sterling, he prohibited all imports and exports of Nigerian currency, and he introduced strict rules of exchange control. The roads between the East and the rest of the country were closed. Many more Easterners, particularly Ibos, who had not already left other areas of the country, now left in greater numbers. Still, some remained.

# CHAPTER 16

# The Civil War 1967-1970

By June 1967 the tongue-lashings between Gowon and Ojukwu had become less frequent, but all were aware of Gowon's promise to use force against Ojukwu if he seceded. Neither side actually declared war against the other, nevertheless the fighting that was soon to start was called the Nigeria-Biafra war by Biafra and the Civil War by Nigeria.

Many countries in Africa that were calling on Britain to use force against Ian Smith's unilaterally-declared independence for Rhodesia in 1964, could not persuade Gowon not to do the same. Besides many of the non-Ibos in the East were themselves imploring Gowon to deliver them from Biafra. Many rushed to join the Federal army. The Yorubas and Edos (Benins), concerned with the plight of the non-Ibos supported Gowon, particularly as Ojukwu had refused to confine Biafra to the Ibo areas of the East.

While Ojukwu and Gowon positioned themselves for the inevitable conflict, observers considered their respective advantages of strength. Before 1914, in the days of the Royal Niger Company in the North, Lugard had used Northern troops in the West African Frontier Force to protect British interests against French threats in the area and in the Ashanti war. From that time until 1950 the military in Nigeria consisted solely of Northerners with British officers. It was after 1950 that a number of Southern graduates were recruited into the army, mainly in the officer ranks. At independence the country had about 7,000 troops in more than ten battalions of which only one was situated in the East and 60 percent of the troops there were Northerners. More than ninety percent of the country's military hardware was situated outside the East and mostly in the North. The North also had more than two hundred miles of common border with the Ibo area of the East. In addition to this, nearly half the population of Biafra were non-Ibos who lived on the coastal areas and could not be counted on to support or fight for Biafra.

From this it was clear from the start that Biafra was severely disadvantaged militarily. In addition, the Ibos, unlike the Hausa-Fulani of the North, did not have a history of warfare even amongst themselves. During the colonial period, like the rest of the South, the East despised the military as purely a 'foreign concern' which they should have nothing to do with. When Easterners did join the Army during the Second World War, it was in the auxiliary sections. Very few joined as combatants. The East had few weapons and less than 600 professionally-trained soldiers of all ranks. In addition to this, the military in Enugu was not in total harmony. Many of the senior officers who returned to the East were not quickly rehabilitated and they blamed that on Ojukwu. Ojukwu retired to the University of Nsukka for retreat and prayer. It was here that he received overwhelming support from the students who formed 'The Young Biafran Revolutionaries'. They swore: "To fight anyone who dared to oppose Ojukwu at this dangerous time in the history of Biafra".

As Biafran leaders miscalculated that Gowon would have the backing of all the other regions, they also got it wrong that most of the international community would rush to support them and pressurise the Federal government, or in some other way, make the secession of ALL of the East a *fait accompli*. Their efforts throughout the crisis were mostly geared towards this direction. Foreign journalists who travelled to Biafra saw only the side which the establishment wanted them to see. In fact it was impossible for them to hear the faint voices of the minorities, many of whom were locked up anyway, or were in their respective villages praying clandestinely for Gowon to succeed, while the determined and jubilant major tribe revelled in Enugu with jolly foreign journalists and visitors.

In Nigeria rumours are often quite reliable. Without any announcement of the beginning of hostilities, the rumour that the war had begun on the 6th July in the old Ogoja province of the East, was spreading. This was not reported in local newspapers due largely to fear on their part. It was only after foreign radio stations had announced fighting, that the Federal government made a statement and said it had begun to use 'Police Action' to crush the rebellion. Of course, Radio Biafra gave a report of fighting but because many were prejudiced about it, only very few tuned-in to it at the beginning of the war.

During the third week of the war, federal troops were already threatening Nsukka, only about sixty-five miles from Enugu, the capital of Biafra. It was a most dangerous situation for Biafra. Its war leaders thereupon decided to do something to distract the federal drive. About sixty miles South of Enugu is Onitsha on the River Niger where there is a bridge that connects the Eastern region to the Mid-West at Asaba. The Governor of the Mid-West had earlier informed Gowon that he was not prepared to get involved with a war against the East. Because of this, Gowon did not garrison the area, leaving the road between Asaba and Benin, the capital, free. From Benin, Lagos was some two hundred and fifty miles.

Biafra decided to take advantage of the position of the Mid-West. Early on 4th August it amassed troops at Onitsha, estimated at around 8,000 men. Victor Banjo, one of the two Yoruba officers whom Ironsi had detained in the January coup, but who Ojukwu had released in April, was one of the four military leaders of the Mid-West operation. The others were Ifeajuna, Alele and Sam Agbam. All these officers were of the Nigerian Army, trained in Britain. With Ojukwu's blessing, they successfully drove their troops, together with several armoured vehicles, and took up positions in Benin City at about 2am.

They easily took control of the radio station and tried to capture the Governor, David Ejoor, but fortunately he escaped. By 4am a contingent of Biafran soldiers was heading for Ibadan, the capital of the West, where they had hoped to be joined by a pro-Biafran group. Another contingent proceeded to Warri and Sapele, 50 miles South of Benin, where they shot five Italian oil rig workers. Soon Biafra Radio was announcing its great victory in the Mid-West and that they were now heading for Ibadan and Lagos. Reaching Lagos would not have necessarily won the war for Biafra, but it would have certainly caused considerable chaos and damage to the Federal action.

At 4am Victor Banjo announced on Mid-West radio:

*"Fellow countrymen and women, this is Lt.Col. Victor Banjo, Commander of the Liberation Army of Biafra, now in the Mid-West State of Nigeria, wishing you a good morning. By power vested in me, I the said Victor Banjo hereby declare the former Mid-West State of Nigeria the Sovereign Republic of Benin. The new Republic will observe all international obligations entered into on its behalf by the former Republic of Nigeria. All citizens of the new republic are advised to carry on their lawful business. My troops are ordered to shoot on sight any person caught looting or causing trouble. There will be a curfew from the hours of 5pm to 7am. May God save the new Republic of Benin".*

Congratulations and approval poured into Biafra from many parts of the world. Some commentators called it: "The Great Biafran Blitzkrieg. Many in Nigeria were frightened at the new turn in events. Gowon, however, seemed unshaken and more cheerful than many thought he should have been when he appeared on television that day and announced to the nation: "The rebels will be routed from the Mid-West within ten days". He also said that he had hoped that the rebels would care for human losses and end the war as both Enugu and Nsukka were being threatened and could be captured within the week.

In Biafra the success of the Mid-West offensive was celebrated by millions of citizens. However, Ojukwu was not so pleased on account of the publicity that his fellow leaders, Banjo, Ifeajuna, Alele and Agbam were getting. Not much credit had been given to Ojukwu for the success of the venture. Ojukwu recalled Banjo and his team on the charge that they failed to continue the success of taking Benin by proceeding to Lagos.

The Biafran command in the Mid-West was taken over by Major Okonkwo who affirmed the independence of the Mid-West and announced that the Oba of Benin had given his blessing to the "Autonomous Republic of Benin" which he said would co-operate militarily with Biafra. Meanwhile Federal troops had begun a retaliatory offensive on the Mid-West and on 20th September Federal troops led by Shuwa Mohammed entered the city. Within a few days the area was secured and the Biafrans had fled back to the East. The people of Asaba on the Mid-West/Biafran border indicated that they would support and fight for Biafra, however their resolve melted fairly quickly when faced with the Federal troops.

The Biafran leadership soon began to look for scapegoats to mollify their people.

"The simple truth was that throughout the war, Biafran top brass were all the time looking for scapegoats in order to cover their inefficiencies and failures".* For the failure to hold the Mid-West and to proceed speedily to Ibadan and Lagos on a walk-over expedition, the scapegoats were Victor Banjo, Emmanuel Ifeajuna, Samuel Agbam and Phillip Alele. "The four officers failed to carry out the grand design to conquer the enemy within twenty-four hours driving from Onitsha to Benin, Ibadan and Lagos." On top of this, they added a charge of treason for: "Plotting to overthrow the Biafran Government". The arrest, trial by a sole judge, conviction and execution of the four men took less than seven days. Thereafter, Biafra continued to decline daily.

It began in Nsukka which is situated about 30 miles North of Enugu. Nsukka and its several villages are on the fringes of a large tropical forest which stretches to the River Benue on the border of Northern Nigeria. The forest is luxuriant, with thousands of colossal trees towering some three hundred feet. There is much wildlife; snakes, monkeys, chimpanzees, baboons and gorillas. It was through this forest that Federal troops had to pass in order to reach Nsukka and thereby threaten Enugu. It was in this operation that Chukwumeka Nzeogwu finally lost his life. He was honourably buried by Federal troops, many of whom realised that "his coup in January had not been motivated by tribalism but rather nationalism, however misguided".

After Nsukka, it was Enugu that occupied the attention

*Bernard Odugwu: No PLace to Hide - Crisis in Biafra, Fourth Dimension (Enugu) Publishers, 1980. Odugwu was Chief Director of Intelligence in Biafra of the Federal forces. The city was pounded by artillery until eventually the residents, realising the imminent fall of the city, began a mass exodus into the dark night. There were chaotic scenes of people, vehicles of all sorts, wagons colliding with each other in the rush to escape the Federal onslaught. By the time the Federal troops entered the city it was empty except for the vultures circling the city. However, they could hear Radio Biafra announcing that: "The vandals from murderous Gowon had been repelled from Enugu with heavy casualties." People were also warned not to travel to Enugu "as it is now a disaster area".

Following the fall of Enugu, Biafra moved its headquarters to Umuahia, 90 miles South of Enugu and about 90 North of Bonny, the oil port on the Atlantic. Within three months of the fall of Enugu, Federal troops led by Brigadier Adekunle had landed at Bonny, and from there began to threaten Port Harcourt. Meanwhile, in Western Biafra, Federal troops with the support of the Mid-West had captured both Onitsha and Nnewi, the home town of Ojukwu.

It was at this stage that civilian leaders and former politicians began to exert pressure on the Biafran military to look for a peaceful solution. One of the earliest peace discussions took place in Kinshasa (Zaire)* under the auspices of the Organisation of African Unity (OAU) on 23rd November 1967. Its chairman, The Emperor Haile Selassie, addressed the meeting and said that the purpose was to explore ways and means for a peaceful settlement whereby the country's national integrity was preserved and innocent Nigerian blood saved from flowing needlessly. He spoke of Ethiopia's firm belief in the national unity of individual African states as an essential ingredient of the larger and greater objective of African unity.

*It later reverted to be called the Republic of Congo, 1997

"It is precisely because of this that we oppose any attempt at national fragmentation on religious or ethnic grounds. That is why Ethiopia unreservedly supports Nigerian national unity and territorial integrity ... We believe a solution needs to be urgently sought to accommodate the varying interests in Nigeria but it must be specific enough to ensure the steady development of the Nigerian State".

At the Kinshasa meeting, Gowon, who had by now been promoted to General, said that his government was convinced that its friends in Africa could help it to solve its difficulties. He said he had removed the greatest obstacle in the country's move towards stability, that was the fear of domination of one section of the country by another. He explained that Federal forces were not fighting the Ibos as a people, and that the Government:

"believes that the Ibos, as a people need Nigeria as much as the rest of Nigeria need the Ibos" and "and we also believe that the Ibos have the same rights as other ethnic groups and that the legitimate needs of each ethnic group can be justly met within the Federal Union of Nigeria."

The Biafran delegation did not address the members; but on 24th November they issued a statement that: "political unification with Nigeria was not practical". Before the close of that year two Papal emissaries, Monsignors Dominic Conway of Ireland and Georges Rocheau of France met with Gowon and Ojukwu separately, and appealed for an end to the hostilities. This was followed by the World Council of Churches, which appealed to African countries to try and persuade the parties to come together and conclude a: "Negotiated settlement". It was difficult for Biafran leaders to consider any settlement that did not include the provinces of Calabar, Ogoja and Rivers within Biafra. This made peaceful settlement of the issues more complicated as many of the people of these provinces did not want to join Biafra which was more than fifty-five percent Ibo.

The next peace initiative came from the Secretary-General of the Commonwealth, Arnold Smith, and was attended by Dr Kenneth Dike for Biafra and Dr Okio Arikpo for the Federal Government. Both men came from Eastern Nigeria; Dike from Awka in the Onitsha Province was an Ibo and Arikpo from Ogoja Province was Ugep. The meeting failed to discuss many of the issues because Biafran leaders would settle only on the basis that all non-Ibos should be included in Biafra as without the delta regions Biafra would be completely surrounded by Nigeria with no access to the sea. More importantly, it would be poor in mineral resources. "By one hundred percent, we do not want to be in Biafra" argued the non-Ibos.

Explaining the British government's policy towards a ceasefire, George Thomson MP, in the Foreign Office, told the House of Commons on 30th January that no request for assistance of any sort had been received from the Nigerian government and that Her Majesty's Government would carefully consider any proposal for a Commonwealth Peace Force submitted by the Nigerian government. On 16th February, Ojukwu was reported to have said that any plan for peace would have to provide a way for Biafra to live in peace: "not in but with Nigeria".

In March 1968, Biafra had been reduced to less than a quarter of its original size. In particular the whole South-Eastern State and Rivers State had been liberated, with their headquarters in Calabar and Port Harcourt respectively. The governors of the two states were now resident in their state capitals which again made peace on Biafran terms more difficult. A further meeting was held in Kampala, Uganda, again under the auspices of the Commonwealth, to discuss a ceasefire and other issues. It was chaired by President Milton Obote of Uganda. In his opening address, he said: "the basic issue as seen by Uganda was no longer the question as to whether the war was just or unjust; but the necessity of bringing it to an end through a formula which should include an early agreement to the cessation of hostilities and a ceasefire at an early stage ..."

On the Biafran side, the meeting was led by Sir Louis Mbanefo, the Chief Justice of Biafra and on the Federal side, Chief Anthony Enahoro, the Federal Minister of Information. Both of them addressed the meeting. Mbanefo set out Biafra's terms for a settlement or an end to the hostilities. He wanted the Federal government to remove its blockade of Biafra and withdraw its troops to the pre-war position; that is out of Biafra altogether and including the areas which the Federal government had re-taken, South-East State and Rivers State.

He said that when that had been done, Biafra would agree to the policing of the ceasefire line by an international force, pending a permanent settlement and in conjunction with the lifting of the blockade of Biafra. They would then be ready to accept supervision at the point of entry into both Biafra and Federal territory to ensure that neither side accumulated arms during the continuation of the talks. Furthermore, once a ceasefire had been achieved, the Biafran delegation would present for discussion the following proposals for a permanent settlement:

1. Maximum economic co-operation between Biafra and the rest of Nigeria, including the sharing

of common services.

2. The division between the two sides of financial assets and liabilities, including the Federation's external public debts.

3. The payment of compensation for the lives and properties of Biafrans lost as a result of the war; and

4. The holding of a plebiscite in disputed areas both inside and outside Biafra.

Sir Louis Mbanefo insisted that: "Only a separate sovereign state could guarantee Biafra's security ... No Biafran could again live with any assurance of safety in Nigeria ... To force Biafra back into the Federation would be like forcing the Jews who fled to Israel back to Nazi Germany".

Chief Anthony Enahoro replied and stated that: "A ceasefire can be concluded only when the talks had produced agreement on the conditions for ending hostilities". He accused Biafra of lying, propaganda and slander abroad, and incitement to tribal hatred at home. "If the argument is that 7,000,000 Ibos in the Eastern part of Nigeria must enjoy the right of self-determination, surely this same right must be accorded to the 5,000,000 Efiks, Ekois, and Ijaws whom the secessionist's leaders wish to force into the so-called State of Biafra. They cannot deny the long-standing demands of these articulate minorities for their own states. There is overwhelming evidence of mass intimidation and brutality conducted by the Ojukwu regime against these people".

Continuing, Chief Enahoro said that:

"The Secessionist's leaders know that they were deceiving the world with their argument for the need of an Ibo state called Biafra. Many of their supporters had privately conceded that such a state would not be viable, and this is why Col. Ojukwu is insisting on the retention of the South-East and Rivers States, on the pretext that he needed an outlet to the sea. In military terms the concept of Biafra is now dead in view of the fact that Enugu, Port Harcourt, Calabar and Onitsha are all under Federal control, and the rebel regime is now confined to two or three towns and their environs in the interior of the so-called Ibo heartland".

While the talks were in progress there was a sudden agitation in the Federal camp. Johnson Banjo, a confidential secretary: "had disappeared with many secret documents". It was feared that he had been abducted, and that put the wind up many of the delegation. The incident embarrassed the Ugandan government and the police were alerted to look for Banjo, but he was not found dead or alive.

When the talks resumed, Chief Enahoro for the Federal government gave the conditions for a ceasefire. Among them were that Biafra should renounce secession, and that observers would supervise the disarming of rebel troops. The Federal government would takeover the areas not yet liberated. Rejecting Chief Enahoro's proposal, Sir Louis Mbanefo said:

"We have not come all this way to indulge in the preparatory discussion for a whole month, simply to surrender in Kampala."

Later Enahoro said in Lagos that: "The realities of war have not been brought home to those Biafrans who live abroad". After the failure of the Kampala peace talks, the British government sent Lord Shepherd to both sides for conciliatory talks. But that too failed. Embarrassed by Ojukwu's claim that bombs used against Biafra were British-made; Lord Shepherd denied the accusation and told Parliament on 29th April that the export of bombs to Nigeria had been forbidden; further that the bombs in question had been examined and found not to be British.

As the fighting continued both sides were reported to be using the services of mercenaries. On the Federal side the London *Times* reported on 8th January 1968 that the mercenaries on the Federal sides were British, Egyptian and South African pilots and a: "small number of Soviet air-training personnel and British and Indian naval-training officers". On the Biafran side, French, German and Italian pilots were serving. On 8th January, Ojukwu admitted that British and French mercenaries were serving with the Biafran forces but he denied that Col. Robert Denard, the famous French mercenary leader, was serving in Biafra. However, another French popular mercenary, Brig. Rene Faulgues, headed a brigade of European mercenaries to fight for Biafra in defence of Bonny. Ojukwu also alleged that Nigerians were using Islamic mercenaries from Niger, Chad and South Africa. Supporters of the use of mercenaries on both sides often referred to the use of foreign troops by the Great Powers such as the French Foreign Legion and the British use of Gurkha troops.

One of the difficulties which confronted Biafra right from the date of secession was foreign recognition. It would buoy her up internally and help her international standing. Biafrans worked very hard in order to gain international recognition. In this way the war would be internationalised. Minorities in the East tried to prevent the recognition of Biafra, however on 13th April 1968, Tanzania recognised Biafra as an independent country. This was quickly followed by Gabon which announced her recognition of Biafra on the 8th May. The Federal government condemned these recognitions, seeing them as: "a stab in the back for African Unity". In less than a week after Gabon announced its recognition, Ivory Coast also recognised Biafra as: "an independent state enjoying international sovereignty". As the announcement was made in Paris, the Nigerian government were concerned that France might also recognise Biafra. The Federal government immediately severed diplomatic ties with the Ivory Coast saying: "It was ridiculous to announce the recognition of a non-existent republic." Zambia also broke off diplomatic relations with Nigeria following its recognition of Biafra.

Ojukwu had performed his hat trick over recognition but unfortunately had not yet been able to convince France to join the group. Very influential in Europe as well as having great influence in the French speaking countries such as Zaire, Congo, Dahomey, and Upper Volta (later Burkina Fasso), France attempted to announce its recognition in steps. The first was on 31st July, when it announced that the Biafrans had demonstrated their will to assert themselves as a people: "and that the civil war must be resolved by appropriate international procedures on the basis of the right of people to dispose of themselves". That day, Chiefs Eyo and Wenike Briggs sped to Cotonue in Dahomey* and sought audience with the Foreign Ministry officials. They handed a long petition to them explaining the situation in Eastern Nigeria since Sir Arthur Richards in 1945 designated the whole area as one region without regard to the ethnic composition of the area. They returned with smiles which expressed success that there would be no more recognition; at least for some time. Also they seemed to be sure that no amount of recognition would remove the State Governors – Col. Eusene and Commander Diete-Spiff, from their headquarters in Calabar and Port Harcourt respectively.

By November, several friendly countries had tried in vain

*Now the Republic of Benin

to intercede. They all realised that the two parties to the conflict seemed too resolved to fight to the end; as was the trait of African leaders. There are abundance of examples in the Congo, Rhodesia (later Zimbabwe), Somalia, Ethiopia, Sudan and Angola. The leaders have hearts made of stone; they never feel sorry for the millions of barrels of blood that were being wasted by their people on account of conflicts founded on their own personal differences. After every country had given up trying to settle the conflict, it was Christian organisations, charities and Red Cross bodies in Europe that sustained millions of lives in the Biafran enclave. Shamefully, no African organisation helped the poor and suffering people.

But the war was not all about liberating rebel-held areas and talking peace; thousands grew rich from it. These included many Italians, French, English, Poles, Americans and even Nigerians. They were arms dealers and runners many of who cheated the Biafrans by selling them unservicable oddments of weapons as old as the Crimean War Period. They presented the old weapons as sophisticated weapons designed and made during the Cold War. Some never supplied any arms at all.

As well as the arms dealers, many Biafran 'ambassadors' were accused of not accounting for donations from supporters in Asia, Europe and America which were intended for the starving and sick, many whom were children. In both Nigerian and Biafran war zones, some businessmen grew rich as they cheated by inflating the numbers of bodies they buried daily. Many women were engaged in the 'attack trade'. With the connivance of some of the lower-ranked officers, women carried goods from nearby Nigerian towns to newly liberated areas and sold them for large profits plus commission to the middlemen.

Biafran currency notes were not accepted in any country outside Biafra, and Biafra had no postal service. Many businessmen took advantage of these hardships and took large sums of Biafran currency to the US where it was exchanged for dollars and then the Biafran currency sent to Gabon (which recognised Biafra). Because the flights were not reliable, many lost their hard-earned dollars.

By the beginning of 1969, many of the older elite of Biafra began to feel that they had enough of the misery and the suffering which had visited them since May 1966. Yet the end was not in sight. The future still looked bleak. Many had run out of ideas that could help to sustain the morale of the masses much longer. Not even the military leaders were now enjoying the confidence of the people and Ojukwu himself did not know what next to do. He had fled his capital twice, and he had reduced his rhetoric against Gowon considerably. Everyone was exhausted and longed for a peaceful solution. However, none of the other countries was willing to intercede, again. Some of them realised that behind the pompous determination, there was weakness and internal conflict in Biafra.

Every day brought bad news for the survival of Biafra. Early in December, Brigadier Obasenjo's Division routed the remnants of Biafra's 58 Brigade and sped into Umuahia and threatened the tiny bit that was Biafran. There the top elite who had not already fled to Nigeria, boxed themselves in, wondering what would happen to them once the Federal troops got to them.

On 6th January 1970, in the village of Etiti which had been the new home of Ojukwu and other civilian and military leaders of Biafra, Dr Ibiam convened all of them for: "Family discussion". He asked everyone to speak without fear and to say whether it was wise to continue the war in view of the fact that they had lost more than 80 percent of the original Biafra. "Can we fight and retake all these places?" he asked. Some borrowed Ukpabi Asika's* phrase and said: "Enough is enough".

*Ukpabi Asika was the Administrator of the East-Central State. Gowon appointed him to succeed Ojukwu after he declared sessession. He moved to Enugu when it was liberated.

Some who believed that several heavy sophisticated weapons were still hidden in the home of Ojukwu at Nnewi, near Onitsha, argued that if those weapons were brought to them, they could carry the war right to the doorstep of Gowon's home. Thereupon even the junior officers who said: "enough is enough" changed their minds and agreed with others that if they were to be provided with sufficient weapons, they could carry on the fight, even in the bush, to the last man. With this Ojukwu concurred, though he appeared absent-minded. He was himself thinking how he could plan his own escape within the next forty-eight hours. All of them knew that they could not at that time be provided with more weapons than they had during the preceding three years. Unlike the junior officers, the senior ones were still afraid that the civilians would think they were cowards, if they spoke as candidly as them.

Ojukwu, who did not say much at the meeting, knew perfectly well that it was not shortage of weapons that had caused the constant defeat of his army. On 6th May 1968 he said: "I started off this struggle in July with 120 rifles to defend the entirety of the East. I took my stand knowing fully that doing so, while carving my name in history, I was signing also my death-warrant. But I took it because I believe that this stand was vital to the survival of the South. I appealed for settlement quickly, because I understand that this was a naked struggle for power and that the only time we can sit down and decide the future of Nigeria on the basis of equality, will always be equality of arms. Quietly I built. If you do not know it, I am proud of my officers". Yet many in Nigeria admired the courage of the East: "for they had courage but no arms". However, as this speech by Ojukwu became popular, too many in the South regretted that he did not make himself understood in the South.

As the Biafran leaders were ending their last meeting, the Federal troops moved into Owerri and threatened Biafra's only airstrip at Ulli. Gowon congratulated them and urged them to observe the code of conduct they had been given and to take proper care of displaced persons. To the Biafrans still wanting to fight, Gowon warned that at this stage it was totally futile and purposeless to continue the fight. He called upon foreign countries not to interfere with the area so as not to cause more serious suffering to the population by prolonging the war.

This was the time, when on the 11th January 1970, Pope Paul VI addressed a crowd at St Peters in Rome and declared that he had made efforts in vain to assist in settling the conflict in Biafra; now he fears: "that the victory of arms will cause torment against the public in Biafra and may carry with it the killing of countless people. There are those who actually fear a kind of genocide. We wish to exclude such a horrendous hypothesis for the honour of the African people and of their leaders who have themselves excluded it with many explicit assurances".

The following day, the Pope again addressed a gathering of the Diplomatic corps at the Vatican and declared:

> "I urge all men of goodwill to try if possible to prevent the Nigerian conflict from becoming a fearful tragedy and from concluding with an epilogue even more cruel than the horror involved in any conflict ...* And he appealed to all governments to prevent 'new bloodshed' and to spare innocent lives in respect for international law ... We know that the Nigerian authorities have again shown their will to assure everybody, including their adversaries, of respect for human and civil rights. This already represents a good sign

---

* In 1935 his predecessor Pius XI had blessed Mussolini's troops for the conquest of Abyssina (now Ethiopia)

and a happy promise. May history tomorrow attest to the magnanimity of all those who have taken part in this decisive event. The Holy See, for its part is ready to do everything to humanize this grievous situation, and with this aim, is ready to bring into play all the means at its disposal".

In Lagos the Federal government responded by accusing the Pope of: "having sustained the rebellion with money and vital supplies and transportation links with the outside world ... and the role of the Vatican in the crisis had had tragic consequences of prolonging rebel resistance leading to deaths of many innocent people and distress for the population in these areas". John Garbar, the Nigerian Ambassador in Rome, told a press conference on 12th January that it was not the intention of the Federal government to carry out reprisals against Ibos and that Nigerians were fully aware of their responsibility for the welfare of all Nigerians including the rebels who laid down their arms.

Early in the morning on 10th January 1970 Biafrans heard what many of them could not believe. It was the recorded announcement by Ojukwu that he had already left the country. He went on to say:

> *"Proud and heroic Biafrans, fellow countrymen and women, I salute you. My Government has been reviewing the progress of the war that has now raged for the best part of two and half years with increasing fury. It is well that at each stage we remind ourselves of the purpose of this war, what we are fighting to safeguard, and why we are so determined to continue to defend ourselves ... Throughout we had made strenuous efforts for*

*peace, taking initiatives of our own to get peace talks going, made compromises in order to get our adversaries to settle our conflict at the conference table. Each condition that we fulfil gives rise to an entirely new one. More recently, some friends of both sides have made some proposals for an arrangement with Nigeria that in our view will offer Biafrans the security to which we aspire. That has been referred to certain forms of union, confederation, association or commonwealth arrangement with Nigeria.*

*"Once more to show our honesty, and in accord with my own frequent affirmation that I would personally go anywhere to secure peace and security for my people, I am travelling out of Biafra to explore with our friends all those proposals further and fully and to be at hand to settle these issues to the best of my ability, always serving the interests of my people. Our detractors may see this move as a sign of collapse of our struggle, or an escape from my responsibilities ... In my short absence I have arranged for the Chief of the General Staff, Major-General Phillip Effiong, to administer the government with the rest of the cabinet to administer the republic ..."*

Baffled military and civilian leaders of Biafra were dumbfounded by the announcement. They hurried to General Effiong who told them that Ojukwu told him he was going for a meeting and would get in touch with him, but had not yet done so. The small group of Biafran elite led by Sir Louis Mbanefo, Chief Justice of Biafra, then met with Effiong. The group then drafted an appeal to Nigeria to afford them an: "armistice to make an orderly disengagement".

Still working on the effort for a face-saving solution, the group settled on the draft which Effiong announced as follows:

*"Fellow countrymen; as you know, I was asked to be the Officer Administrating the Government of the Republic on 10th January, 1970. Since then I know that some of you have been waiting to hear a statement from me. I have had extensive consultations with the leaders of the community, both military and civil and I am now encouraged and hasten to make this statement to you by the mandate of the Armed Forces and the people of this country. I have assumed the leadership of this government ... I am convinced now that a stop must be put to the bloodshed which is going on as a result of the war. I am also convinced that the suffering of our people must be brought to an immediate end. Our people are now disillusioned and those elements of the old government regime who have made negotiations and reconciliation impossible have voluntarily removed themselves from our midst.*

*"I have therefore instructed an orderly disengagement of troops, I am dispatching emissaries to make contact with Nigeria's field commanders in places such as Onitsha, Calabar, Owerri, Aba and Enugu with a view to arranging an armistice. I urge on General Gowon in the name of humanity to order his troops to pause while an armistice is negotiated in order to avoid the mass suffering caused by the movement of the population. I also thank his Holiness the Pope, the Joint Church Aid and other relief organisations for the help they*

*had given us for the relief and suffering of millions. I appeal to all governments to prevail on the Federal government to order their troops to stop all military operations. May God help us all".*

"With sincerity", Brigadier Obasanjo, the Federal Commander in the area, approached the Biafran military and civilian leaders and quickly enabled them to reply to his jokes and humour. Their fears then vanished. Later he flew with Effiong and some other Biafran leaders to Lagos to meet General Gowon, for the surrender, not armistice, ceremony. During that short ceremony, General Effiong resumed his Nigerian rank as Major and said: "I, Phillip Effiong do hereby declare that we are all loyal Nigerian citizens and ... we accept the authority of the Federal Military Government of Nigeria ... and that the Republic of Biafra ceases to exist."

In response, a jubilant Gowon embraced Effiong and said: "We welcome you back into our fold ... We're glad on this beautiful day on which we are re-united with our brothers ... Let us join hands together to build a new and prosperous Nigeria for the glory of our peoples".

Many of General Ojukwu's former admirers were disappointed that he left his people and Biafra in a manner that did not show him as a brave soldier. However, bravery and heroism are not Nigerians' known virtues.

# Chapter 17

# The Peace After the War

"We have been reunited with our brothers". This is the spirit in which Gowon accepted the renunciation of the secession and the surrender of Biafra on 15th January 1970. The date was significant. It was the fourth anniversary of the first military coup in the country. No one could foretell at that time that there would be a long queue of Nigeria's military officers wanting to take positions in the Federal and State governments. The whole country welcomed the end of the secession and of the hostilities. They expressed profound gratitude to Gowon for the manner in which he had handled the conflict, always avoiding rhetoric and measures that would have made reconciliation impossible. Many Nigerians saw the end of the civil war as also being the end of the many internal conflicts that had plagued the country since the Richard's constitution of 1945 and which got to its climax in 1964.

In Biafra, many saw the war as being a necessary evil out of which good would come. The Director of Military Intelligence, Bernard Odugwu, a powerful member of the Biafran government wrote: "A good friend once asked me whether the Civil War was a good thing or not for Nigeria, and was probably shocked when I replied that in my considered opinion it was a good thing; for despite the carnage and the material destruction it entailed, there were many good lessons it taught us as a people aspiring to forge a united, peace-loving, virile nation. Didn't the war teach us a lesson in respect for human dignity, tolerance and re-discovery of ourselves and our potential? For instance, but for the Civil War could it have been possible for us to discover the potential of our national army which was largely ceremonial before then? Today it is possible for Nigerians, and particularly those of the military, to point at a man and say: 'This is a good soldier' and also Nigeria could give a good account of herself in the event of external aggression ..."

Unfortunately a great many Nigerians may not share this view. Colonel Adekunle Fajuyi, who was killed along with General Aguiyi-Ironsi in July 1966, was said to be a good and brave soldier in the service of the United Nations in the Congo, all before the Nigerian civil war. Moreover, it cannot be said that because an army had fought against itself, it can on that experience fight an external war, particularly if that army is not highly disciplined, loyal and patriotic and does not endear itself to its people. An army that is notorious in staging coups and destroying the constituted government of its own country, cannot be said to be patriotic. Not many can seriously say that the Nigerian Army endears itself to the people. Instead, Nigerians accuse their army, saying that: "We have been ruined and plundered by a gang of trigger-happy crooks." Many Nigerians have a love-hate relationship with the highly-politicised military. Since June 12th 1993, many Nigerians have been saying that the country learned nothing at all from the civil war. How much 'respect for human dignity' have any of the military rulers learnt since the civil war?

Bernard's view was, however, not necessarily shared by the country as a whole. Too many people, military and civilian, had been killed over the past years since the first coup in January 1966, including the Prime Minister, state premiers and senior army officers, not to talk of the thousands and thousands of ordinary people.

However, with respect to the end of the civil war, despite Gowon's loud expressions of jubilation and forgiveness, conditions in the East after the war continued to be extremely miserable. A negotiated settlement would have gone some way to avoid the abjectly poor conditions in which people had to live. It would have also protected public servants who later became subjected to compulsory retirement without benefits under a decree promulgated in August 1970. The purpose of the decree was to dismiss and punish public servants throughout the country who had been involved in any hostile and subversive acts or rebellion against any of the governments of the Federation between January 1966 and January 1970. The decree entitled: "Dismissal and Compulsory Retirement of Disloyal Public Officials" also affected those who in any way counselled, aided and abetted any such rebellious acts or whose conduct during the period in question had been such that their further or continued employment would not be in the public interest.

This decree, enacted so soon after the war, completely devastated hundreds of thousands of Easterners as they lost their pensions and gratuities. Many had already lost their homes both in the East and other parts of the country from which they had fled and were unable to repossess them, in some cases for up to ten years. Businesses were destroyed, savings lost or spent, and communications had come to a standstill in the former Biafra. The Biafran currency was worthless both at home and abroad as the Federal government refused to exchange it for the Nigerian currency. This too was later changed "in order to prevent illegal dealing and trading".

On May 20th the International Red Cross and other charities ended their operations in the former Biafra. Their work was taken over by the Nigerian National Rehabilitation Commission but a number of doctors, nurses and other specialists remained in the country for a further six months.

It was agreed by all the official observers from various countries that no inhuman treatment by the Federal government had taken place. As early as 1968 the Nigerian government had invited the UN, OAU, Britain, Canada, Poland and Sweden to send observers to any part of the country including parts of Biafra that were liberated. On 17th September 1969 it was announced in London that Major-General H.T. Alexander, a former Chief of Ghana Defence Staff, had been appointed as a member of the British team of international observers in the civil war. The others were: Maj-General W.A. Milroy of Canada, Maj-Gen Arthur Raad of Sweden, Col. Alfons Olkiewizc of Poland and Brig. Gen. Negga Tegegne, Assistant Chief of Staff of the Ethiopian Army, represented the OAU. Accompanying them was Nils-Goran Gussing representing the Secretary-General of the UN.

After travelling as freely as was possible in the area, the observers wrote a lengthy report which they submitted to the United Nations and to various governments including the British government. In summary the report stated that:

"1. There was no evidence of any intent by the Federal troops to destroy the Ibo people or their property, and: the use of the term genocide is in no way justified.
2. That the Federal troops were taking positive action to obtain the confidence of the local population, and to assist them in re-establishing a normal life.
3. An increasing number of villagers, almost all Ibos, were returning to their homes, and showed no fear of the Federal troops.
4. Food and medical supplies were being given to the civilian population through the combined efforts of the Army, the civilian administration, and the Red Cross. While food supplies had been adequate, those of drugs and medical assistance had suffered

through a shortage of transport, particularly of aircraft, and this situation could become serious if the expected large increase in the number of people requiring such assistance took place."

The team of observers were allowed to continue during the period of the war. In 1969 some of the members were replaced when Brig. Sir Bernard Fergusson, a former Governor-General of New Zealand, joined the team. Later Mr Gussing reported to the UN Secretary-General, U Thant, that: "the Federal troops gave every impression of being alert and well-disciplined and that confidence in their conduct seemed to be reflected in the reaction of those Ibos who had either remained behind or had returned to their villages in the area." He also stated that fear of warfare and natural timidity towards armed soldiers, accompanied by the belief, spread among the Ibo people that the Federal troops intended to exterminate them, had driven most villagers into hiding during the fighting.

These were very favourable reports of Gowon's handling of the war; and they earned a lot of respect and admiration for him all over the world. Many were impressed by his magnanimity at the end of the war. At home, the general public and the lower ranks of the armed forces showered praises on him. But, one or two high-ranking members of his own army, nursed envy and jealousy of him. Full of confidence in himself, in 1972 he promised the country he would restore a civilian government in 1976. To this end, he proposed a nine step plan:

1. Reorganization of the armed forces
2. Implementation of the National Development Plan, which was introduced by Tafawa Balewa; and repairs to the damages of war.
3. Eradication of corruption. This had been

increasing at an alarming rate despite the civil war and often the worst practitioners were senior members of the civil service, military and local politicians.
4. Settlement of the question of the creation of more states.
5. Preparation and adoption of a new constitution.
6. Introduction of a new formula for revenue allocation to the states. As none of the states were able to generate even 40 percent of their budgets, they relied heavily on allocations from the Federal government.
7. A national census of the population. This was a particularly delicate exercise as revenue allocation and seats on the Federal legislature were dependent on population figures.
8. Organisation of 'genuine political parties' that would not be regional, tribal or sectional in make-up.
9. Federal and State elections set for 1976. He called on the elite to try and work out a system of: "distinctive national ideology that can work in Nigeria having regard to our temperament and diversity".

The older politicians welcomed Gowon's proposals; although those of them who had become stoney broke, wished they would come into being earlier than 1976. Many of Gowon's own colleagues in the Army thought that 1976 was too soon. They had not had enough of their share of the national cake, particularly as about this time the oil boom began.

Following much agitation for pay increases by civil servants, the Federal government set up a salary review body for government employees. It was headed by Chief Jerome

Udoji, a senior civil servant. After sitting for about eight weeks, the panel made recommendations for increases in salaries for all grades of public servants by more than one hundred percent. Many were surprised that the government accepted the recommendations. Within two weeks workers had been paid and inflation rose. Workers in the private sector began making similar demands for wage increases with threats of industrial action. Many private firms did pay but many also went out of business. In a country where less than thirty percent of the able-bodied people had jobs of any kind, the rise in prices shown by twenty-five percent inflation became a serious problem for the government. The government's own Price Control Board was unable to cope with inflation which rose rapidly and yearly.

The reaction of Gowon's regime, was to blame: "foreign business monopoly". It then took steps to redress this by legislating on measures that would enable Nigerians to participate in businesses already owned by foreigners. In this regard all business undertakings were classified into three categories. The first, which included professional services, were barred from being undertaken by any foreigners. The second and third categories allowed foreigners to participate on an equity percentage of forty and sixty respectively.*

Nigerian businessmen immediately rushed to take advantage of the legislation. Many foreigners whose businesses were affected sold out and left. Unfortunately, the programme known generally as "Indigenisation of Businesses", was not successful and many businesses taken over from foreigners failed for one reason or another. It was probably the beginning of economic ruin for the country.

Similar legislation was enacted which enabled the government to acquire forty percent shares in each of the foreign banks in the country. These were Barclays, Standard, Bank of America and Bank of India. The government was also entitled

*See The Nigerian Enterprises Promotion Decree 1972-74.

to appoint a chairman to each of the banks and to nominate a number of directors to their boards. They also acquired a majority shareholding in each of the Volkswagen and Peugeot vehicle assembly plants. Within two years of government participation, each of the banks changed its name.* The foreign owners reduced their financial participation over the period of the next three years. This eventually resulted in job losses in many of the large industrial concerns.

Meanwhile, revenue from oil exports grew rapidly and by the beginning of 1974 output amounted to more than 700 million US dollars per year, some 80 percent of the country's total export earnings. This was at the time considered enormous for a country that had hitherto relied on a mediocre income from products such as tin, cocoa, groundnuts and timber. The government began spending large sums of money on developing the infrastructure of urban areas and roads, bridges, hotels, stadiums and so on were built in large numbers. One of the unfortunate results of the oil boom and the money that flowed as a result of it, was that agriculture and other income-generating products were to a great extent ignored.

The prosperity of the country due to the oil boom and Gowon's promise to return the country to civilian rule helped to sustain peace in the country. In December 1973, he confirmed his promise to end military rule by lifting the ban on political parties in October 1974. Nevertheless he stated that the military would not hand over power until they had completed their work. He did not elucidate on the meaning of this statement.

The vagueness of Gowon's promise made many doubt his sincerity about relinquishing power. His regime had earlier published the census result for 1973 in which the population was estimated at 79 million. However, many in the South accused the census authorities of inflating the figures for the

* Barclays to Union Bank; Standard to First Bank; Bank of America to Savannah Bank; Bank of India to Allied Bank.

states in the North in order to give them increased revenue when the time came for deciding on revenue allocation. Many also blamed the regime for the failure of the Indigenisation Decree which induced many states to purchase the assets of foreign firms which they could then not operate and therefore ended up with huge losses. The Udoji salary award had contributed to high inflation.

There were a number of government scandals at the time; one of the more notorious was the 'Cement Scandal', when several Federal and local state agencies ordered hundreds of thousands of tons of cement. This resulted in 'a ridiculous situation' where the port of Lagos was not only congested but there were queues of ships which at the worst period could have been up to 800. Some of the ships waited up to 20 months, by which time the cement was useless. In addition, payments of compensation by the Nigerian government to the ship's crews and other seagoing expenses were huge.

Throughout the conflict with Ojukwu, the people had stood behind Gowon and his leadership. However, by 1974 the country began to doubt his capabilities. Things came to a head when on 1st October 1974 he back-tracked on his promise to hand over to civilians in 1976, by which time he would have been in office for 10 years. He was not the only African leader to have 'over-stayed his welcome'. The same story was being played in Liberia, Guinea, Congo, Senegal, Gambia, Kenya, Uganda, Algeria and elsewhere.

A number of former politicians from the first Republic, Awolowo, Zik, Opara and others began to surface and Gowon feared that another bout of political activity could lead to another crisis. He was thus able to use the excuse that: "to adhere rigidly to the original target would amount to a betrayal of trust, in view of the high degree of sectional politics ... designed to whip up feelings within the country for the benefit of the political aspirations of a few." He added: "What the country and the ordinary citizens wants is peace and stability, the only condition in which progress and development are possible." He did not seem to have faith in democracy.

Further accusations against Gowon centred around his style of rule. Many close to him complained that he made policies with little regard to their opinions. In addition, many of the Army officers that had supported him in his rise to power became angry that they were being excluded from the decision-making process. In some instances this was taken to mean that they were not given: "easy access to the treasury". Senior civil servants became quite powerful, becoming the spokespersons of the government over and above the civilians appointed as Commissioners (Ministers). Journalists who risked exposing the corrupt practices found themselves detained without trial and the perpetrators left to continue their activities.

By 1974 Gowon's regime was so unpopular that had it been a civilian one it would not have even bothered to seek re-election. However, as a military dictatorship it was immovable peacefully. Nevertheless, on the 29th July 1975, exactly nine years after the military coup which put it in power, another coup staged by the very same officers that put him in, removed him. There followed the usual jubilation and welcoming rhetoric by the country's elite, civil servants and so on. Gowon was away in Kampala attending an OAU conference at the time of the coup and thus at least his life was saved. He tried to return to Nigeria but by the time he reached Togo, some 400 miles from Lagos, he had realised the dissatisfaction and indignation against his rule. He feared for his life and was eventually granted political asylum in Britain. The new military head of state was Brigadier Murtala Muhammed.

# Chapter 18

# The Third Military Regime

On 29th July 1975, it was thirty-two year old Joseph Garba, Commandant of the Brigade of Guards, who announced the deposition of General Gowon in a bloodless military coup. Later that week he was appointed the country's Minister of External Affairs.

Garba's announcement stated that: "The Armed Forces have decided to effect a change in the leadership of the Federal Government ... As from now General Gowon ceases to be the head of state of the Federal Military Government and Commander in Chief of the Armed Forces of Nigeria. The general public is advised to be calm and to go about its lawful business. However, in view of the traffic situation in the Lagos area, workers other than those in essential services such as electricity, hospitals and post offices, should observe today as a work-free day. A dusk-to-dawn curfew is hereby imposed until further notice".

As was usual with every military coup, the country's borders and ports were closed. These measures were taken to ensure that foreign troops did not invade the country to aid the toppled leaders. Later that day, another broadcast on the Federal Radio introduced thirty-eight year old Brigadier Murtala Muhammed, as the new Head of State. In his radio broadcast that evening, Muhammed himself gave the reasons why Gowon was removed, when he said that Gowon's administration was characterised by: "indecision, indiscipline and neglect of the administration of the Armed Forces" and that: "many had been disillusioned about the regime as a corrective one ..."

He accused Gowon also of failing to give the country a sense of direction and of refusing to dismiss the state governors, some of whom he said had amassed vast personal fortunes. He said Gowon agreed to dismiss them but failed to do so ... "And that if the situation had been allowed to continue, it could have led to bloodshed". However, he said that Gowon, who was at the time out of the country, was free to return.

As was usual, institutions, market women, students and politicians took their turn in the long queue to shower plaudits welcoming the new regime. In Nigeria the political, social and personal adversaries of fallen politicians were forever ready to acclaim those who topple them, no matter what the reasons were. Very few ever have sympathy for a cause or happening which did not affect them directly or personally.

Muhammed later appointed a Federal Executive Council which consisted of twenty-eight members of whom twelve were civilians, one from each of the twelve states created by Gowon. He dismissed all the former governors and detained them pending investigations into their assets. He appointed new state governors to rule the states, under the supervision of the Chief of Staff, Supreme Headquarters. During Gowon's regime they were all members of the Supreme Military Council of the Federal government. Muhammed also divested the state governors of most of their functions.

Unlike Gowon, Muhammed was not a good mixer. Very devoted in the Islamic faith, he nevertheless did nothing to offend other religious groups in the country. In the military operations in the civil war, he was in command of the Mid-West front that drove through Benin City into Asaba and crossed the River Niger into Onitsha. He was a diehard follower of the Sardauna of Sokoto, and he participated fully in avenging his demise. Under Gowon, he was the Minister of Communications in charge of telephones and their installation and services. More than Gowon, Muhammed always enjoyed the full support of the Northern leadership including the Emirs. He was a dyed-in-the-wool Muslim Hausa, who was the apple of their eyes. In fact, he was one of those Northern youths who benefited from the intense Northernisation policy pursued vigorously by Sir Ahmadu Bello.

Northern leaders are usually quite close to their traditional rulers and to one another on account of their Islamic 'brotherhood'. This usually enables them to exert greater political influence on any matter, than they would have as individuals. In the South there are no such associations or factors which unite leaders. Everyone acts according to his or her personal interest, unless of course, tribal interests supervene.

A week after taking office, Muhammed dissolved all the boards of the Federal and state corporations and any of the boards on which the government had an interest. He did this without regard to the laws under which they were operated. Then he set up panels of investigators to inquire into the assets of all the members. This action earned for him the nickname 'tough man'. As the general public cheered him, he continued his witch-hunting into the civil service, the judiciary and every institution of government. He sacked judges of the Supreme Court and Federal courts without remorse. The Chief Justice of the Federation, Dr T. Oladele Elias, a distinguished jurist who later became a Judge in the International Court of Justice at the Hague, was summarily dismissed. Without regard to civil service, conditions of service and the government's own General Orders, he sacked more than eight thousand civil servants, most of them in the senior ranks. His general reasons for the sackings were centred around inefficiency, indiscipline, low productivity and even: "inaudible speeches".

After dealing this blow to the judiciary and the civil service, Muhammed turned to the universities and hospitals.

There, he also sacked hundreds of senior professors and doctors. Those sacked were accused publicly of: "inefficiency, laziness and failing eyesight". No one dared oppose him, not even in the courts of law or in the press, for fear of retaliation.

Muhammed's hauteur as supreme leader spread throughout the armed forces. Soldiers in uniform insisted on travelling on private owned buses free and even unseated fare-paying passengers so they could sit down. Anyone who challenged them was subject to beatings. As the soldiers became more 'powerful' they were employed by creditors to collect their debts by intimidating or beating up their debtors. Landlords found soldiers handy for ejecting tenants. Very few tenants, particularly expatriate Europeans, were prepared to confront two or three soldiers in uniform and easily gave up possession of the premises.

The courts were too cowed, following the sacking of judges and other civil servants, to enter into matters where soldiers were involved. Bailiffs too were fearful of entering barracks to serve writs as they could be beaten with impunity. With no opposition whatsoever to his authority, Muhammed began the process of demolishing all administrative assets and probity, such as an upright judiciary, a reliable legal system and an efficient public service which was the country's legacy from the colonial system. This process was continued by his military successors.

Only one brave voice dared to criticise him, Dr Cyril Ohabanu, a former law student in Moscow and Cambridge who at the time was a lecturer at the University of Lagos. He suggested that the investigation into assets should include those in the senior ranks of the military, particularly the Supreme Military Council. He was arrested and detained and later charged with sedition. Unfortunately he died while his case was still pending.

Muhammed fully appreciated the burning desire of the politicians and public for a return to civilian government. Within three months of replacing Gowon, he announced a programme for handing power to civilians in 1979. The programme seemed impressive and it convinced many of his sincerity and quickly built up popularity for him.

The programme included the creation of seven more states in addition to the twelve created by Gowon on the eve of the civil war. He also promised to set up a constitution-drafting committee which would complete its work by September 1976 in order that an elected constituent assembly could discuss the draft by 1977. Then there would be a total re-organisation of the local government system, after which the ban on political parties would be lifted in 1978. It would then be more appropriate for the army to withdraw in favour of an elected civilian government, to begin in October 1979.

He warned that after the seven new states had been created, future agitation for more states would not be tolerated as it would end up with a proliferation of states. These states whose names bore geographical references reminiscent of the regions would be re-named in order to help: "people to erase memories of past political ties and emotional attachment". He promised even development and to build a university in each state. Many expected him also to build an international airport in each state.

Muhammed then set up a panel to study the question of founding a new capital for the country in a position which would be central to every part of the country and which had at the same time facilities and advantages of development which Lagos, as an island, did not have. The panel later recommended Abuja, situated about two hundred miles South of Kaduna in the North.

Before the end of 1975, Muhammed had begun working

to fulfil his programme. In October he appointed a fifty-member Constitutional Drafting Committee with Chief Rotimi Williams as its chairman. Chief Williams is an elderly, well known lawyer. He is also the longest practising lawyer in the country. He had been in politics as long as both Chiefs Akintola and Awolowo and worked with them in the Action Group. On this account he had had much experience of the causes of the country's perpetual turmoil and conflict and his appointment gave the committee confidence.

A few days after its establishment, the Constitution Drafting Committee met. Muhammed addressed the group, providing them with the guidelines in which they were to work. These were mainly that they should remove any tribal aspirations from within the Constitution, avoid sectionalism and devise a constitution that avoided a 'winner takes all' principle. Instead, they were to devise a way of limiting the number of political parties and reducing 'cutthroat' activities in politics. The new Constitution should discourage institutional opposition to the ruling party; provide for the independence of the judiciary and public accountability for all persons holding public office. He said that 'the Supreme Military Council' favoured an American system with a President and Vice-President. All appointments should reflect the: 'federal character' of the country. Muhammed hoped that these proposals would solve the problems of tribalism and sectionalism that had plagued the country since its creation.

Later he announced that his government would set up anti-corruption bodies and a Public Complaints Bureau. In spite of the provision for criminal prosecution for bribery and corruption in the Criminal Code, Muhammed enacted a decree in December 1975 laying down penalties of seven years imprisonment or a fine of 5,000 Naira* or both. The fines were later increased to N10,000 and those convicted would in

*At that time the exchange rate was N1=$1.60.

addition refund the amount they had corruptly received or demanded. Many public officers, particularly civilians, were charged with offences of corruption. Later the government reported that it had collected about ten million Naira from such officers. Unfortunately, despite the public outcry, no known serving military officer was charged with corruption.

While the promises for a 'new Nigeria' earned him support from many, some others, whom he had offended by sacking their benefactors, nursed bitter hatred against him. The most notable of these was thirty-year old Col. Bukar Dimka, a physical training instructor in the Nigerian Defence Academy in Kaduna. Like Gowon, Dimka was a Christian and a member of a minority tribe in the North. Dimka found it quite easy to recruit some of his Army friends for an attack against Muhammed. Early in the morning of 13th February 1976, while Muhammed was being driven to his office, Dimka emptied dozens of bullets into his body and killed him outright. He then hurried to the nearby Radio Nigeria office and disarmed the guards there. By 8am he was announcing on the radio as follows:

> *"Fellow countrymen and women, good morning; I bring you good tidings; Murtala Muhammed's hypocrisy has been detected. His government is now overthrown by the young revolutionaries. All the military governors of the states have power of the states they govern. State affairs will be run by brigade commanders until further notice. All Federal Commissioners are now sacked except for the armed forces and police commissioners, who will be re-deployed. All senior military officers should remain calm in their respective posts. No Divisional Commander will issue orders to his*

*formations until further notice. Any attempt to foil this plan from any quarter will be met with death. Fellow Nigerians today is a great day for all of us. All borders, seaports and airports will be closed until further notice. A curfew is hereby imposed from dawn-to-dusk. Thank you; we are all together."*

The thousands who had become Muhammed's adversaries, rejoiced at the news. However, there was still some confusion over the events, particularly as Dimka had sounded nervous as he announced his 'dawn-to-dusk' curfew. Later that day another radio station broadcast that the announcement by Dimka should not be accepted, and that troops loyal to the government would soon capture all the rebel leaders. A spokesman from the 1st Infantry Division, Kaduna, had announced on Radio Kaduna and said: "The general public is hereby informed that what is happening in Lagos has nothing to do with the rest of the country ... and the perpetrators of the rebellion are being rounded up."

This announcement followed another from Calabar that the coup had been foiled. As the day progressed more and more news came in. First street fights amongst soldiers in Lagos; then that troops had landed at Ikeja Airport to assist in the fight against Dimka and his men. At 4pm it was reported that the coup had been crushed. A dusk-to-dawn curfew was announced (this time the correct way round). At 9am the following morning an announcement was made stating that Brigadier Murtala Muhammed and six others, all senior officers, had been killed during the attempted coup. The announcement also stated that the coup leaders were prompted by their belief that 'Muhammed's government was communist-inspired'. An example given was the fact that Nigeria was backing the candidate of the Soviet Union in the Angolan crisis.

Later, in another statement through the radio and television, the government accused the British High Commissioner in Lagos of supporting the coup plotters, and said that Dimka had, on the 13th February at 9am a few hours after Muhammed had been shot, rushed to the British Embassy and requested the High Commissioner to get in touch with Gowon and enable him to return to Nigeria. At that time Gowon had enrolled as a student at Warwick University. The government also stated that one of the coup leaders had travelled to London several times and discussed the plot with General Gowon.

The Federal military government insisted that the British High Commissioner should reveal Dimka's mission at the Embassy. However, he refused, stating it was not in accord with diplomatic practice to accede to the demands of the Nigerian government. Interviewed by the press in London, General Gowon flatly denied any knowledge of the coup, arguing that if it was the intention of some coup plotters to stage a coup and then invite him to return, that was something he could not know about.

Despite the explanation, the Federal military government continued to ask the British High Commissioner to make a request to the British government to force Gowon to return to Nigeria to face charges pending against him before a military tribunal. The military government were informed that in Britain the rule of law was followed precisely and that if they wished Gowon to return they must initiate extradition proceedings in the same way as it was done in 1963 when Nigeria wanted Chief Anthony Enahoro returned. This was something the Nigerian military rulers could not understand. They came to power by breaking the law and it would be too much to expect them to respect the law later.

On March 27th, Brigadier Ya'r Adua announced that the Federal military government would take both: "legal and diplomatic steps to have Gowon extradited from England ... He must come here and defend himself against the allegation of complicity in the coup." On the following day Lt. Col. Joseph Garba, the Foreign Secretary, announced that the Federal government had made a: "formal request to the British government for the return of Gowon." In response to that request, the British government sent Edward Rowlands of the Foreign Office to deliver a letter to the Nigerian government telling them that the British government couldn't accede to their request because: "the questions of deportation and extradition from the United Kingdom are matters for the courts and thus are outside the political sphere". In parliament, the British Prime Minister, James Callaghan, stated that: "For reasons fundamental to the rule of law in Britain, the British government cannot accept the demand of the Nigerian military rulers." But he hoped that the issue would not be allowed to affect adversely the traditional friendly relations between Britain and Nigeria.

Despite the above, on the 15th May, Lt. General Olusegun Obasanjo, the new head of state, told journalists that: "We have made it clear to the British government that any country which harbours Yakubu Gowon ... is committing an unfriendly act towards the government and people of Nigeria ..." He did not address himself to the procedure involved under the rule of law as practised in democracies throughout the world. In Nigeria members of the military government are omnipotent. Their word is the law; and no-one can challenge their actions. On 27th April, the Nigerian government announced that it had suspended all facilities that were granted to Gowon while in Britain. He was also dismissed from the army.*

*This was later revoked during the return of the civilian government in 1979.

Although Dimka, the ringleader of the unsuccessful coup, could not be found, several others were arrested. They included his brother, Isaac Dimka, a senior police officer in Kwara state, and his wife. Others were General Bisalla, who as a Lieut.Col in the civil war had liberated several parts of Biafra and integrated them into Nigeria. His wife was also arrested, together with her brother, the Governor of the then Benue-Plateau State, Police Commissioner Gomwalk and his wife. Seventeen high and lower grade military officers were also arrested. In fact the military was out to arrest any one associated with Dimka by blood or by friendship. Some civilians were also arrested. They included the broadcaster whose microphone Dimka used to make his announcement of the coup. Later a total of thirty six men and women were arrested.

By the 11th of March, that is 26 days after the attempted coup, twenty eight people had been charged, sentenced to death and executed by firing squad. Only one officer was acquitted. The military announced the trial, sentence and execution of the accused men and women a few hours after their bodies had been buried at Attan Cemetry in YABA. The trial was said to be according to 'Military law and Practice'. It was not held in public and there was no appeal of any kind. The whole incident alarmed jurists in Nigeria and abroad. Dimka too was later arrested. His arrest, trial and execution took just three days. Many jurists in Nigeria condemned the trial as worse than "A reversion of the country's justice system to the pre-colonial age and, reminding the younger generation of the forgotten age when human sacrifices flourished in many parts of the country." But it was the way of the military to take the country backward to several centuries behind.

CHAPTER **19**

# Preparation for Return to Civilian Government

On the 14th February 1976 after the attempted coup leaders had been defeated, General Obasanjo promised that, as the new head of state, he would continue the policies of the slain Murtalla Mohammed. Later that year the Constitution Drafting Committee submitted its draft to the military government. Among its provisions the draft stated the way new political parties were to be formed and funded. "In order to avoid too much tribal appeal and patronage."

The draft, for example, recommended that such names as 'Northern People's Congress' should not be allowed as the name of a political party. Emblems and slogans that suggest ethnic or religious patronage should be banned. It also suggested that every political party should have an office in every state. The officers of a political party should consist of persons from at East two thirds of the number of states in the country. Although any person may stand as a candidate for an election, such a person having been elected could not join a political party during the life of the assembly for which he or she was elected. A United States of America type of Constitution was recommended.

Later in October 1977 a Constituent Assembly was inaugurated to finalise the constitution. General Obasanjo addressed the Assembly and reminded its members that "The Assembly provides a unique opportunity to lay the foundation of Nigeria's peaceful future ... Under previous civil rule party politics had produced anxious moments, self-inflicted wounds, chaos and disorder ... Unfortunately, those politicians who led this great country to disaster and near dissolution are once more only a stone's throw away, and they must be tamed so that fresh ideas and approaches are substituted in their places for the good of all. Members were granted 'Parliamentary immunity' to enable them to speak their minds without fear of favour".

The work of the assembly went quite smoothly, and everyone expected the situation was the beginning of a turning point in the political experience of the country. But when the assembly began to discuss the matter of the Islamic Sharia Court, a fierce gust of mutual recrimination took over the assembly as several members became fractious.

As early as Lord Lugard's period, Northern Nigeria had practised the Islamic Sharia system of justice. On the lower grade were the Islamic Mallams or teachers who could be promoted to be alkalis. They were equivalent to Magistrates. They dispensed justice according to the Holy Koran. They did not generally have jurisdiction over Southerners resident in the North. Alongside the Sharia system, a few secular courts also dispensed justice. These were manned originally by British Colonial officers but later by Southern professional lawyers. The fear in the South was that the Sharia Court system was notorious for carrying out brutal punishment and as professional lawyers did not practice in them, they could not be controlled. Unfortunately, up to the time of independence, Northerners were not attracted to the legal profession; and the Sharia system did not advance beyond religion, based on the Holy Koran.

Anyway, several members mostly from the South and Christians rejected any proposal to make Sharia court universal in the country, because several states in the country had no Muslim population at all. These include all the area East of Benin City to the borders with the Cameroons and South to the Atlantic. "We do not have even one mosque in the East" shouted one member continuously as the assembly became uproarious. And there were also shouts of "No Sharia, no Constitution" and "No Sharia, no Nigeria" by Northern members of the assembly. But there were no exchange of blows.

But outside, the argument continued as the non-Sharia group continued to argue that the country has already favoured the Muslims 'too much'. They gave example of the huge amount of money which the government spend each year to enable Muslims to go on pilgrimage to Mecca. The following day, the pro-Sharia group, unable to get the move to make Sharia country wide, walked out of the assembly and they warned that they would not return unless the Sharia issue would be resolved favourably.

A few days later, a committee set up following the intervention of the military, recommended that instead of setting up a Sharia Court of Appeal on the federal level, the Federal Court of Appeal, a court inferior to the Supreme Court, should, where an Islamic matter is in issue, constitute three judges of the Court who are versed in the Koran to adjudicate on the matter.

The suggestion of the committee was rejected by the Northern leaders in the assembly. They wanted Islamic officials designated Grand Khaddi to adjudicate on all matters and in accordance with the Holy Koran. When their argument was not accepted, even by the voting of the assembly, they staged a walk-out in anger. And they resolved to boycott further proceedings.

A few days after many of the boycotting members of the assembly returned to the North, the police advised that there was "fear that the public speeches by some politicians were causing serious ethnic conflicts between Northerners and Southerners in the North." As fighting spread and churches and schools were set on fire in some parts of the North,

Southerners began another exodus out of the North as they did in 1966. This time there were only a few casualties but the country nearly went up in flames again.

General Obasanjo intervened and travelled widely through the North and appealed to members of the assembly to save the situation. Finally, it was agreed that there would be a Sharia court in any state that required it and that on the federal level there would be a Sharia Court of Appeal to be presided over by a Grand Khaddi who would be an Islamic scholar, but he does not need to be a member of the Nigerian Bar, though he would have a standing equal to that of a High Court Judge.

However, despite the settlement, many Southerners who fled the North were afraid to return. The masses were reminded that it now seems that without the military, it would be impossible to keep Northerners and Southerners away from fighting in the North. Very few Northerners live permanently in the South. It is unusual for Northerners to seek employment in the South. They travel to the South generally as traders although since independence many have joined the Federal Public service and are posted to Southern cities, mostly in Lagos. Very few Northerners live ordinarily anywhere in the South.

In October 1976 the military set up the Federal Electoral Commission, popularly referred to as FEDECO. It was headed by Michael Ani, a retired civil servant. All persons, both male and female, above the age of eighteen were eligible to vote. A total of 47,433,757 were registered by 1978.

Before the ban on political activities was lifted the military announced that they would take into account the financial problems which new political parties would likely face. They made huge grants of money to FEDECO to enable new political parties to emerge and organise themselves for election campaign. FEDECO soon became powerful as it was given the power to control the proliferation of political parties; e.g. by requiring that they must set up offices in at East two-thirds of the number of states. If a political party satisfied the conditions, it was entitled to a grant. The grant was calculated on the basis of half of one Naira per registered voter. At that time, one Naira was equal to one and six-tenths of one US dollar. Fedeco was to distribute the money to registered parties in the following way:

(a) Before the election 50 percent of the whole fund was to be distributed equally to the number of registered parties that had established offices in at East two-thirds of the number of states. (b) At the end of the election the balance of 50 percent would be distributed in proportion to the number of seats each party scored in each of the legislatures. A similar arrangement was applicable in the case of the Presidential election. The parties were allowed to use their own funds for the election, provided that they did not exceed the sum of ten Naira per registered vote in the constituency where they canvassed for seats. It was also provided that no association other than a political party would be allowed to canvass for votes; and no association was allowed to make funds available to any political party. However, the members of a party were not prevented from donating to their parties, as long as the amount spent on campaigning in respect of each state did not exceed ten Naira per registered voter in the constituency. In this regard a political party would be bound to keep separate accounts of its expenditure in each state.

While Fedeco staff were busy counting and registering voters throughout the country, press reports stated that many politicians wanting to begin tribal politics were collecting fervent supporters in anticipation of an early lifting of the ban on politics. The military regime noticed this and they feared the likely stampede which would allow a sudden lifting of the ban. Gen.

Obasanjo went on radio on 14th July 1978 and warned the public to desist from canvassing for public support, particularly on tribal lines. He stated that: "the Government has no intention of lifting the ban on politics until the final draft of the new constitution has been formally presented to it on behalf of the Constituent Assembly by its chairman Mr Justice Udoma and it has been approved by the Supreme Military Council." He then advised politicians to be patient and not to repeat the type of politics which nearly ruined the nation. He also gave details of how the military would disengage from politics.

Gen. Obasanjo said that the first step in this respect would be taken in the states. A deputy civilian governor would be appointed to each state and the military governor would be replaced by a junior officer from the local Brigade or by the Garrison Commander. State commissioners would be appointed; but both the deputy governor and state commissioners would be relieved once the civilian government was elected on October 1st 1979. None of the civilians in the government would be allowed to participate in the new regime and all military officers would be retired from service.

In addition, all military officers in the Supreme Military Council and in government at the federal level would relinquish their posts and retire on 1st October 1979. They also would not be permitted to enter politics during the first civilian government.

Earlier in 1979 the regime had promised that it would reduce the strength of the Army which at the time was about 250,000. Civilian leaders headed by Chief Awolowo pleaded that the reduction should be quite substantial in order that money could be saved and spent on education. Many politicians demanded a reduction to about 10,000, while others thought that the country could do without an army, and the military should be totally demobilised, in order to eliminate a possible coup at a later date; although no one at the time had a sneaking suspicion that there would be any more military coup. At the end, there was no dramatic reduction in the strength of the military.

On the 21st of September 1976, the regime lifted the ban on political activities that had been imposed since the 15th of January 1966 by Major Nzeogwu and General Aguiyi-Ironsi. The regime also promulgated the new constitution to be effective from the 1st of October 1979.

The final constitution was a detailed codification of the fundamental rules of governing, including rules for elections, control of political parties, administration of the branches of government and the expected conduct and behaviour of public office holders, having regard, generally, to the multi-ethnic composition of the country. Patterned along the constitution of the United States of America, the Nigerian Constitution is some 20 times more voluminous than the American Constitution. But Nigeria is a country some 20 times more difficult to govern than the United States.

Within two days of the lifting of the ban on political activities, thousands of politicians crowded the offices of Fedeco, fighting to have their associations registered as political parties. There was a price for successful registration of an association. If successful, a registered party was entitled to an advance subvention. This fact might have stimulated many to form associations for registration as political parties. But there were political conditions for registration. An association could not be registered as a party unless it had a: 'federal character'. This meant that, unlike before 1966, every political party must have members from more than two-thirds of the number of states; and that was not possible unless it had more than 60 different ethnic members within it.

Some politicians with a little foresight began to recruit

members even while they were in the Constituent Assembly. This was what the late Alhaji Waziri Ibrahim did. He was a member of the Constituent Assembly and he got one member from each of the nineteen states to form a club he called Club 19. When it was time to have it registered as a political party, he insisted that, being its financier, he should be the chairman of the party as well as its presidential candidate. That created a serious problem. There was also the requirement that the members of an association seeking registration should show tax receipts for at least the previous three years. This condition knocked out several associations.

At the end, Fedeco registered only five associations as political parties. Most of them were like old wines poured into brand new bottles. For example, the National Party of Nigeria (NPN) consisted of the members of the dissolved Northern People's Congress (NPC) led by Sir Ahmadu Bello, the Sardauna of Sokoto and the United People's Party (UPP) formed by Chief Akintola when he broke away from Awolowo's Action Group in 1962. In 1964 the two formed the Nigerian National Alliance (NNA). They were in coalition in the Federal Parliament in 1966 when the first coup struck. Those who survived the coup and the civil war met again at the Constituent Assembly and soon organised to form the new NPN with many other Nigerians from other parts of the country. Their party was led by a most distinguished Southern barrister, Chief Meredith Adisa Akinloye, who later became chairman of the party; while Alhaju Shehu Shagari, a Northerner and a former Minister of Finance in Balewa's government, was its Presidential Candidate.

The Nigerian People's Party (NPP) originated among members of the Constituent Assembly and most of them were members of the banned NCNC. When eventually the party was formed, its members invited Azikiwe to lead it and to become its Presidential candidate. His running mate was Professor Ishaya Adu, a former Vice-Chancellor of Ahmadu Bello University in Zaria. Many of its members were former members of the dissolved NCNC.

But Alhaji Waziri Ibrahim, not able to get his own way in the NPP, quickly formed his own party and called it the Great Nigerian People's Party or GNPP. He was both its chairman and the Presidential candidate. Some said he was also the treasurer. He picked a running mate before any other party did – Dr Ben Nzeribe of Imo State. Like other parties, the GNPP's political ideology was: 'to strengthen national unity in Nigeria'.

The People's Redemption Party (PRP) was formed in 1978 by Alhaji Aminu Kano when he disagreed with th NPN on: 'fundamental differences'. Earlier, in 1950, he had left the NPC also because of 'fundamental differences' and formed the Northern Elements Progressive Union (NEPU). In the Northern Regional Parliament his party was in opposition to the ruling NPC. But in the Federal Parliament the same party was in coalition with the NPC and the NCNC. Aminu Kano survived the coups and civil war. Later he was a member of the Constituent Assembly. He was chairman of the PRP and also its Presidential candidate. The secretary of the party was S.G. Ikoku, an economist who was once a member of the Action Group led by Chief Awolowo. Later he was also a member of the NPN and subsequently, the secretary of the National Progressive Front. He became secretary of the PRP, and Aminu Kano picked him as his running mate for the Presidential election.

Chief Awolowo, who had been organizing an association right from the time the Constituent Assembly was inaugurated, came out with the Unity Party of Nigeria (UPN). At that time, although he was sixty-nine years old, he was as vivacious as a twenty-five-year old youth. He had lost two 'crucial' elections which could have made him the ruler of Nigeria. It was something he had worked for all his life. But the nearest he had ever been to this in the federal government was as the Leader of the Opposition in Balewa's government, and Minister of Finance in Gowon's military regime. This time in 1979, sink or swim, he was determined to win; and many in the country believed he could be third-time lucky. He was by far the most disciplined and the most hard-working politician in the country up to that date. Even as the Constituent Assembly was sitting in 1976/77, Chief Awolowo was controlling more than one-quarter of its members from his home, yet he was not a member.

Within twenty-four hours after the ban on political activities was lifted, Chief Awolowo submitted his association for registration with Fedeco and, simultaneously, he published its manifest which was as comprehensive as any in a more advanced country. Unfortunately it was difficult to remove tribal considerations in Nigerian politics and elections. That consideration favoured Chief Awolowo during his early days in politics when he was the dominant figure in the Yoruba West. In 1979 he thought that the country had been more detribalised and that a good manifesto could help him win votes. That did not happen.

Elections began throughout the country on 7th July for the ninety-five-member Senate; this was followed a week after by the election to the Federal House of Representatives of 449 members; with a deferred election to represent Abuja, the federal capital. Then followed, a week after, the election for the state House of Assembly. On the 28th July there was the election of the state governors. Then came the final election, the Presidential, held on 11th August.

When the total votes for the Presidency were counted, Alhaji Shehu Shagari scored a total of 5,688,875 votes, which was equal to 33.8 percent of the total votes cast. Chief Awolowo scored a total of 4,916,551 votes, which was 29.7 percent of the total votes cast. Dr Nnamdi Azikiwe scored a total of 2,8222,523 votes, equal to 16.7 percent of the total votes cast; Alhaji Aminu Kano scored 1,732,113 votes, which was 10.3 percent of the total votes.

Voting followed ethnic patterns with each candidate scoring heavily in his tribal areas. Alhaji Shagari scored sixty-six percent of the votes in Sokoto state. In Bauchi state, he scored sixty-two percent of the votes; but he only got 4.19 percent in Ondo state and 6.23 percent in Ogun state. He scored only 13.9 percent in Zik's home state of Anambra, and 8.81 percent in Imo, the other Ibo state. He scored more than twenty-five percent in twelve states.

Chief Awolowo got 94.11 percent in Ondo state and 92.06 percent in Ogun state, two Yoruba states. But in Sokoto he only got 2.23 percent and three percent in Bauchi, two Hausa-Fulani states of the North. He scored more than twenty-five percent on only five states. Dr Azikiwe scored 82.88 percent in his home state of Anambra and 86.67 percent in Imo state. He only got 0.86 percent in Ondo and 0.32 percent in Ogun states. He scored more than twenty-five percent in only three states.

On the whole election, Alhaji Shagari won more than twenty-five percent of the votes cast in each of twelve states and won 19.24 percent in the thirteenth state which was Kano. Fedeco therefore declared him elected and that: "the result satisfied the proviso of Section 126 of the Constitution". The section states that:

"(1) A candidate for an election to the office of President shall be deemed to have been duly elected where, there being only two candidates for the election:

(a) he has the majority of votes cast at the election; and

(b) he has not less than one-quarter of the votes cast at the election in each of at least two-thirds of all the States in the Federation.

(2) A candidate for an election to the office of President shall be deemed to have been duly elected where, there being more than two candidates for the election:

(a) he has the highest number of votes cast at the election and

(b) he has not less than one-quarter of the votes cast at the election in each of at least two-thirds of all the states in the Federation."

With respect to sub-section 2: Fedeco held that Shagari had fulfilled the conditions by winning twenty-five percent in each of twelve states, 19.24 percent in the thirteenth state. They argued that two-thirds of nineteen was twelve and two-thirds; that what was required was twenty-five percent of two-thirds of nineteen. Most others interpreted the section to mean just twenty-five percent in twelve states, that is the nearest whole number, since it was not possible to fractionalise in real terms.

Chief Awolowo rejected Fedeco's interpretation. Two other Presidential candidates, N. Azikiwe of the NPP and Alhaji Waziri of the GNPP supported him. Thereupon Chief Awolowo commenced an action under the electoral law. The matter came up in the supreme Court.

Awolowo's main contention was that a state as a corporate body could not be fractionalised and that two-thirds was intended to mean a number calculated to the nearest whole number. Therefore, in order to win under the section the candidate must win in thirteen states of the Federation. He lost the case.

He and his followers were bewildered. They cried slogans such as: "the Presidency has been stolen from us" and they cursed. But they could not reverse the judgement. Henceforth, they resolved not to recognise Shagari as the country's President. As that was not possible for long, all the five UPN governors and their parliaments resolved to confront Shagari as much as they possibly could. Bug Shagari began a new civilian regime on 1st October 1979. It was like another Independence Day. Millions who were not Awolowo's fans rejoiced. Like at Independence Day in 1960, Awolowo and his fans whined along.

CHAPTER 20

# The Second Civilian Regime: 1979-1983

While Chief Awolowo and his followers had not ended their claim that the presidency was stolen from them, 56 year old Alhani Shehu Shagari was installed as the President of Nigeria. He had been a cabinet minister in Sir Abubakar Tafawa Balewa's regime and was also a minister in Gen. Gowon's military government. Like Sir Amadu Bello, the Sardauna of Sokoto, he came from Sokoto in the extreme North-West of the country. Many thought that he was thrust upon the country by General Obasanjo a Southerner wanting to please the North.

His installation took place on 1st October 1979; but without countrywide celebrations. All the five states in which Awolowo's UPN candidates were elected governors, boycotted the ceremonies because: "the presidency is stolen from us", they said openly and seriously; and they resolved not to co-operate with the President, in all the five states as well as in the Federal Parliament. It was the legislature established under the American-style constitution that was to begin, but under the deep tribal settings of Nigeria.

President Shagari needed a majority in the Senate to approve most of his senior appointments to office. But his NPN had only twenty-six members in the Senate of ninety-five members. In the House of Representatives his NPN had 168 members out of the 449 members. The NPN felt uneasy about the threat of non co-operation by the UPN. In Nigeria such a situation of boycott and non co-operation could be more violently expressed, than in the United States. Unfortunately, all the UPN members that were boycotting were Yorubas. The Ibos voted solidly for Zik's NPP and they had sixteen Senators and seventy-nine members in the House of Representatives.

In order to solve the problem, the NPN members began a trading device for support. In the former civilian regime of Balewa and Zik in the 1960s, the NCNC was usually handy to bail the NPC out of difficulties. In 1979, the NCNC had disguised itself as the NPP while the NPC was wearing the mask of the NPN. The two soon recognised each other behind the disguises. They were both happy for a repeat of the compromise which was profitable to both in 1960, particularly in providing jobs for their respective members. The compromise during the early 60s was called coalition. This time both avoided that term. They preferred: 'co-operated agreement', the purpose of which was to enable the two parties to: 'work together in the interests of unity, peace, stability and progress of the country'. The two parties would share offices in the ratio of sixty percent for the NPN and forty percent for the NPP. The compromise enraged Chief Awolowo and his UPN. They became more determined in their confrontation of the President, and they sought the support of both the PRP and the GNPP in the confrontational stance. They resolved never to refer to Shagrari as President. The followers of the PRP and the GNPP also wanted jobs. They would confront until there was a 'compromise'.

Although the elected UPN members were all Yorubas, they were of Awolowo's old Action group. Their adversaries, Akintola's faction of Yorubas joined the NPN, but they were not successful at the elections. The UPN were determined that none of the Akintola faction of the Yorubas should be appointed to a high office by the NPN. That was possible in a Westminster-type of constitution and parliament; but not in the American-style constitution in which the president makes his appointments from members not elected to either the Senate or the House of Representatives.

The two co-operating parties agreed that they should each retain their respective identity, and none should be considered 'the junior' to the other. But: "in the event of the Assembly accepting a definition which confers a *de jure* title of Majority Party to one of the parties, the parties agree to work together to constitute the *de facto* Majority Group in the National Assembly and shall function as such". An inter-party committee was set up in order to facilitate the implementation of the accord on these terms.

Among the first offices that were shared were the Presidency of the Senate and the Speaker of the House of Representatives. The former went to the NPN while the latter went to the NPP. The agreement left the appointment of ministers to the discretion of the President, provided that not less than eight ministerial positions, of which not less than four were portfolios, should be allotted to the NPP. There was also provision in the accord for some financial benefits to be made to Dr Azikiwe, the leader of the NPP who was also a former head of state, as President, while Balewa was the Prime Minister. Zik was to be given a pension under the 'co-operative' agreement'.

But the accord between the NPN and NPP did not last long. It began to weaken when NPN members refused to attend joint meetings with the NPP. Then later an NPP member, Dr Jaja Wachuku, a former minister of external affairs under the Balewa government, and then chairman of the Senate's Foreign Relations Committee, advocated normalisation of relationships with both South Africa and Israel. Then also came the issue of revenue allocation in which the two parties differed seriously. As the accord got weaker, many of the NPP members left the party and joined the NPN. This included Michael Ogon and others. Despite Zik's pleadings for the accord to continue, the parties went on to move asunder.

In other parts of the country, particularly in Kaduna and Kano states, there were serious conflicts between the governors of the states and the members of the State Assemblies. In both these states, the governors were from the People's Redemption Party (PRP), founded by Aminu Kano and said to be radical, while the large majority of the members of the Assemblies were NPN. The governors joined Chief Awolowo's confrontational movement against the NPN federal government and President Shagari. In retaliation the members of the Assemblies in each of the states, refused to allow every name submitted by the state governor for appointment to his cabinet. They insisted that he must accept a list submitted by the Assemblies.

In Kaduna the conflict went on until the House of Assembly successfully impeached the Governor, Balarabe Musa, and removed him from office. His deputy, Abba Rimi, succeeded him. Unlike Balarabe Musa, Abba Rimi co-operated with the Assembly and the government carried on smoothly.

In Kano, before an impeachment could be set in motion, the Governor, Abubakar Rimi, a former journalist, and as radical as his colleague in Kaduna, threatened to dismiss the Emir of Kano. But he did not succeed. Just then, the Governor's house caught fire and burned down. He luckily escaped and was quiet in view of a more serious incident in the State.

While the conflict between the Governor of Kano and his House of Assembly was raging, a religious 'fanatic from an Islamic fundamental movement', started to kill and maim Christians in Kano. The killings, religious abuse and burning of churches, caused widespread riots in many parts of Kano. Its Islamic leader, Maitasine Mohammed Marwa, resolved to wipe out the Christians in the state, all of whom were Southerners and foreigners from outside the country. At the end, armed troops were used to dislodge him from his power base in the heart of Kano. A tribunal of inquiry estimated the deaths at 400 but rumour put it at more than 4,000.

Shagari's regime, as many people had expected, was fairly peaceful by Nigerian standards. In response to the rule of law and its inherent fundamental rights, the regime released all those who were the victims of Obasanjo's obnoxious laws such as the Foreign Exchange (Anti-Sabotage Decree) under which several innocent people were imprisoned. Shagari also withdrew the names of Gowon and Ojukwu from the list of wanted persons.

However, the regime's good name was tarnished when on 17th January 1983 the Minister of Internal Affairs, Alhaji Ali Baba, suddenly announced that: "all illegal immigrants should leave the country within two weeks or face imprisonment and deportation". The Minister spoke on the television in English which, though it is the official language, is understood well by less than twenty percent of the population. Later the order was translated and read in several of the more than two hundred languages in the country. In almost all of these languages, there is no difference between the meaning of the words 'stranger' and 'foreigner' or even 'visitor'. All of them refer to a person who is not a native of the village. An Ibo from one village is a foreigner or stranger in another. The same applies to Yoruba or Effik. A person whose native home is only ten miles from Lagos is a 'foreigner' in Lagos according to most Nigerian languages. That was how many understood the order of Alhaji Ali Baba. Added to these problems, more than half the population do not even know the name of the country. They learn it at school. If they do not go to school, there is no way they could comprehend that they are Nigerians.

Right from the night when the Minister spoke, panic gripped many homes and families. They had witnessed many exoduses in recent years; it was not very easy to convince them that this was not another one; particularly as many mothers, on hearing the radio announcement, travelled long distances to warn their children to leave their sojourns. Many foreigners and Nigerians, who thought that they were definitely Ghanaians or Cameroonians, began the move out of the towns and cities. Within the ten days that followed, lorries and trucks were conveying foreigners as well as Nigerians criss-crossing the country for their homes of birth or their roots.

The government sent hundreds of people to explain that it did not apply to Yorubas, Ibos, Ijaws, Tivs, Urhobos, Kururukus, Munshis or Hausas and countless others that were fleeing. But it affected Togolese, Ghanaians, Nigers and Several others who were not in the territory which the British made into Nigeria, only about sixty-four years earlier.

At the regional meeting of the consul de l'Entrente* held in Togo in February that year, the heads of states of Togo, Niger, Ivory Coast and Upper Volta condemned Nigeria for the action. They said: "They should have been notified on the matter before the Nigerian authorities took the drastic step so that they could prepare to receive their own nationals and this is not a way to treat your neighbours."

It was estimated that the order affected about two million Ghanaians resident in Nigeria. Massive relief materials from the United Kingdom, China, France and other parts of the world, except Africa, were hurriedly sent to help the situation of refugees in the affected countries. The expulsion order, which tarnished Nigeria's name for a long time after Shagari, solved nothing for his government.

It was believed that the Minister of Internal Affairs, Alhaji Ali Baba was compelled to announce the expulsion of illegal immigrants in consequence of the regime's sudden realisation of the huge financial burden caused by the limitless expenditure for administration and profligacy. Like the military regimes before it, Shagari's administration did not show much respect for budgetary control.

*An association or community of French-speaking countries in West Africa.

The president's office alone had more than 60 top officials. These excluded the Ministers with and without portfolios. Each of the Senators and the members of the House of Representatives was provided with fully furnished accommodation in Lagos. Each was entitled to a: 'suitable car' and a driver as the perks of office. They had limitless free use of electricity and telephones, and they travelled at government expense, even by air, within the country. A large majority of them had touts and thugs they used as security men. In each state the same thing was repeated for the members of the Houses of Assembly. The governor in each state, apart from his house-keeping expenses, was entitled to large sums of money for security purposes, which he did not have to account for.

On top of all these expenses was the burden of maintaining the military whose equipment and outfits, including shoe laces and shoe polish, were imported from Europe.

All this expenditure depended on oil revenue which accounts for ninety-seven percent of the country's foreign earnings. With unaccountable numbers of people unemployed, only workers in government offices, professionals and employees of corporate companies paid any tax. None of the governments in the country bothered themselves with collecting taxes efficiently; not even revenues from customs and excise were properly collected. Then suddenly at the end of 1982, oil revenue declined. Oil production, which averaged 1.5 million barrels a day, declined to 700,000 barrels a day. And the price reduced to $29 a barrel. Shagari's regime now had revenue only half of what it enjoyed at the beginning of its term of office in 1979. With the propensity for corruption and profligacy unstoppable, the regime began to face problems of maintaining government workers inside and party supporters and thugs outside.

On the last day of December 1983, the regime was swept

out of office three months after the beginning of its second term. The coup was the fourth successful one in the country; and it was staged by officers whose only purpose was to gain access to the country's treasury. As coups continue in the country, the intellect of coup makers regressed. This last set were not Sandhurst or Aldershot graduates like those in January 1966. They were local products led by General Alhaji Mohammed Buhari.

# Chapter 21

# A Military Regime that Harried Politicians

The abrupt termination of Shagari's civilian regime by a bloody coup staged by Northern troops, confounded many observers of Nigeria's problems. Shagari belonged to the Northern establishment. In fact they accepted him as a 'little Saduana of 'Sokoto' who would seek their interest. Northern elite and leaders were pleased with him.

"What must have gone wrong?" The position was that by 1983, many in the military had become so thirsty for power and the wealth which flows from it, that they were ready to seize any available opportunity to stage a coup. There are always present in the country such evils as corruption and profligacy that they could give as their reasons. Also, many of the elite and the intellectuals are ever ready to support them, hoping for jobs for themselves. The country produces many more mechanically unskilled and qualified people than it can absorb, there being comparatively few businesses.

However, early in the morning of December 31st 1983, a radio announcer gave his name as Brigadier Sanni Abacha, Commander of the Ikeja Cantonment, and said:

> "In furtherance to the discharge of our national role as promoters and protectors of our national interest, the military has decided to effect a change in the leadership of Nigeria, and to form a National Military Government ... and the new government hereby decrees the suspension of the constitution and the offices of the president, state governors, senators and all legislators in the Federal legislature and states ..."

And he gave all of them seven days within which to vacate their premises and surrender their vehicles and other articles belonging to the government. The announcement was repeated every thirty minutes. Later it was known that the officers who were killed included Brigadier Ibrahim Bako and five others. They were all Northerners. The President and the Vice-President were arrested and detained.

Abacha's announcement gave the impression that many in the Nigerian Army seemed to have arrogated to themselves the right to judge the conduct of any civilian government in order to decide when to remove it from office and rule. It is a most dangerous situation which has become impossible to stop.

Anyway, later that day another voice came through the radio. It introduced itself as General Mohammed Buhari, a fifty-three-year old former petroleum minister in General Obasanjo's government. After the usual greeting he said: "The object of the coup is to save the nation from total collapse ... and the change has become necessary in order to put an end to the serious economic predicament and the crisis of confidence that is afflicting the nation ... The government of President Shagari has mismanaged the economy ... and they have been unable to enforce and cultivate financial discipline and there has been widespread rigging of votes during the last elections; corruption and misuse of public funds have been the order of the day during the past four years ..."

As was usual after a coup, many of the adversaries of the victims trooped out in jubilation. In this case, millions of Awolowo's UPN supporters were out in full force, dancing and revelling all over Lagos, Ibadan, Akure and other cities. Many carried slogans saying: "We welcome the military saviours of the constitution". Some strongly believed that General Buhari would: "Hand over the government to Chief Awolowo". This notwithstanding that within the next twenty-four hours, Buhari had sacked all the state governors including the UPN governors. He also dissolved the legislatures.

The state governors were immediately replaced by military officers. A day later General Buhari announced that he would set up special military tribunals to try all the politicians for economic sabotage, corruption and many other offences. Then followed the stampede to flee the country. But all the exits – sea, land and air – were closed, with hundreds of Buhari's troops guarding them. Yet several escaped in circumstances that many Nigerians attributed to be supernatural and 'juju'. Fortunately, at that time, it was quite easy to travel to the UK, which was the haven, even with expired passports.

But, like a lion on the trail of its prey, Buhari pursued them, even to London. His aim was to catch them and bring them back to Nigeria to appear before his special courts, for sentencing, before he killed or, at best, jailed them. There were no provisions for appeals from the decision of the special tribunals which were presided over by members of his troops, and which had power to impose the death sentence on conviction.

In March, Buhari proceeded to enact new laws creating more new offences with severe punishment for acts committed as long as four years ago, retrospectively. Under the Recovery of Public Properties Decree, he established more special courts to investigate properties acquired during the lifetime of the accused politicians. In some cases he provided for a High Court Judge, serving or retired, to preside over the matter. But in all cases there would be present on the adjudicating panel one or more military officers. The military in Nigeria always pretended that the presence of a judge on the panel of a tribunal or special court lent respectability to it, even though such a tribunal was not allowed to observe the rules of evidence, and also its decisions could not be appealed against for any reason.

Unable to understand that civilized, democratic and stable countries are ruled strictly by law, Buhari's regime thought that it could easily obtain the extradition of those who fled the jurisdiction of their special tribunals. They demanded that Great Britain should send the refugees back to Nigeria to face trial. They were advised to follow the procedure for extradition. But they blamed the UK government for 'wasting time'.

Of the many refugees, they particularly wanted Dr Alhaji Umaru Dikko quickly. He was Shagari's Minister in charge of Transport, but his bigger job was as head of the Presidential Task Force, a quango which many businessmen believed could award them profitable contracts. While Dikko was in the UK, the story about him in Nigeria was that he was so wealthy, he could raise an army to invade the country, and that he could also, once within the country, instigate a coup against Buhari and his military colleagues. On this account the name 'Dikko' made many big men shiver.

Before the military government began the extradition proceedings, something happened on the 6th July 1984 at lunchtime on a bright summer afternoon, right in the heart of London on a working day. Dikko was walking leisurely in a busy street when suddenly three men kidnapped him and bundled him into a moving van. Quickly they drugged him and pushed him into a cage like a wild hyena. The cage was then put inside a diplomatic bag while the van kept on moving at great speed. There were five men in the van and their destination was Stansted Airport, where a Nigerian 'plane was waiting to take off.

London police were alerted and followed the van at breakneck speed. They intercepted the large bag with Dikko inside it, before it could be loaded into the 'plane. They released Dikko and sent him to hospital for treatment. Fortunately for Dikko, the 'diplomatic bag' in which he was confined did not have the: "usual visible diplomatic markings and proper documentation to qualify it for un-impeded passage under the Vienna Convention on diplomatic relations".

Later four men were charged with kidnapping and drugging Dikko in order to abduct him to Nigeria. Two of them were Israelis with business connections in Nigeria. In London, the High Commissioner, Major-General Hananiya, said that the government knew absolutely nothing about the incident. The Nigerian Airways 'plane and its crew were stopped from returning to Nigeria. Whereupon, in Lagos, the Nigerian military government retaliated by detaining a British Caledonian 'plane and its crew and passengers bound for London. But the 'planes and the crews were later released. Dikko and the rest of the refugees fought hard to remain in the UK. Many did not return to Nigeria until after Buhari's regime had been toppled. The rest of them left only after Buhari's successor General Babangida had been forced out of power in 1993.

Dikko's attempted kidnappers, Alexander Barake, an Israeli business executive and three other Israelis and a Nigerian were convicted at the Central Criminal Court in London and were each sentenced to fourteen years in jail in February 1985.

In 1984, while still fighting tirelessly for the return of Umaru Dikko, whom he had painted so horribly to the world as the cause of all the economic miseries of Nigeria, Buhari imposed severe restrictions on the country's import trade. Still justifying his bloody coup, he accused the civilian regime which he topped of: "Fraudulent administration of the import-licensing system. The system was so corrupt that they denied licenses to genuine importers and manufacturers, only to be given to middlemen whose only interest in those licenses was to hawk them about ... and they committed fraudulent acts of every description and arson, smuggling, armed robbery and other evils".

He listed many offences which carried death penalties on conviction. They included drug trafficing or possession, stealing electric cables or wire, counterfeiting currency, bunkering of petroleum products and economic sabotage. Many other offences carried twenty-one-year jail sentences. They included copying at examinations, leaking of examination questions or results, tapping electricity fraudulently and cheating.

Several state governors and other politicians were 'tried' by his special tribunals and sentenced to terms of imprisonment ranging from twenty-one to twenty-five years. Later, in October 1984, he told a press conference that his government had recovered a total of N112,129,482, which at the rate of exchange at the time was equal to £1,688,185. He also said he had recovered the unspent money from Fedeco and the National Assemblies. He said the numbers of persons detained: "were only 500". On 24th September, Buhari had set up a commission to control the press and other media. The chairman was Capt. Emeka Omeruah. Under him the press and other media were reduced to reporting only news; it being difficult to comment on any matter without being detained.

Several civilians who jumped for joy when Buhari seized power, soon became disenchanted with their hero. He did not hand over the presidency to Chief Awolowo. He kept it for himself. Then he detained more than 1,000 politicians, including several UPN governors and legislators, including Alhaji Lateef Jakande, the Governor of Lagos state and Awolowo's alter ego. Some he detained without trial; others he jailed for long terms after his special tribunal had found them guilty of corruption and other offences.

As Buhari and his military regime engrossed themselves in harrying politicians, to the delight of their adversaries, the economy was neglected. Inflation mounted weekly as the ban on imports began to create economic depression and endanger the few jobs available. Armed robbery cases increased, despite the death penalty imposed on convicted persons. Teachers in schools did not receive salaries for several months and the hospitals were closing rapidly for lack of drugs and equipment. When doctors and other hospital workers protested, Buhari responded by proscribing the Nigerian Medial Association. But, he did not think that the action hurt the doctors sufficiently; he passed a decree that no doctor who resigned from any hospital should be given a job in any other undertaking, medical or otherwise. Still on the offensive, he detained the President of the Nigerian Medical Association, Dr Thompson-Akpabio and his deputy Dr Beko Ransome Kuti. Then on 24th July, he reminded the public that his decree No. 2 of 1985 – The State Security (Detention of Persons) Decree was still alive and ready to clamp down "On any person big or small". Then he declared: "Any political discussion in public will be considered as an action contrary to the public interest and prejudicial to state security and to be punished accordingly".

As the media in the country was totally beaten down, news of the regime's brutality emanated only from foreign press or local rumour. In November 1984 the foreign Press reported that a coup which was planned for the First of October that year had been foiled and that forty-two Army Officers were executed. The Military alleged that the coup leaders had planned to stage a coup during the Independence Day Parade. Later it was rumoured that another ninety six military officers were executed while more than eight hundred troops waited their turns for execution. Under the military in Nigeria, rumours enjoy greater credibility than they do in democracies where the press is free subject to actions for libel.

Buhari's deputy in the Supreme Military Council was more feared. He was Brigadier Idiagbon. In 1984 he set up a quango which he called "War Against Indiscipline". He said the regime had "Identified Indiscipline as the bane of the Nigerian Society". The programme was "To instill discipline through campaigning because Nigerians clearly manifest indiscipline and they are vulgar, corrupt, fraudulent, bootlicking, un-gallant and unpatriotic. W.A. I. will remedy all these vices."

The regime also accused "The so-called educated elite for assuming meaningless highfaluting titles and chieftaincies only to impress gullible foreigners, particularly Europeans, in order to defraud them. And they cannot realise that these foreigners return to their own countries and give Nigeria a bad name".

The regime alleged that several top politicians and civil servants had hidden lots of the country's currency in cemeteries and bushes. In order to defeat 'these evil men', it suddenly announced that every denominating of the currency, the Naira, would be changed in colour and format. He then gave the people two weeks within which to exchange all their old currencies for new ones. Soldiers were stationed at all ports of entry to prevent smuggling in old currencies 'feared to have been hidden abroad.' The purpose of the operation was 'to render useless the huge amounts of Naira, corruptly acquired and hoarded in homes and in some cases hidden in family vaults and graves'. By the time the operation ended, millions had been rendered penniless, because they could not meet the deadline or were afraid to bring out large quantities of notes for the exchange.

On 27th August, 1985, General Buhari was toppled in a military coup staged by some of his own colleagues in the Supreme Military Council. There was countrywide rejoicing. But some who enjoyed the ruthlessness that did not affect them, were saddened by Buhari's exit. Many expected that the coup leader General Ibrahim Babngida who ousted him would be a more benevolent dictator.

CHAPTER 22

# The Regime with a Star-Crossed Election

The 27th August 1985 was an Islamic festival – Id Al Kabir (Festival of the Sacrifice). Like Christmas and Easter, it was a public holiday in Nigeria. The day ended the month-long period of fasting by devout Muslims. Those who can make it, usually go on pilgrimage to Mecca. Buhari was unwell and did not go on pilgrimage on that occasion. His deputy in the Supreme Military Council, Brigadier Babtunde Idiabong, went. That was the day on which his fellow Muslim, Alhaji General Badamosi Ibrahim Babangida, 44-years old, toppled his regime.

The first announcement of the coup was made by a predecessor, Joshua Dogon Yaro, a Christian who was also a member of the Supreme Military Council.* Buhari was immediately detained. All the ports, including airports and borders, were immediately closed. Even if he wanted to, Brigadier Idiagbon would not have been able to return to Nigeria. When the new junta had got itself settled, the ports were re-opened and Idiagbon flew to Lagos airport, only to be arrested and taken to his place of detention.

In the afternoon that day, Babangida, the new head of state, went on the radio and gave the reasons for the coup. He said Buhari's administration had been: "too rigid and uncompromising". He accused Buhari's deputy Brigadier Idiagbon of using the: "machinery of government to further his personal ambitions". He promised that his new administration would repeal all these obnoxious decrees which Buhari had enacted, and also that he would release all those jailed under those decrees. He condemned Buhari for causing the economic

*Under Babangida's regime it became the Armed Forces Ruling Council.

depression which had brought the country to the brink of decay and for nepotism, despotism, corruption and other ever-present evils in the country. In this regard Babangida followed the pattern of earlier military coup makers in the country. They always made their debut on the radio and television by trying to justify their actions with the hackneyed condemnation of the rulers they had toppled.

Within two days of the coup which brought him to power, Babangida decreed that he should be styled President instead of military head of state. It was the first time that a military ruler had insisted on being called President. Later, many visitors to the country took him for an elected President. This was what he wanted. But only a few Nigerians could discern his dissembling ambition to convert his position into a civilian President in the long run. Yet he looked an insipid character, and not aggressive as his predecessor, Buhari. He got his military training from Kaduna under the instruction of Major Nzeogwu, but he did not buy Nzeogwu's idolization of Nasser, Castro and Nkrumah. Later he fought in the civil war and also took part in the defeat of Dimka in 1976. Though a Northerner and Muslim, he did not belong to the Hausa-Fulani establishment. He is a Tappa from the Niger State and his wife Marian is an Ibo from Asaba, as was Nzeogwu.

Babangida had not been six months in office when his government announced on the 20th December that they had foiled an attempted military coup. The plotters of the coup included Babangida's own clansfolk, General Mamman Vasta and twenty five others. Some weeks later a special tribunal was set up to try them. Their trial and execution took less than two weeks. But of the twenty five men accused, only three were sent to jail. Others were executed by firing squad but not in public. By this time, trials by special tribunal and execution within hours of the persons accused, had been too frequent in

Nigeria so that not many were shocked. Those who came to power by means of the sword, always used it to destroy those who dared to try to unseat them. The victors never showed mercy. At least in Africa.

However, notwithstanding the penalty that awaited a failed coup, there were on the average two attempted coups each year. The coup leaders always knew that if they failed, death awaited them; but if they succeeded, the country's treasury was their trophy. It is commonly thought in Nigeria, that many soldiers think that the risk in coup making is not greater than drug trafficking, yet a million times more rewarding.*

In 1986 Babangida attended the 16th convention of the Organisation of Islamic Conference (OIC) in Morocco and, on entirely his own decision, committed Nigeria to be a member of the Organisation. That was the usual behaviour of a military dictator. He runs the country like a domestic establishment.

The news sparked off widespread resentment throughout the South. There were protests and demonstrations everywhere. Babangida was emphatically reminded that Nigeria is not an Islamic country and it is also not a Christian country. Individual Nigerians belonged to either of the two world religions and many belonged to purely local beliefs that must be tolerated.

Because of the distinctive spread of the two organised world religions, i.e. Christianity and Islam, it is impossible for the country to be committed politically to either religion. In the Northern areas of Sokoto, Kano, Zaria, Katsin and Bauchi, every indigene is probably a Muslim and this continued further Southwards to Ilorin and Kaba. But in other areas of the North, the number of Muslims is small; particularly South of Jos to the River Benue where there are less than ten percent Muslims.

In the Yoruba areas of the South, i.e. in the former Western Region, Muslims are about forty percent in Abeokuta

*In Buhari's military regime drug trafficking was punishable by death by firing squad.

and from there it gradually decreases eastwards to Ondo where there are less than ten percent Muslims. From there Islam fades away to Benin. East and South of Benin to Asaba and across the Niger and what was formerly the Eastern Region there are no indigenous Muslims whatsoever. In this type of situation it seems to many that the country cannot fit politically into any religious group.

In the South, Muslims and Christians have all the time lived together. Among the Yorubas, Muslims and Christians exist within the same family even in monogamous families. There are known monogamous families of about six in which both parents are Muslims but two of the children are Muslims, four Christians; of the Christians, one is Methodist, two Catholic and one an Anglican. Most parents send their children to Christian mission schools without bothering about their conversion, particularly before the government took over schools from the religious missions in 1973.

During the past decades the country has witnessed widespread religious riots and disturbances in the North where several churches and mosques have been burnt down and people killed. The South is for ever concerned about the growing religious bigotry. In 1993, the former Biafran leader Col. Ojukwu wrote:

"When somebody says that this country should be an Islamic state, we should give him the right to think that way. That is how he sees it ... The only thing is that being a Roman Catholic, I don't agree with him. Simple; you want it to be an Islamic state, I don't, if you insist, then I will insist on a Roman Catholic state. But if I am not going to have my Roman Catholic state, you must not have your Islamic state. Therefore, let us agree that religion should be out of it. We will now have a secular state ... And when someone says: 'My ambition is to dip the Koran into the waters of the Atlantic' his followers clap for him. The unfortunate thing is that to do so, you have to pass through my area; and I ain't gonna let you; simple."

In July 1987, Babangida and his followers, more used to grandiose utterances than their predecessors, launched what they titled: "Directorate of Mass Mobilisation for Self-reliance, Economic Recovery and Social Justice", otherwise known as MANSA. Later a decree in December the same year changed the title to Directorate of Social Mobilisation. It was one of the several quangos through which several adherents of the military regime got corrupted or obtained money indirectly from the treasury.

The preamble to the decree stated that: "Despite these transmutations in name, MANSA will remain one of the greatest innovations along with the Directorate of Foods and Rural Infrastructure (DFRRI) and the Directorate of Employment (NDE) of the present administration". And in continuation of the statement they said: "The purpose of these bodies are:

(a) to establish an appropriate framework for positive mobilisation and education of all Nigerians towards economic recovery, the development of new political order, and national integrity;
(b) to inculcate in all Nigerians the value and spirit of social justice and economic self-reliance through mobilising and harnessing of their energies and natural resources into productive use;
(c) to sensitize, induct and equip all Nigerians to fight against internal and external domination of

our resources by a few individuals and groups;
(d) to re-orient all Nigerians to shun waste and vanity and to shed all pretences of affluence in our lifestyles."

When some newspapers asked for clarification of the many difficult words and phrases jumbled together to explain the purpose of MANSA, the regime warned that any criticism of MANSA would not be tolerated and asked the public to be patriotic. The military regime's understanding of patriotism is not necessarily support for the nation's way of life, or obedience to its constitution but rather unreserved veneration of the military as a Godsend to remedy the evils of the country. Criticism, however moderate, stings them.

After setting up more quangos, including the National Institute for Democratic Studies, Babangida set out to form political parties for the country "because the people in general are too tribal and incapable of forming national parties with a countrywide outlook". The regime claimed that they wanted a system that would cement the various heterogeneous communities together to make a peaceful nation.

For this purpose he set up a panel to form political parties. The panel decided that the number of political parties must be limited to two. To them, the experience of 1979 when more than a hundred parties sought to register as political parties, was unacceptable. The panel also decided that each of the new political parties must have a moderate ideology. In this respect, they regarded fascism as: "too much to the right" whilst the British Conservative Party was: "Only a little to the right". Also Communism is regarded as: "too much to the left" whilst the Labour Party was only: "a little to the left". There are similar arrangements in other democracies but, the two main parties in Britain were taken as models. In the peculiar tribal nature of the Nigerian communities, they thought it imperative to ignore the fact that in democracies other parties can be formed and that there are no rigidly enforced limitations.

The regime therefore formed two political parties for Nigeria. The one which was: "a little to the right" was called the National Republican Convention (NRC). The one: "a little to the left" was called the Social Democratic Party (SDP). The regime also gave to each party its manifesto written by the same panel. The government then appointed the officers that would run each party as well as the funds for running for office, including all necessary equipment, such as vehicles, stationery, etc. The party officers were paid by the government which put the government in the position of having the exclusive right to discipline, promote and dismiss party leaders, as well as party functionaries.

Like other military rulers, Babangida enjoyed sycophants singing his praises. That usually gave them the false impression that they were popular. Having executed General Vasta and others at the beginning of his regime, he thought he was out of harms way. But suddenly on the night of the 12th April 1990, the Lagos radio boomed out the familiar announcement that usually introduces a military coup. "Good morning to you all good people of the Middle Belt and Southern Nigeria ... We have good news to tell you. We have today got rid of the corrupt regime of Ibrahim Babangida ...", and it accused him of several evils that were unprintable. It also announced that the: "Sudan North will be cut off from Nigeria". In a later announcement, the coup leader was introduced as Major Gideon Gwarzo Orka, from the non-Islamic or pagan area of the North.

The jubilation in the South was short-lived. Babangida's troops in Lagos and other loyal troops from the North, fought fierce battles in the streets of Lagos and in the end Major Orka's troops were defeated. Orka himself escaped. Those arrested and executed included Majors S.D. Mukoro and G.T. Edoja. This time none of the coup leaders was Hausa, Ibo or Yoruba. Babangida was not killed but many troops including his guards were.

After the leaders of the attempted coup had been dealt with, the regime paid attention to the series of steps it had planned for the coming of a new civilian regime to be headed by an elected President. The first step was the election of the chairman of each local government. The 449 chairmen were all elected on the same day in their respective areas. This followed the election of members of the Councils. By the beginning of 1992 all the state governors and the members of the state Houses of Assembly had been elected, and they were 'functioning' under the military.

Later, members of the Federal House of Representatives and the Senate were elected. According to the plan published by the NEC,* the election for the President would be on Saturday 12th June 1993. The military regime appeared ready to relinquish power. It made many believe that it would leave government, particularly as it appointed a new set of members for its executive council or cabinet. They included some former politicians like Matthew Mbu who had served in Balewa's government, and others; Chief Ernest Shonekan, a lawyer by profession, and who was head of the largest and oldest business concern in the country, the United Africa Company Ltd. From thence the government was called the: 'Transitional Government'.

Towards the end of 1992, the two political parties established by the government were busy over their American-style conventions for nominating presidential candidates for the election. The conventions ended early in 1993 and each of the two parties had selected its presidential candidates. The SDP selected fifty-six-year old Chief Mojeed Abiola, a

*National Electoral Commission headed by Professor Humphrey Nwusu.

Southerner and an accountant by profession and a wealthy businessman. The NRP also selected a businessman, Alhaji Bashir Tofa, a Northerner. Both names were submitted to the military government and the NEC for vetting. They were both accepted as suitable candidates for the Presidential election. Because, six months earlier, the government had rejected two candidates submitted to them by the parties, everyone became convinced that the government would now allow the elections to proceed as planned.

Thereupon, the parties continued their campaigns for the support of their respective candidates. Of the two candidates, Chief Abiola was better known, at least in the South. Being a Muslim leader, he was quite close to the Islamic leadership in the North. He was also much closer to the military leaders than the average Nigerian. He claimed a close friendship with General Mohammed and later General Babangida.

The NRC candidate, Alhaji Bashir Tofa, was a Northern Muslim who lived and carried on his business in Kano. He was forty-six in 1993, and had earlier completed academic studies in business in London. His running mate was Sylvester Ugo, an Ibo Christian. This fact, it was suspected, would not endear him to fundamentalist Muslims who are known to be widely active in the North. If the voters in Kano were tribal, Tofa would not have much chance in the city, unless, like Abiola, he had the strong backing of an extremely popular Hausa-Fulani Muslim. Abiola had one such person, he was retired General Yar'adua, probably the most influential politician in the whole of the North at the time.

By the middle of May, beside referring to his new cabinet as the Transitional Government, Babangida had not done much to convince people that he would leave in June. In the case of Obasanjo in 1979, he travelled to each state and bade farewell to the people. Babangida did not do that; instead he was still planning ahead for the continuation of the civil war in Liberia over which the country had already spent a fortune.

As the 12th of June approached, a sombre feeling of uneasiness gripped millions of Nigerians on account of the widespread doubt that he would leave, despite the oncoming Presidential election. A few people known to be his supporters had been writing to the newspapers suggesting that he should continue. But the pro-democracy movement was demonstrating that he should leave and that there should be an end to military governments.

On the 9th June, i.e. three days before polling day, Chief Arthur Nzeribe, leader of the Association of Better Nigeria, (ABN), a new movement, brought an action for an injunction to restrain the Electoral Commission from conducting the election on 12th June. Millions were surprised that the injunction was granted. The news was reported widely on the 10th. Half-disbelieving the news, many did not bother going to the polls, but the election went on.

Within twenty-four hours from the end of voting, the results began to be announced. Many glued themselves to the radio and television as the results came in. Then, suddenly the military government ordered the Returning Officers to stop announcing the results. Many were baffled and the politicians were dumbfounded. Later the SDP politicians commenced actions in various courts in Benin and Oyo, praying the courts to compel the Returning Officers in those states to continue announcing the results. Whereupon, other politicians in other states commenced actions praying that the Returning Officers in these states be restrained from announcing the results. By the second day of the election, writs and orders opposing one another were flying out from the courts to the offices of Returning Officers and the Electoral Commission. It blamed the cancellation on the courts and on the conduct of the elections which they said was fraudulent and corrupt. But observers both local and foreign reported that it appeared peaceful and fair.

The SDP, claiming that it was winning the election when it was stopped, spearheaded demonstrations in Lagos and other parts of the former Western region. The following day demonstrations and riots began as thousands shouted slogans such as: "Babangida must go; it is time for the South to rule the country; It is the turn of the Yoruba to rule". The police, unable to end the rioting, called in the military. But thousands of furious crowds chanted war songs and the troops opened fire. It was unofficially reported that eighteen died.

The following week a 'Sit-down strike' that lasted nearly a whole week paralysed business in Lagos while politicians and the military continued to engage in rhetoric inveighing against one another; sometimes with threats of secession. Frightened masses began the exodus in search of the tribal and clannish roots once again, as they did in 1966 and early 1967.

News of the incidents flashed all over the world. Britain led the European Community and the US in warning the military government that if they did not respect the aspirations of the people for democracy, sanctions would be imposed on the country. But the military ignored the warning. The EC issued another statement that they had stopped granting visas to military officers and their families. In Nigeria, this was embellished to mean that the next possible step would include freezing the accounts of military officers abroad in these countries. That did the trick. Frightened military officers now pressurized Babangida to quit.

Under pressure from his colleagues, Babangida thought of a face-saving manner of escape. He suggested another election to be held before the 27th August, the day on which he promised to leave. The parties did not support him. Also, this time the NRC was contending that it was it that would have won the election if the results were all announced. Both parties rejected Babangida's suggestion for another election. As the 27th August fast approached, Babangida invited the two parties and a third party, the military, to discuss the best way out of the deadlock. The three parties decided that a government of civilians and military should be formed in order to administer the country for eight months and to organise a presidential election at the end of the period. They called the government the Interim National Government. Not provided for in any constitution, it was an ad hoc arrangement probably as unconstitutional as any military regime.

Nevertheless, it seemed to be a practical solution that could usher in a civilian regime quickly and peacefully. On that account alone, many welcomed it. Chief Shonekan, who was already a member of Babangida's Transitional Government, was chosen as its head, while General Sanni Abacha, the military officer next in command to General Babangida became his deputy. Finally, Babangida handed over power to the Interim National Government on the 26th August and left.

## CHAPTER 23

## A Civilian Government that was not Elected

*"One talks about the amount of blood we have sunk into the unity of this country, Nigeria, but it is a fact; sentimentally, we think a break up would be a loss. It would be starting all over again ... but if that is what Nigerians want, I hope they would choose Czechoslovakia and not Yugoslavia."*
Odumegbu Ojukwu speaking in July 1993.

In order that the country did not sink more blood into the unity of the country, millions of Nigerians accepted the Interim National Government headed by Chief Ernest Shonekan. Shonekan and Abiola are both Yorubas; they are also from the same town – Abeokuta. It was thought that these facts would satisfy those who were tribally motivated to fight for Abiola. But even here, some saw some differences between the two men. It was not in respect of their tribe alone but in the tenure of the office. Abiola, if he had been allowed, would hold office for four years and possibly for eight years. The maximum for Shonekan was seven months. The election that he would organise might bring in someone of another tribe. On this account Shonekan, though a Yoruba, was not a satisfactory substitute. It was the Yorubas that would now fight him more fiercely and discredit him. Of course there were also some others who had invested in Abiola and could not count on Shonekan for patronage so easily as they thought they could with Abiola. Not having been a politician, Shonekan had no fans or others that had invested in him.

Many Nigerians considered Babangida's annulment of the June 12th election as a military coup against the favourite likely to win. In this respect there is also the argument that Babangida's coup against Abiola, his 'close friend' is not as hurtful in dimension as Buhari's coup against Shagari in 1983, because unlike Abiola who was only "very likely to win the election," Shagari had won, and had been sworn in as President, and had been actually in office. The argument was advanced by those who felt nauseated with the prolonged bickering about the June 12th annulment instead of treating it as another coup and moving forward, in order to end, once and for all, military interference in the politics of the country.

However, in his inaugural address Chief Shonekan said:

"Following the annulment of the June 12th election the formation of the Interim Government became necessary as a most viable stopgap arrangement pending the time a fresh Presidential election could be held to complete the transition programme initiated by Babangida's administration ... our recent wrenching experience remains a most painful reminder of our civil war which lasted three years with most traumatic consequences. Keen observers of the events of the last few weeks would wonder whether we learnt any lesson from the civil war ... The existence of the Interim National Government terminates on March 31st 1994 which makes a seven month tenure ..."

A few weeks after his inauguration, Shonekan decided to visit the state capitals. Babangida had, a year earlier, allowed all state assemblies and state governors to be elected. Of the five Yoruba state governors, only one, the Ondo governor, was prepared to welcome Shonekan to the state. Almost all the prominent men of the Yoruba states boycotted the visit. Shonekan and some other Yoruba elite who were seen as supporting the adversaries of the tribe had their houses burnt down. Many Yorubas saw the annulment of the June 12th election, which Abiola was 'winning' as hurtful as the pogrom against the Ibos in 1966. They expected that the tribe should close ranks as effectively as the Ibos did in 1966. The more vocal adversaries of Shonekan pretended that they were against him: "Because he was heading a military regime camouflaged as a civilian regime". This type of rhetoric swayed a lot of people to think that the anti-Shonekan group was also inflexible in their anti-military coups and regimes.

Some weeks before his visit to Ondo state, Shonekan had set up a panel to inquire into the circumstances of the annulment of the June election. Many used the inquiry to open up old wounds. Many supporters of Abiola in the name of pro-democracy insisted that, if the inquiry found that the election was peaceful and fair, then Shonekan must invite Abiola to be President. To this the Northern leaders contended that the inquiry was not necessary; that the panel should recommend that Alhaji Shehu Shagari who was elected President and was serving as such, before he was toppled by Buhari's coup, should be recalled to complete his term. The leaders in the East also contributed their voice, saying they would not accept any decision that was made under tribal influence.

Then as rhetoric and strikes continued, the country began to move towards another round of clashes as many got prepared for another exodus to their roots. The situation worsened when, despite the threatening turmoil, the government increased the price of petrol by more than 500 percent. It said it was: "removing the subsidy" as was the case in other countries.

As head of state, Chief Shonekan lived and worked in

the uncompleted new capital of Abuja, a dull city which had no other activity besides political meetings, intrigue and government. His neighbours were ambitious military officers, who envied him his job. Many of them fully knew how easily they could snatch it from him. He had no following and none knew him sufficiently well to get close enough to him in expectation of favours. It was the sort of situation in which only the most tenacious or iron-willed person could survive; and Nigerians are a most difficult people and not known to be valiant.

  On the 17th November 1993, a few military officers walked into the office of Chief Shonekan. They had no prior appointment for a meeting, and they were not announced before entry. Shonekan suspected the military were up to their usual tricks. He was right. They demanded his resignation and his quick agreement made it unnecessary to use the tanks and other military hardware they had left outside the premises of his office. It was the most peaceful coup in the country. Later an officer read out the resignation letter on the television. General Abacha, who at the time was next in command to Shonekan, gave his full support to the coup leaders and later took up the mantle as Head of State.

# Chapter 24

# The Failing Struggle

"One curious phenomenon of Abacha's coup was the flurry of enthusiasm with which it was received by those whom it was thought would oppose it ... Coup or no Coup, Abacha's triumphant entry, or return to power should be seen for what it is worth – a balm on our jaded nerves. It brought relief to a land ravished by drums of war, of the fear of Armageddon, social upheaval worse than the combination of Bosnia and Somalia ...", thus wrote *Newswatch* on 13th December 1993.

Chief Abiola himself and his running mate in the annulled Presidential election, Dr Kingibe, led the scramble to congratulate General Abacha right on the very day of the coup. Then followed several of the 'Pro-Democracy' activists and their leaders, including the most vocal such as Chief Lateef Jakande, a former chief priest of the Action Group, Dr Onaguruwa and Chief Babatope; all rushed to register their support for Abacha and his new military junta. Millions of their dumbfounded followers watched the stage helplessly as they remembered who Abacha was.

Abacha was the officer who announced the coup that brought Babangida to power in 1985. He and Babangida had been hand in glove for many years and throughout Babangida's government, Abacha had been second in command and a member of the cabinet. Also, it was Abacha who had led the fight against the attempted coup of Gideon Orka and saved Babangida in 1990. He appeared to many to be exactly the same as Babangida as far as his ambitions to rule the country. General Obasanjo spoke of the two of them, saying: "General

Babangida is the main architect of the state in which the nation finds itself today, and General Abacha was his eminent disciple, faithful supporter and beneficiary".

Within twenty-four hours of his coup, Abacha did what Shonekan or an elected civilian head of state could not do. He dissolved all the elected legislatures in the states and sacked all the elected governors and appointed military officers as governors for the states. He then convened a meeting of senior officers of the rank of major and above and asked them to advise him on how best he could rule the country. To many of these officers, the military had been a: 'stealing club'. While they listened to Abacha, many of them were busy planning how they could enrich themselves with their new positions. "Normally when people steal money, they hide it. In the case of the military in Nigeria, they flaunt it with reckless audacity."*

Before he appointed his cabinet, Abacha went on television and said:

> "All through the past decade or so, the nation's economic foundation and cherished values have been badly shaken and subverted. In all this, our people found solace in the expectation of a new political order ... and in the believing in the sage who said: 'seek ye first the political kingdom and everything else shall be added on to you ... † For eight years our country has been drifting in the manner that threatened its very existence as an entity ... it is in the midst of this dangerous drift that we found it necessary to step in to check the incipient chaos and secure the integrity of Nigeria as an indissoluble nation. The move towards democracy

---

*Professor Chuba Okadigbo in *Tell* Magazine, 14th February 1994. Okadigbo was a senator in Shagari's government, 1979-83.
†The sage he referred to was understood by many to mean Kwame Nkrumah.

must be handled with care, and we must lay a very solid foundation for the growth of democracy, and avoid any chaotic temporary solution".

To many millions of his listeners, the speech had no value whatsoever. Abacha himself was involved as the second person in command in the government during the decade he referred to. He and Bangida set up and introduced the 'temporary solution' he mentioned. Since 1966, the military had not been able to lay the foundation for the 'growth of democracy'. But in Nigeria, military dictators hear only their own voices. With haughty resolve they always choke any voice that differs from theirs. Hardly do they appreciate that is not the way to 'lay the very solid foundation for the growth of democracy'.

On the 19th of November, the junta further confounded the followers of Pro-democracy movement and others agitating for the end of military rule, when they offered jobs in military cabinet to several of their most militant opponents. Alhalji Kingibe became his Minister of External Affairs. Lateef Jadande became Minister for Works and Housing, Olu Onaguruwa became the Attorney General and Ebeniza Babatope was appointed Minister of Transport. However as events happened later, they were only the junta's catspaw while it got itself well on the saddle of dictatorship.

Meanwhile, the followers of Pro-democracy movement helplessly endured the frustrating apostasy of the weak leaders, but lamented and grouched "Instead of Abiola and others whose voices were so loud during the 12th June debacle continuing the struggle for the people's mandate of restoring democracy, they turned round to support Abacha's military regime".

However, Abiola soon realised that Abacha did not stage his coup for the purpose of enthroning him as the president of Nigeria. On the other side his own followers in the party continued to berate him for his 'cowardice' and they goaded him 'to do something'. For a time he was imprecise about his next step, except to leave the country. That made it worse for him within the country, as it confirmed the accusation of cowardice. But abroad, he found much sympathy for his cause among his fellow countrymen and the press. That buoyed him up to a determination to fight for the end of military rule in Nigeria. In this, he was supported by a veteran politician, Anthony Enahoro, and a well-respected fellow countryman, Wole Showinka, the Nobel laureate.

Returning to Nigeria in May 1994, Abiola was impelled by his supporters mainly the Yorubas and the workers in the oil industries 'to take up his mandate'. By this they meant that he should declare himself President of Nigeria. By early June Abiola had been completely convinced that he should do so. Now the die is cast: and he seemed prepared for the consequences.

On the 11th June 1994 at the Eleganza Sports Club in Lagos, amidst slogan-chanting pro-democracy activists and motorcycle outriders in uniform, Chief Abiola declared himself 'President And Commander In Chief of Nigeria'. Then followed a prolonged thunderous applause and cheers. He did nothing more than to return to his home and entertain his supporters and well-wishers.

A few days later, the rumour began that he had been arrested and taken to appear in court at Abuja, the new capital of the country. In Abuja he was charged with treason which carried the death penalty. But after a few appearances in court, he was not seen in public any more. Despite world intervention and call for his release or trial, he continued to languish in detention with thousands of other Nigerians.

Ignoring Abiola's issue, later in the year 1994, the junta, following the example of earlier successful coup makers, set up a constitutional assembly to discuss yet another constitution for the country. Members of the Assembly were partly elected and partly nominated by the military regime. Among the members elected was Odumegbu Ojukwu, the erstwhile Biafran leader. Among the members nominated by the military to represent some Northern interest was Dr Umaru Dikko, who under the military regime of Mohammed Buhari had taken refuge in the United Kingdom, where an attempt to kidnap him and fly him back to Nigeria was foiled. Under General Abacha's military regime, Dikko returned to Nigeria as a hero, and took a grand seat at the Constitutional Assembly. Dikko's return under those circumstances reminded Nigerians of the saying in the country that 'No condition is permanent' and 'Never count a Nigerian off until he's dead and buried'. But, it sickened many Southern Nigerians.

The Assembly was presided over by Mr Justice Karibi White, a judge of the Supreme Court. It did not however have the full backing of the Yorubas. At a Conference of Yoruba Traditional Rulers held at Abeokuta in April 1994, the members did not address themselves to the issue of June 12, over which the masses in the South, particularly the Yorubas, were concerned. Instead they called on the Yorubas to support the military and also prayed the Military regime to provide a place for them in the proposed constitution by creating a House of Chiefs. That would give them money and status.

In 1951, Chief Awolowo in imitation of the British House of Lords, created a House of Chiefs in the Western Region. But many of the traditional rulers and chiefs were soon accused of being fawning stooges to politicians. Later constitutions did not provide for them. A good many became abjectly poor.

In contrast to the conference of traditional Rulers, the All Yoruba Leaders Conference, held at the Premier Hotel, Ibadan in August the same year, 1994, called on all Yorubas in Abacha's military regime, including the civil servants and the constitutional assembly, to withdraw their services. They resolved that "unless June 12 was actualised, we the Yoruba race will never recognise any President that emerges in any other election'. But only a few Yorubas took notice of the resolution which many expected that it would test 'a Yoruba resolve".

However, several Yoruba vented their grievances when the properties of some leading Yorubas, who did not support the 'June 12 debacle' and Abiola's cause, were set on fire.

Also in September that year a number of Yoruba elite and university dons had an audience with a traditional ruler and requested him to convene a meeting of Yoruba elders and 'leaders of thought' in order to consider secession of the Yoruba area of the country. Frightened of the military junta, the traditional ruler asked the group to see him again on the subject in ten days time. But on the fourth day, he did a bunk. He remained in the United Kingdom until long after Christmas that year. However, the group met again and resolved "Come hell or high wind, we shall work with other groups in Southern Nigeria to save the Yorubas from perpetual domination by the North". One of the group's leaders, a professor in Ife University, had urged that "We Yorubas must find a leader that can bring out the courage and the determination hidden inside us".*

Still, a good many Yorubas do not support the All Yoruba Leaders Conference and the group of dons. In October the following year, another faction of Yoruba leaders surfaced. This called itself Egbe Omo Yoruba; that is An Association of Yoruba sons and daughters. Its first conference was held in Lagos under the chairmanship of Chief Kola Balogun, a long-standing barrister and an erstwhile high apostle of Zik's NCNC from

---

*Unlike the Ibos in 1966-67 who were under one military leadership in one region, the Yorubas in 1994-97 were in five different States and different military rulers. It is more difficult to lead such groups in the Nigerian setting.

its beginning. At the conference which was its first outing, the Egbe condemned the All Yoruba Leaders Conference held in Ibadan and "All other Yoruba reactionary movements which are only antisocial movements full of antisocial elements who want to turn Yorubaland into a battleground". And it called upon "all Yorubas to support the Abacha military regime wholeheartedly". Then it requested the military regime to create four more states in the Yoruba speaking areas. In a whole page advertisement in the *Daily Times* of the 19th October 1995, the Egbe listed the names of its seventy-two member inner executive and referred to itself as "a social organisation".

Many Nigerians did not share the fear of the Egbe Omo Yoruba that if they supported Abiola or merely discussed secession, Yorubaland would be turned into battleground. Instead, there is a general belief that the military regime, or even a civilian Federal Government, cannot justify a fight against the Yorubas if they decided to secede within their 1966 area. In 1967, Gowon justified his war against the Eastern Region for declaring secession, on the ground, principally, that the non-Ibo area, particularly the Ijaws and the Effiks, did not want to secede with the Ibos. And this was why most of the world supported him in the prosecution of the war. Understandably, the Ibos, surrounded by non-Ibos, did not want to secede alone. The Yoruba area with the Atlantic in the South and the Republic of Benin on the West are not so surrounded. This area excludes Ilorin which is disputable.

It was not only the Yorubas who considered the question of secession since 1993. Easterners at home did not generally contemplate any new Biafra. But abroad, particularly in the United Kingdom, the London based Biafran Association became lively in 1993, with the rallying cry "We cannot adopt a 1914 amalgamation that is inimical to us". Its fifty-six years old leader, who hails from the Cross River area, assiduously spread the gospel for a new Biafra.

Preaching his gospel for the new Biafra, to some Nigerians near a public library in London, the leader of the Association said: "The new Biafra will be the most peaceful nation in Africa. This time it will be achieved peacefully because the time is right. It will not be an Ibo dominated affair; every tribe East of the Niger is involved in the struggle. No state in the new Biafra will be too large and every linguistic community however small will have the right to have its own autonomous state. The government will not be engaged in any contract or business and all minerals will belong to those on whose lands they are exploited, subject to special taxation, like in the civilised countries. Only offshore minerals will be entirely owned by the nation." It was later rumoured that some of the members had travelled to the Baltic states to study how those states got out of the Soviet Union peacefully. But that is thought to be unnecessary as no part of Nigeria annexed the other. They were all merged together by Great Britain.

In Lagos one of the most popular advocates of splitting the country into North and South is Adebiyi Olumono, a well known barrister who was a political activist during the years before independence. Like Adebiji, many in Lagos think that it would not be difficult to convince both Southern and Northern leaderships that splitting would be beneficial to both sections of Nigeria. In a friendly situation the North could continue to use Southern ports, as if the two were the same country. "The North and the South definitely need separate administrations" he insisted. In the mid-West, Chief Anthony Enahoro,* before his detention by the Military regime in 1995, campaigned for the country to be grouped into eight confederate regions if that would be acceptable to the majority in each of the areas. But a great majority in the Mid-West express a preference for a North/South division.

*In 1996 he escaped to the United States of America. Like Wole Soyinka he continues to keep away from Nigeria under military rule.

It was in the light of the feeling about splitting that many received the news of the 1994 conference to discuss a new constitution. A good majority considered the discussion on a new constitution to be cliched. The country has spent more than fifty years of its eighty-years existence discussing, making, amending and drafting 'new constitutions' that have not helped it to settle in peace. They now looked for what they called: "A National Conference" to discuss splitting the country. "A National Conference is eighty-years overdue ... the British did not consult us before the amalgamation of the North and South in 1914 ... now we need a conference to determine whether what they did 80 years ago, when we did not know one another, is what we really want ... We need to sit round a table and talk about the unity and future of this country so that the forces of mutual distrust among the various ethnic groups will be laid to rest."*

Unlike in the days of the NPC and up to 1975, the Northern military generally do not support splitting up the country in any form, not even on the basis of confederation. Many in the South think that is because they are ruling it and have seen greater personal advantages than their predecessors. However, in this current discussion some Northerners do support the idea of reverting to the pre-1914 position. Alhaji Lawan Dambazua, a leader of the erstwhile Northern Elements Progressive Union and disciple of Aminu Kano, is the leading advocate of the topic. In February 1994 he told *Tell* magazine: "I will suggest that we sit down peacefully round a table and ask one another in every section of Nigeria if they will like to belong to Nigeria. Those who want to go, should be allowed to go in peace, instead of us deceiving one another over a non-existent concept of ONE NIGERIA". Some others in the North see reversion desirable because it would enable them to develop at their own speed, make the practice of the Islamic

*From *Tell* magazine, 13th December 1993.

religion more easily universal with its Sharia system of law unrestrictively accepted.

Anyway, Abacha's constitutional conference ended with few amendments to the American-style constitution, but it suggested that the office of the President should rotate between the North and the South. No one, however, believes that alone is likely to end the conflicts and move the country to real unity. The people in the South and those in the North just can't find a modus to live in harmony. As late as February 1995, the problems still continued to the extent that General Obasanjo, addressing the students of the Ahmadu Bello University, Zaria, Northern Nigeria, said:

> *"In Nigeria the Settler/Stranger syndrome aggravates the sense of belonging and stake in the country. It is pathetic and most lamentable that after forty-long years of residence in any part of Nigeria, a non-indigent is still regarded, and still regards himself as an alien in that part of the country. Worse still are the institutional and procedural mechanisms that accentuate, amplify and reinforce such a feeling of alienation. I refer in particular to such instruments as discriminatory school fees, and appointments and promotions in the civil services of states. It is important that we regard any Nigerian who had lived in a particular area for upwards of twenty years OR who has been born into that area as qualified for all the rights of an indigene of the area ..."*

The several different languages in the country present one of the most serious handicaps to its social progress and understanding among the general masses. In most European countries everyone speaks the official language; and contact among the peoples is not difficult. This is not so in Nigeria. In some parts of the country, there is a different language at every ten miles or less. English, the official language, is not spoken at home or in social gathering; only at schools and offices. Even so, only the educated few can read and write fairly well in English. In many parts of the country radio news are given in five different languages; yet some languages are left out. No Nigerian school teaches a language other than English and the language of the district in which the school is situated.

Ethnic division and distrust are more obnoxious in Nigeria than racism is in some other countries. For example, it is exceptional in Nigeria for a Nigerian to get employment in a Local Government or a state government establishment, other than in his ancestral local government or state government. This applies also to employment in schools and colleges run by local governments and state governments. Few of them will employ an 'outsider' unless there are no 'sons of the soil' available. The situation has been made more painful since 1973 when during Gowon's regime, the military took over Religious Mission schools and Colleges and gave them over to local governments and state governments.

The takeover of Mission schools and colleges was a serious blow to Southern Nigeria where some of the schools and colleges taken over, such as the CMS* Grammar School in Lagos and NDP† schools in the Niger Delta, were more than one hundred years old. It was European Christian missionaries aided by their home charities that introduced schools in the South as early as during the era of the Consuls in the middle of the last century. These schools were flourishing in Southern Nigeria before the Amalgamation and when Lugard

*CMS refers to Church Missionary Society, an imprint of the Church of England.
†NDP refers to Niger Delta Parsonage, a branch of the CMS in the Niger Delta.

was preventing Christian Missionaries from founding schools and colleges at all in the North. At the time of the takeover in 1973, Eastern Nigerians were still burdened with the miseries of the civil war and could do nothing. The rest in the South did not fight against the takeover. Yet the whole of Southern Nigeria treasure education highly.

Anyway, with regard to jobs in Nigeria, federal government jobs are available to all, regardless of tribe and state of origin. But here the quota system monitored by the 'Federal Character Commission' ensures the even spread of federal jobs among the various tribes and states indigenes in a fair proportion. The purpose is to prevent the practice of nepotism with regards to federal jobs. But the system is hopeless for job-hunting candidates whose tribes or states have overproduced qualified candidates'.

In 1984 the story was told in Nigeria that a number of Nigerians resident in the United Kingdom were elected into various local government councils including Lambeth, Hackney and Brent boroughs. Many in Nigeria could not believe the story, because such a thing could not happen in Nigeria. Here, everyone wanting to stand election for any position must do so, only in his ancestral constituency. Up to this day in 1997, no Nigerian gets a professional or similar job outside his own ancestral state or local government. Casual or unskilled jobs under foreign companies may be possible.

General Agui-Ironsi, in 1966, tried to end references to state or tribe of origin for jobs and other matters but the military regime that succeeded him re-introduced tribalism and kept it alive. Foreign businesses in the country do not practice tribalism but Nigerians in management positions in foreign businesses are often accused of practising nepotism.

## CHAPTER 25

# The Military's Final Solution Against Ogoni

In the 19th century explorers and colonisers won over the natives of the Niger Delta with gifts of colourful beads and fine clothes. Today (December 1995) the goodwill of the indigenous communities comes a little more expensive – but not much more, when you consider that Shell is earning more than half a million dollars a day from the region."*

The years 1994 and 1995 witnessed some of the most unpopular acts committed by military regimes in Nigeria. The sixth regime went wild in the fear that a coup was being plotted against it. They set out to confound their opponents by all means, and in particular by intimidating them unto submission and passivity. They could not tolerate even a demonstration by a few civil servants wanting an improved condition of service. In Makurdi, capital of Benue state, a few local government workers who attempted to strike were stripped naked in public and flogged a dozen times each.

As the regime continued to clamp down on dissidents, they closed several newspapers and magazines which they considered not favourable to them. They included the African Concord, the Guardian, Punch and Tell. Many of their editors were detained without trial. Later three hundred troops swooped on a meeting of Pro-democracy activists and arrested several of their leaders including Gani Fawehimi, the most respected lawyer in the country. In Abeokuta, home of the detained presidential candidate, Chief Mojeed Abiola, the

*The Independent, London 1st December 1995

military detained several outspoken members of the elite who had not escaped from the country.

Within Nigeria, opposition to the military has never really been concerted, only sporadic, here and there. Fortunately, the urge for democracy gained support abroad. Even this frightened the military junta. Suddenly, they cried wolf as a pretext for clamping down on frequent travellers whom they feared were destroying their image abroad by influencing foreign opinion against them.

Early in 1995 they announced that they had foiled a conspiracy to stage a coup against them. They immediately arrested several ex-military leaders and more pro-democracy activists. They included General Obasanjo, a former military head of state. In 1995, he was the junta's gadfly, and he accused them abroad of 'spending money like drunken sailors'. Others arrested with him were Dr Beko Ransome Kuti, a medical practitioner and a pro-democracy activist who, like Mojeed Abiola, hailed from Abeokuta. Others included journalists Miss Anyanwu, an editor and mother of three young children. They were charged with treason. For their trial, a Special Military Tribunal was set up. The fifty-two of them were tried in just four weeks. Twenty-nine of them were sentenced to death. But a timely intervention by world leaders, including Mr Jimmie Carter, an ex-president of the United States, saved them from execution within three days of their sentence. The death sentences were commuted to life imprisonment.

In Nigeria, Tribunals also called military tribunals since 1976, are courts with omnipotent jurisdictions and a hundred times more powerful than the Ordinary Law Courts. They differ from the Tribunals of the colonial period or civilian governments.

During the colonial era and before 1976, the government usually set up tribunals or other bodies for the purpose of inquiring into or investigating the causes and circumstances of incidents and other matters in order to avoid their re-occurrences. They were subject to the supervision of the Judiciary and they were bound to observe established rules of evidence, particularly those related to the rules of natural justice. In every case their decision could be appealed against and they never had jurisdiction to try criminal matters or to punish by restraint of liberty or property. If a tribunal during its proceedings found that in its opinion an offence had been committed, it could only refer the matter to the police. The system continued until 1976.

In February that year, General Murtalla Muhammed was killed during a military coup which was subdued by street fighting, and failed. Several military officers and civilians were arrested. Under General Obasanjo, who succeeded Murtalla, a military tribunal was set up to try the accused persons. Their trial, conviction and execution took less than one month. Their bodies were buried at Attan Cemetry at Yaba, near Lagos, before the news of their trial and execution was released to a shocked public.

A few months later, under the same regime of General Obasanjo, the same type of military tribunal was set up. This time, it was to try offenders of the newly created retrospective crimes relating to foreign exchange trafficking. It was given power to convict and jail for fifteen years; yet it was not bound by any rules of evidence whatsoever; and there could be no appeal against its decision on any ground whatsoever.

Unhappily, as far as the Bar was concerned, some High Court judges agreed to sit on the panel of the military tribunal with military officers in uniform. All the accused that were brought before it were civilians. In its first week of sitting, the tribunal convicted several Nigerians and foreign business men. They were all sentenced to long terms of imprisonment. The military were so pleased with these convictions that they set up many more of the type of tribunals as factories for turning innocent people into convicts.

At that time the Nigerian Bar Association was a strong body. Together with other organisations that championed the principles of justice, it struggled in vain to throw out the 'barbaric tribunals'. The Association unsuccessfully urged its members not to practise in tribunals that did not have rules to guide it and in respect of whose decisions there could be no appeal at all. It insisted that the law must be practised as an art and that it could not be so practised without abiding rules. The lawyers who practise in the sort of tribunals, the Association argued, merely lent respectability to them before the ordinary folks in the community. A defence lawyer in such a tribunal is like a soldier without weapons; he would be utterly useless. However, all the arguments failed to stop the use of military tribunals being used to try civilians and executing them. As has been said earlier, the military came to power by breaking the law, it seems impossible to convert them to respect the law and the justice that springs from it. So, military tribunals continued to be used by subsequent military regimes.

The most notorious use that has been made of military tribunals was in the case of Ken Saro-Wiwa and other Ogoni leaders fighting to end the destruction of their land through oil exploration by the Shell Company of Nigeria. In most parts of the world oil exploration and oil business mean big money. In Nigeria they also mean big trouble. Ninety-seven percent of the country's revenue that gets into the treasury comes from oil; and Shell is the largest producer from its vast wells in Ogoniland. To every military group that successfully staged a coup, and established a military regime, the treasury is the prize. Without Shell's business in Ogoniland, there would be very little money in the treasury and Nigeria's military officers would not be fabulously wealthy. To the military therefore, Shell is the most vital organisation in the country. They cannot touch Shell, but they can very easily subdue Ogoni and have their land exploited mercilessly for the wealth it produces. And they cannot allow Ogoni to continue to disturb Shell as they had done during the past three years. They now looked for a final solution to the 'Ogoni problem'. Final solutions usually involve fatal measures.

The Ogoni people are one of the smallest tribes in the Rivers State of Nigeria and they occupy the entrance to the Niger Delta with one of the worst terrain in the country. The struggles for the improvement of their area were conducted under The Movement for the Survival of Ogoni People, led by fifty-four year old prolific writer, Ken Saro-Wiwa, who was during the civil war the Administrator of Bonny. Like many others from the Niger Delta, during the civil war, he fought actively against the inclusion of the area in Biafra.

As the leader of the Ogonis for the purpose of redressing the injustice to them, Ken had been the sharpest thorn in the flesh of the military junta since Babangida's regime. The military found him a much more principled fighter for what he believed to be right and just than the average Nigerian. In a country that breeds an ingratiating and timid elite, and where many adjust to difficult circumstances very easily, Saro-Wiwa was a one off. He was known as a brave man who could not compromise his course venally. Many elite such as him, even in the Niger Delta, easily drop their principles and tussle for money to become village chief or for other megalomaniac pursuits.

So when on the 21st of May 1994, during a meeting of the Ogoni Movement, a fight took place and four leading members of the Movement unfortunately lost their lives, the military regime did not allow the state police to complete their investigation of the matter and refer it to the Ordinary Courts as was usual. Even as the police were investigating the matter, the military government took it over. They cited the precedence for their action from a decree of General Obasanjo's regime, titled Federal Civil Disturbances Tribunal, 1977.

By early 1995, the military regime, having taken the matter over from the police, had set up its Special Military Tribunal at Port Harcout, capital of the Rivers state, and where the junta had appointed a Northern officer, the Administrator, following the coup in 1993. The tribunal was 'special' in every way. It was not to be bound by any rules of evidence or law whatsoever; and there could be no appeal against its decision, but the military must confirm any sentence passed by it.

The press reported that many of the intended witnesses for the prosecution declined and asserted by affidavit that they had been promised money to give false accounts of what happened, but were disturbed by their respective conscience to withdraw. The accused themselves put up the defences of alibi. But all such defences were for a law court, not for the special military tribunal, in which the panel included some military officers of the rank of major.

When their judgement came on the 1st November 1995, it was Guilty. The sentence was Death. Four days later, the military junta at their headquarters in Abuja, confirmed the sentence. Five days later, despite worldwide outcry for a stay of execution, Ken Saro-Wiwa and eight other accused were hanged at Port Harcourt Prison only fifteen miles from Ogoniland. As he was led to the gallows, Ken exclaimed: "Lord receive my soul and let the struggle for justice in Ogoniland continue and bear fruit."

After the military junta had silenced the Ogoni leaders, they proscribed their Movement and prevented their compatriots from mourning them by attending church services to pray for their souls. The Ogoni people were not allowed even to dress in black as a sign of mourning.

In other parts of the Niger Delta, the dumbfounded folk believed that the military killed the Ogoni leaders to please Shell, and as the final solution of 'the Ogoni problem' and also to teach the rest of them a lesson.

Elsewhere in the country there was not much condemnation for the act of the military junta. There were very few public demonstrations on account of the execution. The heterogeneous nature of the Nigerian communities and the general heart-burnings among them, make it unusual for one tribe to feel concerned with the tribulations of another. In the same way as only a few non-Yorubas felt concerned with the ordeal of Chief Abiola, the detained Presidential candidate, so too, a few non-Ogonis (in Nigeria) condemned the military. Of course, some Yorubas openly did not support Abiola. They argued that "Abiola is not the Messiah" and that he was "too close to the Northern Military leadership and religious establishment to be of much help to the Southern cause". Nigerians abroad usually feel quite differently.

On top of the basic distrust among the various ethnic groups, there is in particular, no love lost in relation between the two large ethnic communities in the South. These are the Yorubas in the West and the Ibos in the East. Though there has never been any physical clash between them, the Yorubas continue to feel that the Ibos had not forgiven them for not supporting them in their Biafran cause in the civil war. The Ibos considered the war 'as a struggle to end Northern domination of the South.' That argument became popular at the end of the civil war. But the Yorubas too continue to remember that during the Balewa regime, 1958 to 1965, "The Ibos ganged up with the North to vanquish the Yorubas and their leader, Chief Awolowo".

The same feeling of bitterness exists between the Ibos

and the rest of the tribes in the former Eastern Region, particularly the people of the Niger Delta. Most of the victims of the Ogoni execution were among the foremost opponents of Biafra. Many in the Niger Delta say they could overhear the Ibos saying of them "It serves them right".

There has never been any incident or issue in the country in respect of which the various tribes have acted across ethnic lines or consideration; not even the 'struggle' for independence. That came as Zik said 'On a platter of gold'. However, it is likely that a future generation of Nigerians may be so highly developed that they will concern themselves with society problems no matter who is affected. Then the people will organise movements such as Greenpeace, Amnesty and Charities.

# CHAPTER 26

## 'Judicial Murder' that Provoked World Anger

"The death of Saro-Wiwa is only Nigeria's most recent wound. She will receive many more until she is delivered from a dictatorship so contemptuous of the well-being of her people and of world opinion."*

No incident in Nigeria has shocked the outside world so horribly as the hanging of Ken Saro-Wiwa and eight other Ogoni leaders by the Nigerian military junta on the 10th of November 1995. During the eight days between the sentence of death and their hanging world leaders and international organisations had passionately pleaded with the military to spare their lives. But the junta did not care a straw about world opinion and intercession. It was the most primitive nature of the so-called trial and the brutal execution that outraged the civilized world.

Many of the Commonwealth leaders at their Auckland, New Zealand conference were horrified by the sentence of the tribunal. Even at that stage, Mr. Robert Mugabe of Zimbabwe demanded stiff measures against the Nigerian military government. In South Africa, Archbishop Tutu, in a powerful speech, urged the Commonwealth to expel Nigeria until democracy was restored. But as some of the leaders hesitated, Her Majesty, the Queen, in an unusual manner, implored the Commonwealth to be seen to have some moral values.

While the Commonwealth leaders vacillated, millions of Nigerians abroad felt hopeless that sufficient indignation might not be vividly expressed to condemn the brutal action of the

---

* Chinua Achebe, leading Nigerian novelist, writing in *The Guardian*, London 11th November 1995.

Military. That would confirm the general impression of many Africans that "The Commonwealth is truly a mere extension of the OAU to include our brothers in the West Indies; and it will soon be as worthless as the OAU".

The OAU would condemn an evil and fight to end it only when it was perpetrated by the apartheid South Africa in those days, or when it related to what they saw as racism. That is why they usually had very little to discuss at their conferences since the end of apartheid. The organisation is known to be 'too soft' on brutality committed by African rulers even on tribal grounds. If the Commonwealth behaves in the same way, it too will be held contemptuously. It is immoral for a people or an organisation to condemn an action or a policy only when they are victims of it.

Anyway, after the death sentence had been carried out, the Commonwealth leaders blazed up. The British Prime Minister, Mr John Major, called the hanging 'Judicial Murder'. Mr Nelson Mandela, the South African President, became more inflamed and pledged to help Nigeria overcome its misfortune. At the end, they suspended Nigeria for two years unless democracy was restored. They did not say why they gave the military two more long years to continue when Mr Mojeed Abiola, who was considered to have won the last Presidential election, was still alive and ready to take up his mandate; though he was still in detention without trial.

Even before the Commonwealth Prime Ministers decided on what they would do, the governments of the United States of America and the European Community countries had withdrawn their ambassadors from Nigeria in expression of their anger for the brutal execution. And they also threatened to impose sanctions on the country unless democracy was restored. The action gladdened many Human Rights Activists around the world, even though the withdrawal was short-lived.

In some parts of the world, particularly in Europe, there was much public sympathy for the Ogoni cause. Several Human Rights and pro-democracy organisations condemned the execution and demonstrated against the brutality by the Nigerian military. Foremost among these were Anita Boddick's Body Shop organisation, Amnesty International, The Greenpeace Movement and World Council of Churches (WCC) and writer's organisations.

In January 1997, as a follow-up, the WCC published a report of the situation up-to-date in Ogoni, and it accused the military in Nigeria of "widespread oppression in oil-rich Ogoniland". It also accused Shell "of causing environmental devastation in the region". The report also stated that "a quiet state of siege, even today (January 1997) on Ogoniland ... intimidation, rape, arrests, torture, shooting and looting by soldiers continue to occur ... it is no wonder why Shell has been the target of international sanction. Its environmental record in Ogoniland and other minority oil producing areas is distasteful".

Despite world outrage over its brutal violation of Human Rights, the military junta did nothing to remedy the situation. Instead, they tried to mollify foreign governments and businesses with sweeteners of some sort. They repealed the regulations that required foreign businesses to have local participation as imposed by earlier military regimes. They also relaxed the restrictions on repatriation of profits imposed in 1972.

However, probably because of the depth of instability, the high crime rate and the pitiable state of the damaged economy, foreign businesses did not rush to the country on that account and Nigeria continued to be isolated, while the public industries continued to grind to a halt.

Even before 1990, almost all the public utilities had broken down or were on the verge of breaking down. There is probably no other country in Africa where electricity supply is so absolutely unreliable as in Nigeria. No household or corporate consumer can rely on the uninterrupted supply of electricity for seven days. To ensure a regular supply of electricity, everyone in the village, town and city requires a generating plant imported from distant countries. The situation is the same with regard to water supply. Everyone who can afford it constructs a bore hole or private well for water. The bad roads all over the country make travelling extremely hazardous. The two thousand single track line railways constructed at the beginning of the colonial era have not been increased by one inch. It is used mostly for cattle transportation from the North to the South. More than forty percent of the country's hospitals and clinics have closed down for lack of staff, medicine, equipment, maintenance of building and other factors. The only class of people who ever have medical treatment are the military and public servants. They are usually flown abroad for treatment. The most painful institution destroyed by the military is the country's educational system. Good schools and colleges are now things of the past.

CHAPTER 27

## Conclusions

"One of the greatest paradoxes of Africa is that its people are for the most part poor while its land is extraordinarily rich."*

No other country in Africa or even in the whole world has been as coercively dominated for so long a period by their own military as the people of Nigeria. Out of thirty-seven years since Independence, twenty-eight have been spent under various military despotism. During these twenty-eight years, the people have been prevented, under pain of detention without trial, from discussing in public the problems of their own country. Yet the military are by no means the most intelligent class in the community. If they are good soldiers, they cannot be good statesmen or politicians; for no-one can be jack of all trades. But they keep the country backward.

So Nigeria, a country blessed with natural resources of iron, gold, silver, petroleum, columbite, tin and with a variety of cash crops including palm oil, cocoa, groundnuts, timber and several others, today ranks as one of the poorest countries in the world. In the Seventies the income per capital was said to be two thousand and six hundred dollars. Today it is one hundred and fifteen dollars. It is still regressing.

There have been more than a dozen coups during this period of twenty-eight years. Out of these, only six succeeded to establish regimes. The suffering of the people caused by the incessant, sudden and violent changes of government by coup is beyond imagination. The situation is usually worsened by

*Nicholas Krislof in *International Herald Tribune*, May 27th 1997.

the ever increasing restrictive measures that follow every coup.

Within minutes of the sudden announcement of a coup, on the radio, a dawn to dusk curfew is imposed on the whole country; then the radio goes silent for days. All radio stations are government-owned and controlled. As the curfew is imposed, all the country's land, sea and air borders are closed too. No-one can lawfully get out or get into the country. Road blocks and searches are mounted in places, usually at intervals of every ten miles, so travel even within the country is impossible. There are hardly any railway passengers in the country.

In the administrative sector, every coup is followed by changes in the senior staff in every department. The same changes are made in all businesses in which the government has financial interests or equity shares. And in Nigeria, government has interest in every big business. Probably there is hardly any business that employs more than one thousand workers in which the government has no interest. Government therefore appoints a number of directors as well as the chairman or woman for the business. Each time there is a coup all these appointments are directly affected. Also as every transaction in land and property, whether leasehold or freehold or tenancy, requires the written consent of the government, a coup affects every transaction in land. The required consent has nothing to do with payment of taxes on the transaction. They are additional to such transactions. Following a coup, every programme and plan of the ousted government is dumped overboard and businesses connected with them are totally frustrated. In some cases they begin again under corrupt dealings.

In addition to these measures, following every coup, troops in battle readiness are stationed in every town and city, making the country look like an enemy territory just conquered by an invading army. Yet under these situations, fawning elite and intellectuals rush to applaud each incoming military junta in the hope of jobs and bounties. Some psychologists have warned that the general traumatic and frustrating conditions in Nigeria cause subhuman instinct among the intellectual class.

Then also the unstable situations caused by coups step up inflation which substantially reduces the value of everyone's income. In the effort to overcome the lowering of income and living standard, a great many become sycophants to the military junta. Many others are attracted to corruption. These include the military itself, judges, lawyers, accountants, public officers, licensing officers, revenue collecting officers and others. The bureaucracy in every section of the administrative machinery greases the wheels of corruption and fraudulent practices that are totally peculiar to Nigeria. Here in Nigeria corruption really is a combination of unjust enrichment and pure fraud. Now they are so widely practised that only a very few see them as wrong-doings. But they shock foreigners right from their first transaction in the country. The clumsy ways in which business is sometimes transacted show up corruption.

There has always been corruption in Nigeria; but the trauma and instability caused by twenty-eight years of military dictatorship have grossly multiplied it. Now it seems impossible to eradicate it. In August 1997 the Berlin-based Corruption Watchdog, Transparent International, (TI) published its report shameful of Nigeria, when it stated that Nigeria is the most corrupt country in the world.

It is sometimes argued that many other countries in the world are also corrupt. That may be true. But the leadership of several countries are not corrupt at all. It is always better to follow the examples of good countries with honest leaders. The situation in Nigeria is made worse by military despotism and the consequential denial of human rights. In order to end instability, the military must first de-commission itself like any other terrorist organisation.

Every constitutional conference or assembly since the end of the civil war has urged the military to reduce its strength or even disband completely. As pro-democracy activists put it, "No-one in Nigeria is afraid of a potential invading enemy and at any rate a military that is deeply involved in governing a complicated country like Nigeria cannot be a good fighting military force".

More important is the common knowledge in the country that only a very few Nigerians join the military at any time on purely patriotic grounds. Before 1958, many joined the military for the jobs it provided. Later several joined the army as a stepping stone to political power and big money as some of the officers themselves later admitted, as in the case of Major Ademoyega, already referred to in this work.

In December 1965, when the rumour of an impending military coup was in the air, the Prime Minister, Sir Abubakar Tafawa Balewa, was duly warned of it by his Intelligent Officers. But he disbelieved them. According to un-printed news or rumour Abubakar told his Intelligence Officers not to bother themselves about the young officers whom they were suspecting at the time. "We have lots of information about the remnants of Chief Awolowo's Action Group Party; they're the trouble makers, not these poor young officers who are enjoying themselves, knowing that Nigeria will never go to war. All around us are ants; we're the elephant. The British established an Army which we're obliged to take over. We don't really need an army".

Sir Abubakar was probably wrong to think that Nigeria was obliged to take over the Army. Unlike Great Britain in Europe, Nigeria in Africa does not require a balance of power in international politics. It was regrettable that he did not know that many of the young Nigerians he was encouraging into the army at the time were not joining the army to become professional soldiers. To many of them, the military was a short-cut to political power; as some of them later admitted and as events exposed.

In this respect, one can begin with the case of Major Ademoyega, who wrote "I came to the army with a heart pointed towards finding a solution to Nigerian political problems ... I had met and established a solid relationship with two young officers in the army, Nzeogwu and Ifeajuna, whose hearts point in the same direction as mine ... The political trend in most parts of the world in the late 1950s and early sixties was towards military take over of governments in which the soldier statesman emerge from the barracks during a political tension to restore his country to social and political peace, as well as economic stability."* The fact is that this thought and desire have not changed among a good many who have joined the military since Balewa's time.

On the fifteenth of January 1966, in his first radio broadcast, Major Nzeogwu† said "Our enemies are the political profiteers, the swindlers, the men in high and low places that seek bribes and demand ten percent, those that seek to keep the country divided permanently so that they can remain in office as minister and VIPs and the tribalists, the nepotists, those that make the country look big for nothing ... We promise that you will no more be ashamed to say you're Nigerians."

Major General Aguiyi-Ironsi snatched power from Nzeogwu on the 28th of January 1966, and in his first radio broadcast he said 'The Federal Military Government will stamp out corruption and dishonesty in our public life with ruthless efficiency and restore integrity and self respect in our public life ... An end will be put to extravagance and waste in public expenditure.'

---

*Already cited in Chapter 11 Major Ademoyega was trained in the British Military Academy at Aldershot. See his book titled *Why We Struck*, published by Evans Brothers Ltd., Ibadan 1981.
†He led the first coup in January 1966. See Chapter 11.

On the 4th of August the same year, Colonel Yakubu Gowon took over power from General Aguiyi-Ironsi following a military coup; and he said in his radio broadcast "I have the responsibility thrust upon me and I have to accept it in the national interest ... I like to add that meanwhile no constitutional or other change will be made without the fullest consultation with the people of this country".

On the 29th of July 1975, Brigadier Murtalla Muhammed staged a coup and took over the government from General Gowon. In his radio broadcast he said "Nigeria has been left drifting. The situation if not arrested would inevitably have resulted in chaos and even bloodshed ... The armed forces, having examined the situation came to the conclusion that certain changes were inevitable ... The leadership, either by design or default, have become insensitive to the true feelings and yearning of the people". He was second-in-command in Gowon's cabinet and in the Supreme Military Council.

On the 13th of February Muhammed was killed in an attempted coup and General Olusegun Obasanjo succeeded him. In his broadcast on the radio, General Obasanjo said: "I have been called upon against my personal wish and desire to serve as the new head of state. All policies of the Federal military government will continue". He was 'called upon' by the military to rule Nigeria.

On December 31st 1983, even as millions of Nigerians were celebrating the old year turning into the New Year of 1984, General Muhammed Buhari staged his coup and toppled President Shagari, who was installed President in 1979. In his first radio broadcast, Buhari said: "It is true that there is a worldwide economic recession. However, in the case of Nigeria its impact was aggravated by mismanagement ... While corruption and the indiscipline have been associated with our state of under development, these twin evils in our body politics have attained unprecedented heights in the past four years ... This new government will not tolerate kick-backs, inflation of contracts and over-invoicing of imports, etc., nor will it condone forgery, fraud, embezzlement, misuse and abuse of office and illegal dealings in foreign exchange and smuggling. Corruption has become so pervasive and intractable that a whole ministry has been created to stem it. This generation of Nigerians and indeed future generations have no other country than Nigeria. We shall remain here and salvage it".

On the 27th of August 1985 General Ibrahim Babangida staged his coup and toppled General Buhari. In his radio broadcast General Babangida, who insisted that he must be styled President, said on the national radio and television that: "The initial objectives which were to make fundamental changes, did not appear on the horizon. Because of the present state of uncertainty, suppression and stagnation resulting from the perpetration of small groups, the Nigerian Armed Forces could not, as part of this government, be unfairly permitted to take responsibility for failure ... The last twenty months have not witnessed any significant changes in the national economy. Contrary to expectation, we have been so far subjected to a steady deterioration in the general standard of living and intolerable suffering by the ordinary Nigerian has reached unprecedented heights." He was a member of Buhari's regime.

On the 18th of November 1993 General Abacha toppled the Interim National Government headed by Ernest Shonekan. In his first radio broadcast Abacha said: "Under the present circumstances the survival of our beloved country is far above any other consideration. Nigeria is the only country we have. We must therefore solve our problems ourselves. We must lay solid foundation for the growth of democracy. We should abhor or avoid any temporary solution. Drug trafficking and other economic crimes such as 419,* must be eliminated. We cannot afford further dislocation and destruction of our economy ... This regime will be firm, humane and decisive. It will not condone or tolerate any act of indiscipline. Any attempt to test our will, will be decisively dealt with".

The types of rhetorical support claimed by millions of Nigerians that "the country's military have been reduced to an evil political movement since 1966". Each batch that succeeded in setting up a regime, nourished on the timid and ingratiating vice of the more enlightened species: and they took advantage by saying that "Nigeria is the only country we have" – a basic statement which applies to almost every man and woman in every country. Yet millions of Nigerians have fled the country because of repressive military regimes, particularly Abacha's.

Military regimes in Nigeria have gone on for so long that the young and middle-aged Nigerian do not know anything better. The older ones know of only nine split years of the practice of democracy. This was why everyone looked forward to the Presidential election of June 1993. They had thought that it would be a turning point in the country's unending crises that began in 1945.

Always looking for a solution that would end the crises, the 1994 constitutional conference considered what they called 'Rotational Presidency' meaning that Northern Nigeria and Southern Nigeria should alternately present two candidates for election as President for four years term. It was later seen not to be satisfactory. Every tribe in each section would want to have a turn; and it would take some tribes more than eight hundred years to have a turn. The ridiculous proposal was therefore abandoned.

*Section 419 of the Nigerian Criminal Code deals with fraudulent practices. These crimes reached an alarming proportion during Babangida's regime and the term 419 was used to nickname it.

Following the example of earlier military regimes, the Abacha regime, in 1995, announced that it would consider the creation of more states "out of the present thirty states". Within four weeks of the announcement, more than one hundred tribes and clans had applied for separate states from the one to which they belonged. The common reason was the usual "freedom from the domination" of larger tribes in the same state. After considering the numerous applications for states, the military created only six new states, three in the North and three in the South. By the creation of the new states, the indigenes of the new states were moved from the former states to their new states. This affected all the members of the staffs in the public services of the states concerned. In consequence, a few new jobs in all grades were created. This will be followed in due course by the establishment of new universities, airports and all other facilities which other states enjoy. As more than ninety percent of the country's revenue is derived from oil, all these schemes depend on the 'revenue allocation' shared to all the states and local governments by the military. No state generates much money outside this fund.

Measures such as the creation of new states and appointments to quangos usually mollified peoples despair and even make them acquire smug attitudes in the depressive state of affairs.

With respect to the matters of Human Rights and Democracy about which the regime had angered the international community, in April 1996 a delegation of the Commonwealth Action Group consisting of high level officials and politicians, visited Nigeria. The delegation included representatives of Great Britain, Ghana, South Africa, Canada and Zimbabwe. They had gone to see the programme for democracy and Human Rights, but the regime refused to meet them. On return to London, the Group reviewed the development as they saw it in non-official circles.

In its review, the Group stated that: "Although the military had organised a 'non-political local government elections' in the preceding March, the general human rights situation in the country continues to deteriorate. For example, not only had political detainees not been released, but further political detention has occurred".

The so-called 'non-political election to the local government' was described by pro-democracy activists as "an attempt to deceive observers of Nigerian problems into thinking that an election of some value had occurred". The system was used as far back as 1947 when 'Electoral Colleges' were established to form assemblages in villages. From the assemblage, candidates were selected to Regional Assemblies, under the Richards Constitution. Since that time, the country had abandoned the practice, and had progressed far beyond that atavistic procedure that bred nepotism, corruption and other malpractices.

Unlike South Africa during the apartheid regime, Nigeria under military rule, presents some difficulties with regard to the imposition of sanctions. Apart from the fact that Nigeria is too underdeveloped to survive any severe sanction, the undemocratic regime in Nigeria is imposed by the military and the general public cannot remove them. In South Africa, the apartheid regime was elected by a section of the community and they could remove it in order to introduce a democratic regime.

The Commonwealth group probably had examined the situation before they agreed on the type of measures that might not cause unnecessary hardship on the general public.

In April 1996 they recommended the following measures for application by members of the Commonwealth and others sympathetic with the situation in the country.

1. Visa restriction on members of the military and their family.
2. Withdrawal of Military Attaches.
3. Cessation of Military training.
4. Embargo on sale of weapons to Nigeria.
5. Denial of Educational facilities for members of the military and their families.
6. An immediate visa ban on all sporting contacts.
7. Downgrading of cultural links.
8. Downgrading of diplomatic missions.
9. Ban on airlinks.
10. Freezing of financial assets and bank accounts of members of the regime and their families.

Anyway, as the struggle for the restoration of democracy continues, Nigerians are reminded of the several issues that frequently generated conflicts among the regions, states and local governments. One of the most notorious of these is Population Census. Since 1947 it has frequently caused riots and confrontations among the various local as well as regional governments.

Because population is used to determine the amount of revenue to which a state or local government is entitled, every state and local government became nervous at census periods; and everyone accused the others of inflating its number in order to cheat on Revenue allocation. "As long as population continues to be used as the basis on which to divide revenue, no matter the weight attached to it, Nigeria will never in the future be able to conduct a reliable and acceptable population census."*

If the local governments and state governments in Nigeria continue to accuse each other on census inflation and fraud,

* See Professor Adeotun Phillips: Nigerian *Financial Times* Survey. Spectrum Books Ibadan 1981.

the world will soon begin to disbelieve Nigeria for its population claim.

In 1961 an inter-regional conflict over census nearly caused the first civil war. Fortunately, the then Colonial Governor, Sir James Robertson, had not left office. He controlled the situation quite effectively and peace was maintained.

Nigerians who are old enough to know the early civilian governments of Sir Abubakar, and later Alhaji Shagari, are consumed with the awful memories of the unending ethnic conflicts and strife that distinguished those two periods. During those periods, democracy ushered in all the freedom including the right to free expressions and of assembly. In the exercise of this freedom, Nigerians exhibited some of their worst traits of tribalism, profligacy, blackmail and egocentrism, even in the running of political parties. In the general disquiet that followed the expected peace and development were not achieved.

However, notwithstanding all the past and presently unresolved problems, some Nigerians are still hopeful for the country's future. They say that it is likely that the experiences of the three decades of military rule marked by repression will help any new civilian government to behave diligently and prudently and make democracy grow in the country. They were pleased with the British Foreign Secretary, Malcolm Rifkind, when he said on the 28th of November 1996 that "the desire for democracy is alive across Africa".

Unfortunately Africans do not seem quite ready to fight for it. They have totally lost the twentieth century and they do not seem ready to board the fast moving train and join the rest of the world into the twenty-first century of peace, democracy and technology.

In Nigeria, if the Amalgamation continues, the twenty-first century will be lost to the people to an extent worse than the twentieth century has been. The people in Northern Nigeria and those in Southern Nigeria are still 'incompatible' today in 1997 as they had been in 1914. It must be admitted that the grand idea of One Big Great country of Nigeria has failed. "The basis for unity is not there," said General Gowan in 1966. He and others tried to restore that basis, even by force, but they failed. Any continuous effort to keep the country alive in its present amalgamated form will only prolong the misery and the waste of lives which the younger generations are experiencing.

A simple evidence of this is the fear which many young Southerners entertain in taking up, even temporary residence in Abuja, the new capital of the country, situated in the North. A good many young Southerners resign their reliable jobs instead of being transferred to Abuja. "It's difficult to imagine that any Southerner will ever think of making a home in Abuja. This military, they should have left us in our own Lagos," lamented a top senior civil servant in April 1997. But few Northerners ever make their homes in Lagos or other parts of the South. At best they only sojourn while engaged in trading. As has been discussed earlier in this work, after more than eighty years since the amalgamation, the two sides of Nigeria are still as divided as ever. As some put it: "We Nigerians cannot be the first people on earth to run a Nation of Babel successfully".

The world has several precedents of territories that have split to become smaller countries with great advantages to all its peoples. Some examples of this have been discussed earlier in this work. One was the Central African Federation which consisted of Northern Rhodesia, Southern Rhodesia and Nyasaland. In 1963 they separated and later became Zambia, Zimbabwe and Malawi respectively. They have since become the best of friends and good neighbours, and they are developing faster than Nigeria.

The worst handicap to national development of every kind is instability caused by social and political conflict due to distrust, tribal ambitions and other such evils. These have plagued Amalgamated Nigeria during the past fifty-two years. If the North and the South split, each of them may endeavour to begin anew. As has been discussed earlier, the main advantages to both sides would be that the number of different tribes would reduce in each of them and the conflicts arising from religion might also disappear in each of them. Each of them might break up further if necessary until they got settled like the states of the former Soviet Union. In this regard the international community must help the people of Nigeria to accept splitting peacefully, because it is that alone that can enable the people to move peacefully into the twenty-first century with the rest of the world.

CHAPTER 28

# The Commonwealth Failed Nigerians*

"Despite outspoken worries by African leaders, the heads of states decided to turn the Ministerial Group into a permanent Human Rights watchdog to report on any other members" wrote Michael Binyon of the London Times on 27th October 1997.

At the end, the Commonwealth conference held in Edinburgh 1997, saddened Nigerians when it decided to take Nigeria off the hook by not expelling it. Possibly Mr Tony Blaire, the British Prime Minister was frightened by the threat of the junta to pull Nigeria out of the Commonwealth. But he should have known that, all those countries, even with elected legitimate governments, that pulled out of the Commonwealth, soon returned to the fold. In Nigeria with the imminent disintegration hanging over it, pulling out of the Commonwealth appeared irrelevant for the time.

However, the expulsion of Nigeria from the Commonwealth might not have removed the junta and introduced democracy. It could only have damaged the junta's conceit and sharpened the courage of the pro democracy movement towards victory and quickened the disintegration of the country which appears extremely unavoidable in the long run.

Anyway, other Nigerians agree that it was sufficient that the Commonwealth did not reverse the suspension of Nigeria, despite the efforts of some African leaders in that direction. Some of these leaders had in the dark coven of the moribund O.A.U sworn to support the junta and keep Nigeria in continuing instability.

*The Commonwealth decided to continue the suspension of Nigeria until October 1998; and to expel it thereafter unless democracy is restored.

To many of them, the term "Human Rights" represents a denunciation of themselves. They climb to power by making coups and toppling legitimate governments. The O.A.U is full of such men. And they quite easily plague good men. "Even the South African President, Nelson Mandela, who once led attacks on General Abacha, fudged on Nigeria this time" Wrote Mary Braid in the Independent of 28th October 1997.

Understandably, Nelson Mandela is still feeling some gratitude to all those who fought to free him from Apartheid prison. In the case of Nigeria, he could better express his gratitude by fighting to free the people from repressive regimes. Also it was General Obasanjo, now held in prison by Abacha that led the struggle against Apartheid in the nineteen seventies and eighties.

Like the O.A.U the Commonwealth is getting to be full of leaders unloved by their own people. And as it continues to behave like the O.A.U it even opened its Edinburgh Conference with a display of native dances. Then it closed with self complimentary speeches. In order to be credible and liked, the Commonwealth must show that it has some basic principle which can give some hope, some times, to the people.

Looking at it optimistically, all these have happened in order for Nigerians to appreciate that the struggle to liberate themselves from the conflicts that began since 1945 is entirely on their own hands; with support from good people around the world.

The future continues to look worse, as the military continue in their ambitions to rule the country. Sometime it was "Buhari Must Go" then later it was "Babangida Must Go" Now the shouts are "Abacha Must Go". Still no one in Nigeria believes that Abacha's regime will be the last of the long relay of military regimes. The end of the amalgamation can also end military coups. The two sections will compete with each other to develop itself by itself alone. And the amalgamation can possibly end by peaceful actions pursued with unflinching determination by the masses on both or either section to end it.

It does not seem realistic as many think, that because the amalgamation was inflicted on the people by an earlier British Government, succeeding British Government, even today, has the obligation to terminate it. This notwithstanding that an earlier British Government had supported the North in rejecting even a secession clause for insertion in the constitution as proposed by Chief Awolowo during the London Conferences earlier referred to. Later, every one probably thought that a sort of Modus Vivendi might be found to enable the North and the South to share a common destiny. "After more than fifty years of trying, its time to revert to the position before the amalgamation" the people now cry.

## Chapter 29

## *Dedication to Wasted Lives*

*This chapter is dedicated to the thousands of Nigerians young and old whose precious lives have been wasted by the acts of various Military Regimes since 1966. Many of these victims of inhumanity were executed outright; that is without trial at all. Some were executed a few days after the 'judgement' of Military or special tribunals. Many were imprisoned outright. Others were imprisoned after the 'judgement' of Military or special tribunals. There is always no appeal against the judgement. A good many of them have died in prison. And thousands have escaped to foreign countries. The names of all these highly qualified and talented lives that have been destroyed to keep the Military in power can fill a volume larger than this book. It's everyone's moral obligation to strive that their number does not grow larger.*

# APPENDIX I

Reproduced by kind permission of Frank Cass & Co. Ltd. London.

## REPORT ON THE AMALGAMATION OF NORTHERN AND SOUTHERN NIGERIA

by Sir F. Lugard

### PART I. INTRODUCTION AND PRELIMINARIES TO AMALGAMATION

#### THE GENERAL CHARACTER OF NIGERIA

1. *Geography, area, and climate*

Before dealing with the amalgamation of the two separate Governments of Northern and Southern Nigeria, it will perhaps serve a useful purpose if I sketch briefly the character of each country, and indicate the causes of their divergent forms of Administration and the reasons which led to the necessity of amalgamation.

The area of 'Northern Nigeria' was about 255,700 square miles, that of 'Southern Nigeria' including the Colony, being about 76,700 square miles. The former consisted for the most part either of open prairie and cultivation, or was covered by sparse and low forest of the deciduous 'dry zone' type. The central portion—Zaria and Bauchi—forms a plateau varying from 2,000 to 4,500 ft. in altitude, with a bracing climate. The dry desert wind—the 'Hamattan'—which prevails in the winter months causes the temperature to fall rapidly when the hot sun goes down, so the nights, especially on the plateau, are often very cold. The rainfall is small, decreasing towards the confines of the Sahara, which forms the northern boundary.

Southern Nigeria, on the other hand, is situated in the zone of equatorial rainfall. A great part of the country is, or was till recently, covered by primeval forest. It is low-lying with the exception of the water-parting, which traverses it from East to West, and divides the watershed of the Niger and Benue to the North from that towards the sea in the South. The southern portion is intersected by a network of salt-water creeks, bordered by mangrove-swamp or vegetation so dense that it forms almost a wall of giant trees and undergrowth interlaced with creepers.

Horses, donkeys and vast herds—aggregating millions—of cattle, sheep, and goats flourish in the North, but animal life is scarce in the South, where the yam fields of a dense population cover every acre reclaimed from the grassless forests, which are infested with tsetse and other biting flies. There are, of course, exceptions to these generalities. Districts in the South from which the forest has disappeared tend to resemble the open character of the North, and there are districts in the North on the banks of the Niger and Benue which approximate to the characteristics of the South. These two great rivers are a prominent geographical feature of the country. The Niger, flowing North and South, divides the Southern Protectorate roughly into

293

halves. Some 250 miles from its mouth its course lies with a sharp inclination to the West, and the Benue, which joins it here, forms with it a continuous waterway of some 700 miles from the Cameroon frontier in the East to Jebba in the West, where the Niger, bending northwards again, is broken by rapids almost to the point where it first enters Nigeria from French territory. The River in the extreme East is the only other river which is navigable by large steamers, with the exception of the creeks and the affluents of the Niger Delta.

2. *Ethnography, population, religions, etc.*

The population of the North—described 60 years ago by Barth as the densest in all Africa—had by 1900 dwindled to some 9 millions, owing to inter-tribal war, and, above all, to the slave raids of the Fulani. But these dreaded horsemen could not penetrate the forests of the South, where a population estimated at 7¾ millions (probably an over-estimate) found refuge. These tribes are of purer negro stock than the Hausas and other negroids of the North. Though in the more open areas they show themselves to be admirable agriculturists, many of the delta tribes live a semi-aquatic life in their canoes, fishing and collecting the abundant sylvan produce (especially of the oil palm), both for their own sustenance and for trade with the middlemen who carry it to the coast merchants.

From a very early date the influence of Islam had made itself felt in the North, and the religious revival of the early years of the nineteenth century had formed the motive for the Fulani conquests, which swept the country from Sokoto in the north-west to Yola, 1,000 miles to the East, and from the Sahara to the confines of the Equatorial Belt. The social and religious organisation of the Koran supplemented, and combined with, the pre-existing, and probably advanced, form of tribal administration handed down from the powerful Songhay Empire, which had extended from Chad to Timbuktu. The courts were served by judges erudite in Moslem law and fearless in its impartial application. The system of taxation was highly developed, and the form of Administration highly centralised.

A rapid deterioration had, however, followed the decay of the religious zeal which had prompted the Fulani *Jihad*, and at the time when the Administration was assumed by the Imperial Government in 1900 the Fulani Emirates formed a series of separate despotisms, marked by the worst forms of wholesale slave-raiding, spoliation of the peasantry, inhuman cruelty and debased justice. The separate dynasty of Bornu on the Chad plain had fallen before the armies of Rabeh from Wadai, who at this time was looting and ravaging the country. The primitive Pagan races held their own in the inaccessible fastnesses of the mountainous districts of the plateau or in the forests bordering the Benue river. Others had come under the domination of the ruling race and lived a hard life.

The South was, for the most part, held in thrall by Fetish worship and the hideous ordeals of witchcraft, human sacrifice, and twin murder. The great Ibo race to the East of the Niger, numbering some 3 millions, and their cognate tribes had not developed beyond the stage of primitive savagery. In the West, the Kingdom of Benin—like its counterpart in Dahomey—had up to 1897 groaned under a despotism which revelled in holocausts of human victims for its Fetish rites. Further West the Yorubas, Egbas, and Jebus had evolved a fairly advanced system of Government under recognised rulers. The coast fringe was peopled by negro traders and middlemen, who had acquired a smattering of education in Mission schools, and who jealously guarded the approaches to the interior from the European merchant. In the principal towns (Lagos, Calabar, etc.) there were some few educated native gentlemen who practised as doctors, barristers, etc.

### 3. *The advent of British Rule*

The British Government, which had maintained a Consul at Lagos since 1852, obtained the cession of the island in 1861 with the sole object of putting an end to the overseas slave traffic. In the following years the abandonment of all West African settlements was contemplated, and any extension of responsibilities with the interior was vetoed. It was not therefore until the 'Scramble for Africa' which followed the Berlin Act of 1885 that any steps were taken to secure the coast line from Lagos to the Cameroons and to establish a claim to the hinterland as a British 'sphere of influence'. This area was then placed under the Consular jurisdiction of the Foreign Office (under the name of the Oil Rivers Protectorate), to whom also the Royal Niger Chartered Company, who were endeavouring to open up the districts bordering the Niger, were responsible. Colonial Office control remained limited to Lagos Colony. It was not until 1893–4 that, in consequence of friction with France, the Foreign Office was compelled to champion the cause of the Niger Company and to declare a Protectorate over the Niger territories. The Oil Rivers then became the Niger Coast Protectorate. With the advent of Mr. Chamberlain to the Colonial Office in 1895, British West Africa entered on a new era. British influence was extended into the Lagos hinterland. The 'French crisis' was brought to a close by the Convention of June, 1898, and steps were taken to buy out the Charter of the Niger Company. This was completed on January 1st, 1900, and the Governments of Northern and Southern Nigeria were created. The former included all territory North of Lat. 7° 10' (approx.) and the latter the old Niger Coast Protectorate, with the addition of such parts of the Company's territory as lay to the South of that line. Lagos formed a third Administration.

### 4. *Character of British Administration*

The divergent conditions which I have described—geographical, ethnographical, and climatic—together with the very different manner in which the two countries had come under the direct control of the Crown, had, as was to be expected, profoundly influenced the form which British Administration took in each. The early Administrations in the South were confined to the Coast area, where a large revenue was at hand from the duties imposed on imported trade spirits—small though the duties were at that time. Access to the interior was the first desideratum, the creation of roads through the primeval 'Bush', the clearing of waterways blocked with sudd, and, later, the creation of a port at Lagos and the commencement of a railway. Any coherent policy of Native Administration was well-nigh impossible in such circumstances, and the material was very unpromising except among the tribes in the interland of Lagos. Gradually the wall of opposition which barred access to the interior was broken down. Systematic penetration of the almost wholly unexplored country East of the Niger began in 1900, and in

E

1902 the Aro Fetish, whose ramifications extended throughout the eastern portion of the country—a cult of human sacrifice and slavery—was crushed by force of arms.

The inauguration of British rule in the North was in strong contrast. Here the Chartered Company, restricted by financial considerations, had been compelled to confine their depots chiefly to the banks of the Niger and Benue Rivers. The very existence of any organised Government was threatened by the haughty insolence of the Fulani armies. The condition of Bornu—where the French had intervened—compelled immediate action. Nothing could be done until a force strong enough to cope with these powerful Emirates had been created.

The West African Frontier Force was raised in 1898-99, and on its return from its successful campaign in Ashanti, the task of dealing with the Moslem Emirates was undertaken, in 1902-3. Kontagora, the noted slave-raider, who had boasted that, like a cat with a mouse, he would 'die with a slave in his mouth', was the first to be coerced. Nupe, who had also threatened the existence of the new Administration, followed. Bornu, overrun by Rabeh's army from the Egyptian Sudan, which in turn had been defeated in British territory by a French force, placed itself under the Government, and General Morland's force, *en route* thither, brought Bauchi under control, and its Emir was deposed in reprisal for his ruthless massacre of the people of Guaram. Zaria offered no opposition to peaceful occupation, but the murder of Captain Malony, Resident at Keffi, precipitated hostilities with Kano. The fall of this great city and that of Sokoto in March, 1903, was followed by the submission of the minor Emirates, and convinced those which had already submitted that their belief that the British would be exterminated by these powerful Emirs was vain.

When this had been accomplished, and the forces of disorder had been broken, the British Administration was faced with the insistent urgency of creating a new organisation and of developing a native policy without delay. The system evolved will be described in a later paragraph.

The necessity of securing means wherewith to carry on the Administration was no less insistent than the reorganisation of the Native Administration. There was no revenue to be got from spirits, which were wholly prohibited, while the cost of the large force necessary for the control of the country absorbed the greater part of the wholly inadequate grant from the Imperial Government.

5. *Necessity for Amalgamation:* (a) *Finance*

Such in brief were the antecedents which had given to the North and South their divergent characteristics and policies. In 1906 a further step in amalgamation was effected in the South. Southern Nigeria and Lagos became one Administration under the title of the Colony and Protectorate of Southern Nigeria. From this date the material prosperity of the South increased with astonishing rapidity. The liquor duties—increased from 3s. in 1901 to 3s. 6d. in 1905—stood at 5s. 6d. a gallon in 1912, and afforded an ever-increasing revenue, without any diminution in the quantity imported. They yielded a sum of £1,138,000 in 1913.

The North, largely dependent on the annual grant from the Imperial Government, was barely able to balance its budget with the most parsimonious economy, and was starved of the necessary staff, and unable to find funds to house its officers properly. Its energies were concentrated upon the development of the Native Administration and the revenue resulting from direct taxation. Its distance from the coast (250 miles) rendered the expansion of trade difficult. Thus the anomaly was presented of a country with an aggregate revenue practically equal to its needs, but divided into two by an arbitrary line of latitude. One portion was dependent on a grant paid by the British taxpayer, which in the year before Amalgamation stood at £136,000, and had averaged £314,500 for the 11 years ending March, 1912.

6. (b) *Railways*

To the financial dilemma there was now added a very pressing difficulty in regard to Railway policy and control. The North, to ensure the development of its trade and to secure its Customs duties, commenced a railway from Baro, a port on the Niger, to Kano in 1906.\* The South responded by pushing on the Lagos Railway to the frontier, and obtained the Secretary of State's sanction to carry it on in the North, to effect a junction with the Baro–Kano line at Minna. In the opinion of Sir John Eaglesome, Director of Railways, the line, when it reached the Northern Nigerian frontier at Offa, should have crossed the Niger at Pateji, traversing a well-populated country and tapping the great trade centre at Bida—thus avoiding the extremely costly and difficult bridge at Jebba, and the uninhabited country to the North of it—the distance to Minna being precisely the same. But no single railway policy had been possible, and the two outlets to the sea were now in acute competition. Major Waghorn, R.E., was sent out to report on the two railways, and propose some system of joint use and control. He animadverted very strongly on the needless cost which had characterised the construction of the southern section of the Lagos line. It was full of sharp curves and dangerous gradients, which had to be rectified at an expenditure of £200,000. It was stated that the section to Ibadan, which presented no special difficulties, had cost two millions (over £15,000 a mile). Immediate unification of control with a view to checking extravagance was recommended. The advent of the railway, moreover, accentuated the need for a revision of the apportionment of Customs duties collected at the port. The growing divergence of administrative methods, as the interior became opened up in the South, also called for a common policy. In a long memorandum, dated May, 1905 (while still High Commissioner of Northern Nigeria), I advocated amalgamation, a policy supported by the then High Commissioner of Southern Nigeria and the Governor of Lagos, and there was increasing evidence that it could no longer be postponed.

7. *Decision to Amalgamate*

Towards the close of 1911, Mr. (now Viscount) Harcourt, Secretary of State for the Colonies, invited me to undertake the task. I was at the time Governor of Hong Kong, having previously been High Commissioner of Northern Nigeria from its inauguration in 1900. I was therefore intimately acquainted with the method of Administration there, for the creation of which I had indeed been responsible. Reaching England in April, 1912, I was

\* This had been pressed by me in 1905, not only on these grounds but in order to render possible the realisation of the direct tax paid in kind, which was in danger of failure owing to the difficulty of finding a market for it, and to cheapen Administration.

appointed Governor of the two separate Administrations simultaneously, and after spending several weeks in England, to acquaint myself with the current views on some important matters, I proceeded to Africa in September, 1912. I returned in the following March, and submitted my proposals for amalgamation in May. They were accepted in September, when I returned to Nigeria, and on January 1st, 1914, the new Government of Nigeria, as set up by fresh Letters Patent and other Instruments, was proclaimed.

## 8. Nature of the Task

It was clear that so large a country as Nigeria, with an area of 332,400 square miles—of which the North and South were connected only by a single railway and the uncertain waterway of the Niger, while no lateral means of communication existed at all—must be divided into two or more dependent Administrations under the control of a Central Government. The first problem therefore which presented itself was the number of such Lieutenant-Governors, their powers, and relations to the various departments, together with the subordinate Administrative units throughout the country, and the control of such departments as the Railway and the Military Forces, which were common to the whole of Nigeria. The functions, and future constitutions, of the Executive and Legislative Councils, the unification of the Laws and the Regulations based upon them, and of the Executive 'General Orders' and other instructions, the Judicial system, the methods of Taxation direct and indirect, and the disposal of the Revenue so as to benefit the country as a whole, without creating jealousy and friction, the assimilation of the policy of Native Administration—these, with many minor problems, had to be solved by any scheme of amalgamation which should have any prospect of permanency. In every one of these matters the systems of the two Governments differed essentially as I shall show in discussing each in detail. The alarm and suspicion caused among the native population of the South by the appointment of a Committee to enquire into the question of land tenure added to the difficulty of the task. Amalgamation in my view was 'not a mere political, geographical, or more especially a financial expression'. I regarded it rather 'as a means whereby each part of Nigeria should be raised to the level of the highest place attained by any particular part'. Thus regarded each of the two Administrations had much to learn from the other. The North—a younger Government—was capable of improvement in its departmental organisation, and backward both in the development of its material resources and of the facilities (such as roads) required for the purpose. The South required a better organisation of its Native Administration and of its judicial system.

## PART II. METHOD OF AMALGAMATION
GENERAL SCHEME. DIVISION OF THE COUNTRY—CENTRAL DEPARTMENTS

## 9. Amalgamation, January 1st, 1914

On January 1st, 1914, the former Governments of Southern and Northern Nigeria were formally amalgamated with some fitting ceremonial. After the oaths of office had been taken at each capital—Lagos and Zungeru—by the

Governor-General, the Lieutenant-Governors, and the Chief Justice, etc., a Durbar was held on the great plain at Kano, which was attended by all the chief Moslem rulers from Sokoto to Chad, who met for the first time in common friendship to swear allegiance to His Majesty, and by representatives of the principal Pagan tribes. Though the retinue of the chiefs was necessarily limited by considerations of food supply, etc., it was estimated that not fewer than 30,000 horsemen took part in the picturesque display. Each in turn marched past and then gave the Salute of the Desert, charging at full gallop with brandished weapons. Nor was the gathering a mere ceremonial. Hereditary rivals met as friends. The Shehu of Bornu was the honoured guest of his quondam enemy, the Fulani Emir of Kano, and no friction or dispute for precedence among their somewhat turbulent following disturbed the harmony of this remarkable gathering, which undoubtedly had a very beneficial effect. A uniform time for Nigeria (viz., $7\frac{1}{2}°$ meridian)—half an hour fast of Greenwich—was established for railway and telegraphic convenience. A single weekly Gazette, with a supplement containing all ephemeral matter, superseded the former publications. The 'General Orders' of the former Administrations were cancelled, and replaced as soon as possible by Standing Orders common to all Nigeria. The printed forms in use in all departments were revised and largely reduced. A new Colonial badge was introduced consisting of the interlaced triangles known as 'Solomon's Seal'.

\*

### 10. The Governor-General

The whole of Nigeria—the size of which approximates to one-third that of British India, with a population of 16 or 17 millions, the largest of the Crown Colonies and Protectorates of the Empire—was placed under the control of a Governor-General, but it was intimated that the title was personal to myself. The Letters Patent and other Instruments setting up the new Government omitted the usual provision that when the Governor was absent from Nigeria his Deputy should administer the Government, for it had been decided that the Governor should spend four months of each year *on duty* in England. The object of this somewhat startling departure from precedent was to preserve continuity of Administration, to keep closer touch, by the personal presence of the Governor, with the Colonial Office and the commercial and other interests in England, and to give the Governor some time to carry through the heavy work of re-drafting laws, etc., while relieved of the onus of comparatively unimportant daily routine in Africa. He was when absent from Nigeria represented by a Deputy, fully empowered to deal with all matters of urgency, with whom he was in telegraphic communication. It was not desired to decrease the responsibility of 'the man on the spot'—the change, as Mr. Churchill expressed it, consisted rather of a definition of 'the spot' due to the rapid means of transport and communication which steam and telegraphy had introduced. A room was provided at the Colonial Office for the use of the Governor and his Private Secretary and clerk.

The system served its purpose, and without it I doubt if the work could have been accomplished. It presented obvious difficulties, and the Secretary of State decided to cancel it in 1917. It demands only a brief reference here, as an integral part of the method by which amalgamation was carried out.

\*Author's Note: The ceremony described in paragraph 9 was not attended by Southerners. A ceremony at Tinubu Square in Lagos was attended by civil servants to mark the event.

## Appendix II

Maps showing the restlessness of the Nigerian tribes and clans. Each of them struggles for a secure place. They force the three regions created in 1945 into thirty-six states by 1996, and many more states are in demand as every tribe and every clan believes

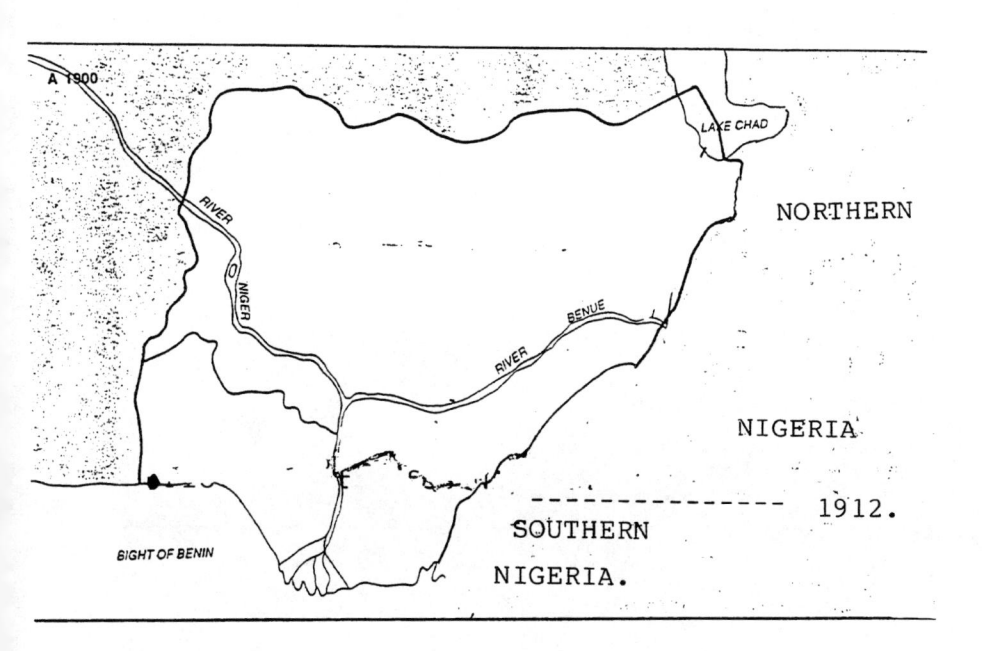

### 1914 Amalgamation

1. Protectorate of Northern Nigeria
2. Colony of Lagos and Protectorate of Southern Nigeria

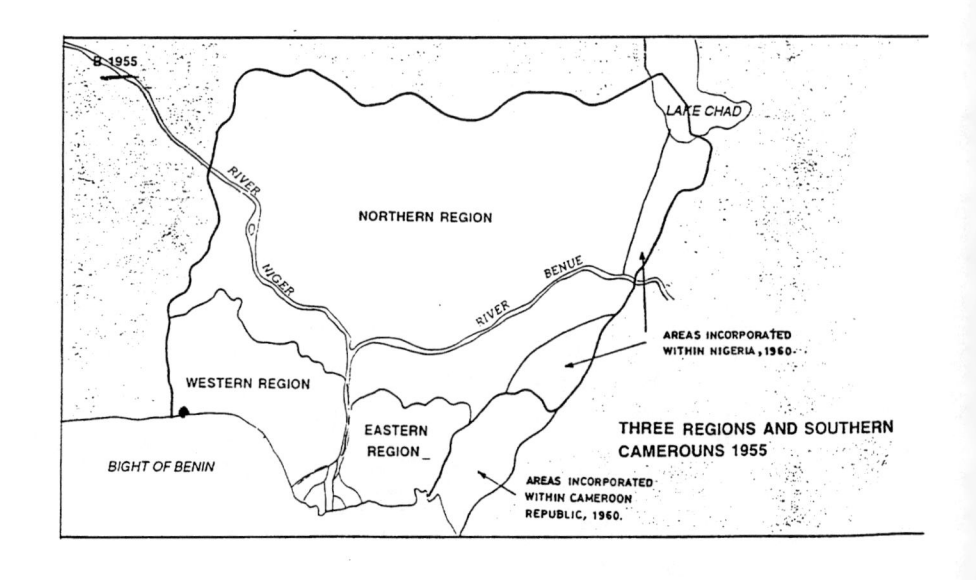

### Three Regions 1945-63

1. Northern Region  2. Western Region
3. Eastern Region

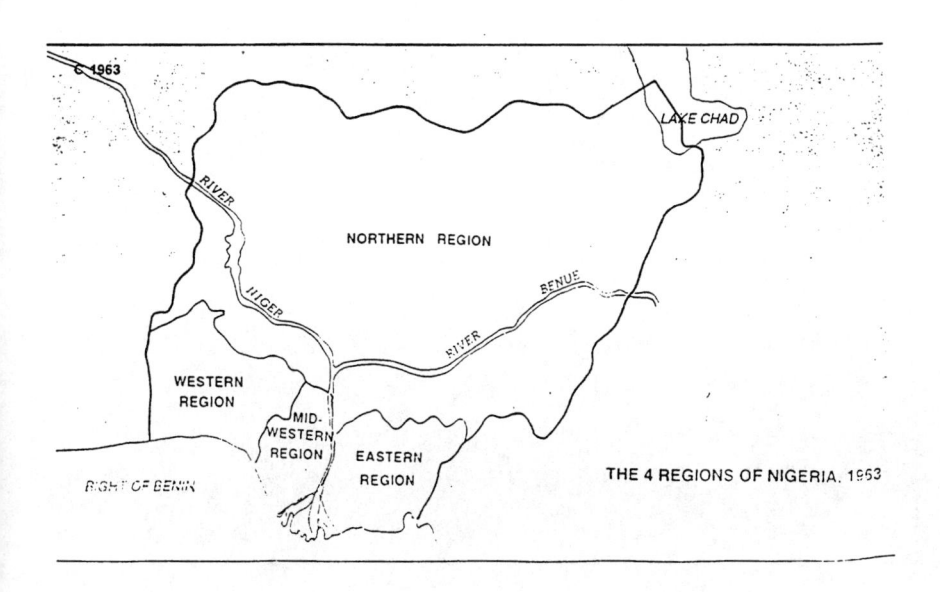

## Four Regions 1963-67

1. Northern Region
2. Western Region
3. Mid-Western Region
4. Eastern Region

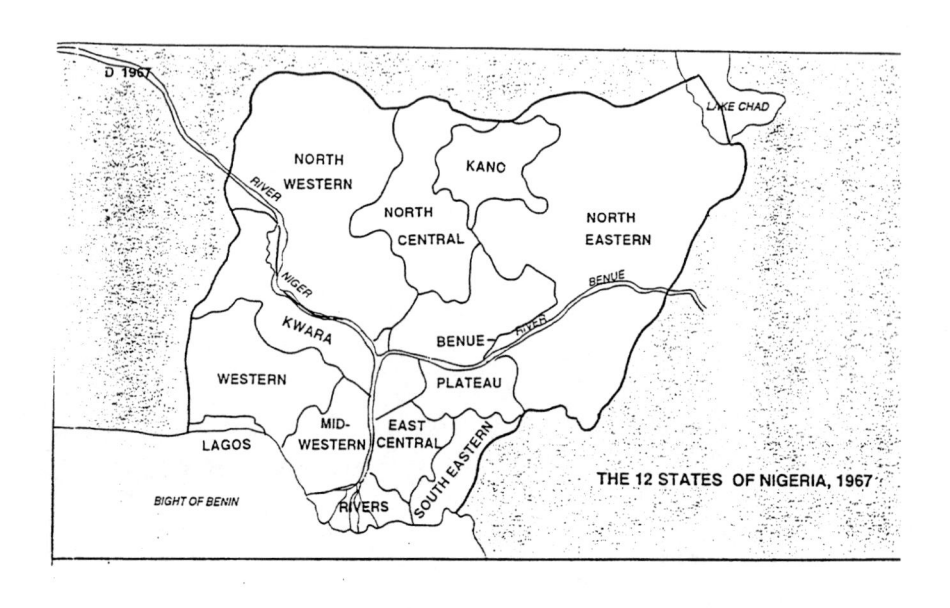

## Twelve States 1967-75

1. Western State
2. Kwara State
3. North Western State
4. Kaduna State
5. Kano State
6. North Eastern State
7. Benue Plateau State
8. South Eastern State
9. River State
10. Mid-Western State
11. East Central State
12. Lagos State

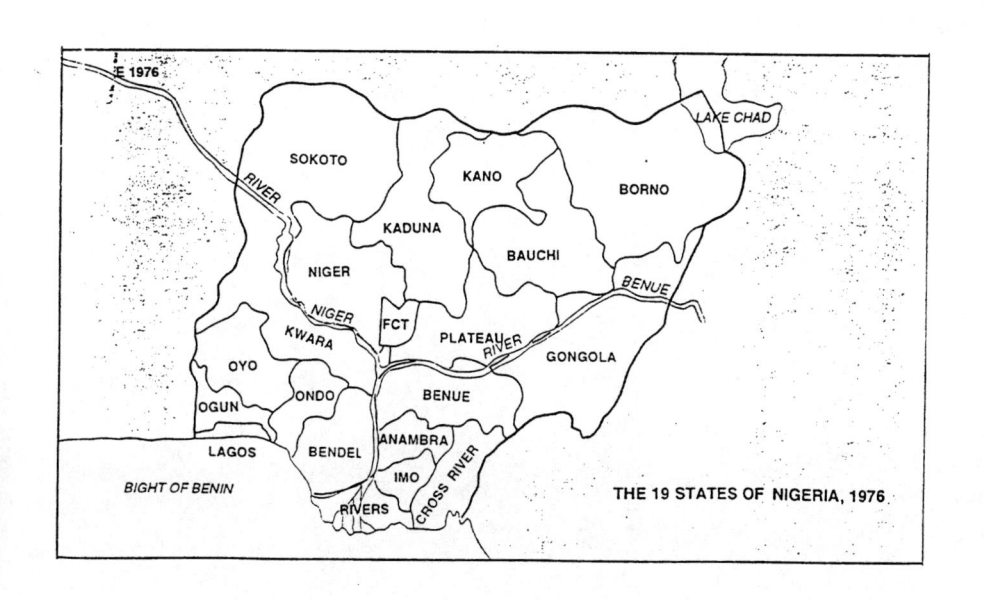

**Nineteen States in 1976**

THE 21 STATES OF NIGERIA, 1987.

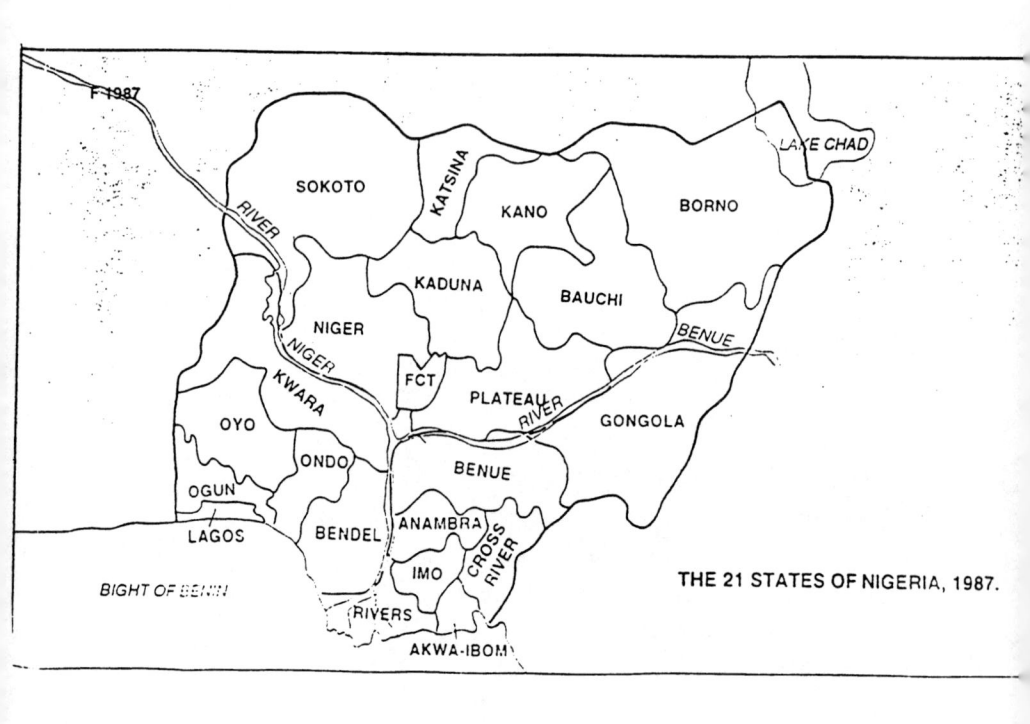

**Twenty-one States in 1997**

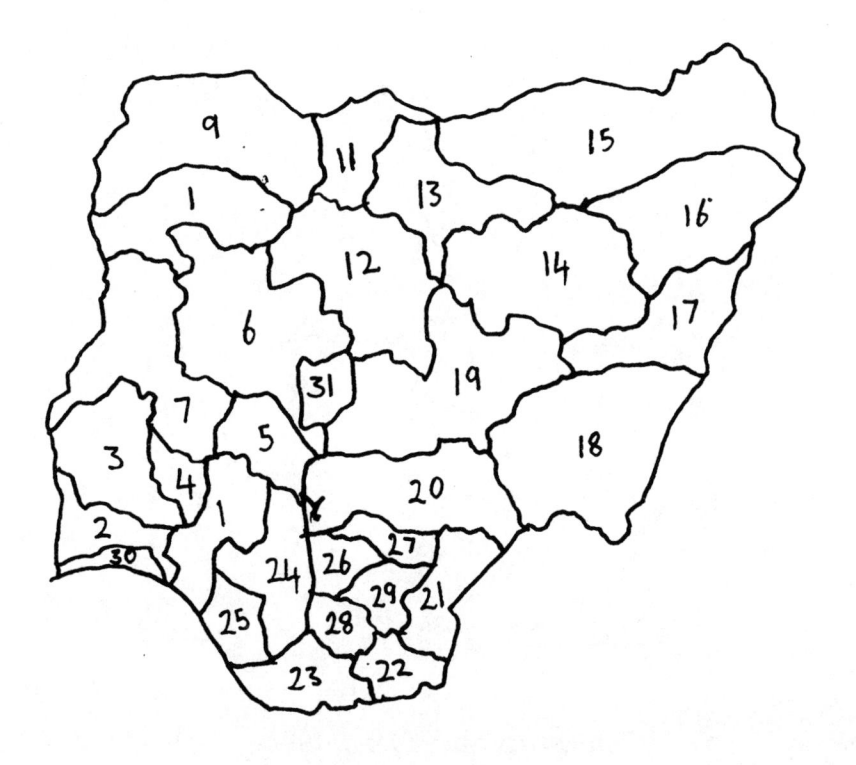

## Thirty States 1992-96

1. Ondu State
2. Ogun State
3. Oyo State
4. Osun State
5. Kogi State
6. Kebbi State
7. Kwara State
8. Niger State
9. Sokoto State
10. Kaduna State
11. Katsina State
12. Jigawa State
13. Kano State
14. Bauchi State
15. Borno State
16. Yobe State
17. Adamawa State
18. Taraba State
19. Benue State
20. Plateau State
21. Cross River State
22. Akwa-Ibom
23. River State
24. Edo State
25. Delta State
26. Anambra State
27. Enugu State
28. Imo State
29. Abia State
30. Lagos State

*@ Federal Capital Territory 31

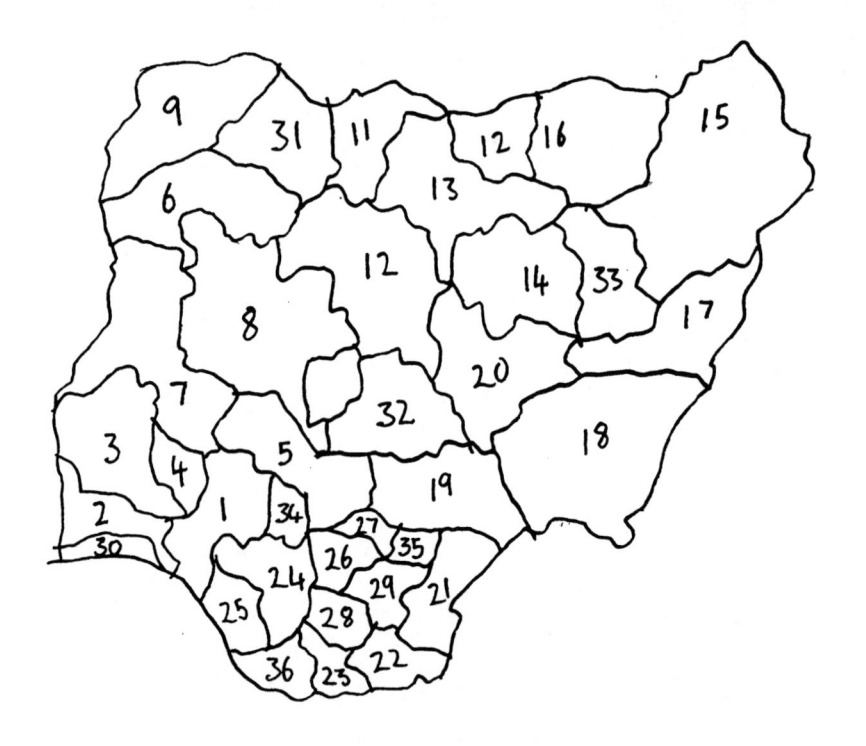

**Thirty-six States from 1996**

1. Ondu State
2. Ogun State
3. Oyo State
4. Osun State
5. Kogi State
6. Kebbi State
7. Kwara State
8. Niger State
9. Sokoto State
10. Kaduna State
11. Katsina State
12. Jigawa State
13. Kano State
14. Bauchi State
15. Borno State
16. Yobe State
17. Adamawa State
18. Taraba State
19. Benue State
20. Plateau State
21. Cross River State
22. Akwa-Ibom
23. River State
24. Edo State
25. Delta State
26. Anambra State
27. Enugu State
28. Imo State
29. Abia State
30. Lagos State
31. Zamfara State
32. Nasarawa
33. Gombe State
34. Ekiti State
35. Ebonyi State
36. Bayelsa State

*@ Federal Capital Territory 31

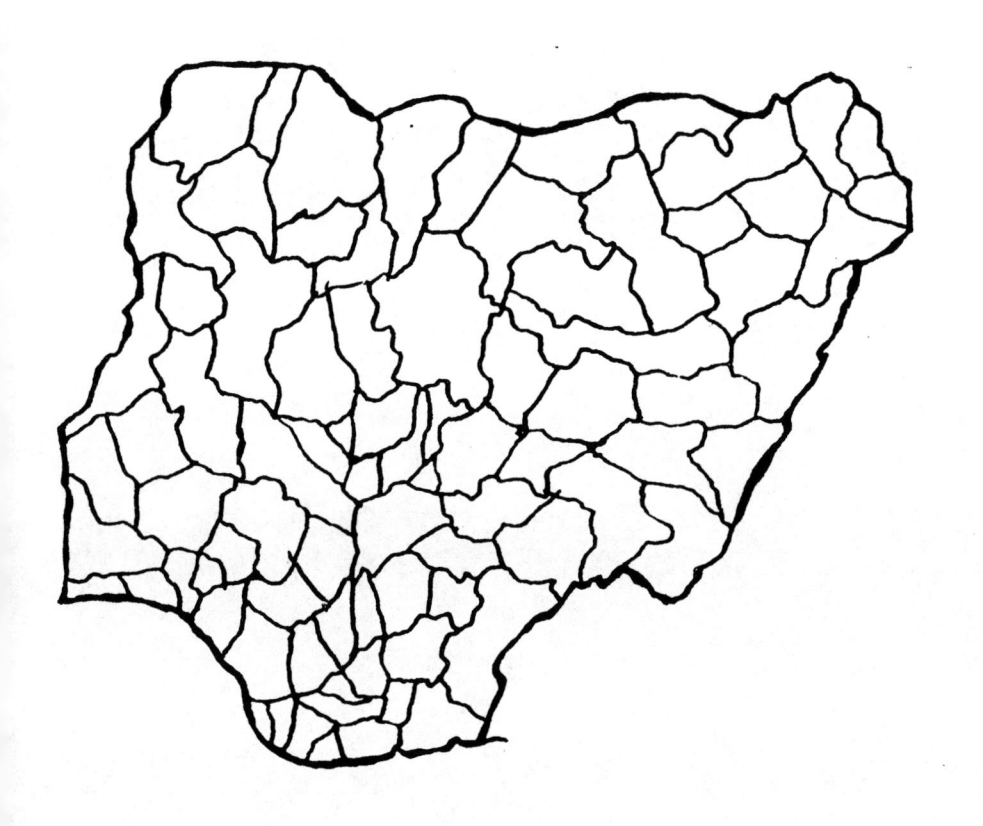

This map reflects the creation of new states
which are in demand

# Index

## A

Abacha: Brig. Sanni 225, 226, 244, 248, 249, 250, 251, 253, 255, 257, 279, 280, 288
Abiola: Chief 241, 245, 246, 247, 249, 251, 252, 254, 255, 261, 262, 267, 270; Chief 9, 10;
Abiola: Mojeed 240
Ademoyega: Maj. 92, 98, 276, 277
Adeyinka: Lt. Col. Adebayo 128
Adu: Prof. Ishaya 210
Agbam: Samuel 161, 163, 164
Agu: Emman 135
Akinloye: Chief Meredith Adisa 210
Akintola: Chief Samuel 40, 66, 72, 75, 81, 82, 83, 84, 85, 86, 87, 88, 89, 90, 91, 94, 96, 97, 102, 103, 105, 106, 113, 196, 210, 218
Akitoye; King of Lagos 16
Akpata: Dr. Bankole 65
Akran: Gen. 145, 148
Alakija: Sir Adeyomo 53
Alele: Phillip 161, 163, 164
Alexander: Maj.Gen.H.T. 184
Alexandra: HRH Princess 78
Ani: Michael 206
Anyanwu: Miss 262
Arikpo: Dr. Okio 167
Awolowo: Chief Obafemi 40, 42, 48, 52, 53, 60, 62, 63, 65, 66, 67, 69, 72, 73, 74, 75, 81,
82, 85, 86, 87, 89, 97, 131, 140, 141, 145, 153, 154, 189, 196, 210, 211, 212, 213, 214, 215, 217, 218, 220, 226, 230, 253, 267, 276, 289
Azikiwe: Dr.Nnamdi 210, 213, 219 37, 66, 214

## B

Baba: Alhaji Ali 222
Babangida: Gen. 229, 233, 234, 235, 237, 238, 239, 241, 243, 244, 245, 246, 249, 265, 279, 288
Babatope: Chief Ebeniza 249, 251
Babngida: Gen. Ibrahim 232
Bakare: Chief 115, 116
Bako: Brig. Ibrahim 226
Balewa: Sir Abubakar Tafawa 6, 35, 48, 59, 60, 62, 65, 72, 78, 87, 88, 90, 92, 101, 106, 113, 131, 145, 185, 210, 212, 217, 218, 219, 240, 267, 276, 277
Balogun: Chief Kola 254
Banjo: Johnson 161, 162, 163, 164, 170
Barake: Alexander 229
Beecroft: John 15, 16, 17
Bello: Sir Ahmadu 6, 48, 57, 70, 90, 95, 100, 102, 104, 106, 113, 117, 119, 193, 210, 217, 258
Bevin: Ernest 45
Bey: Shitta 97
Biriye: Chief Harold 90, 139
Bisalla: Gen. 201
Bismarck: Otto van 18, 80
Boddick: Anita 271
Boro: Isaac Adaka 6, 90
Briggs: Chief Wenike 130, 138, 139, 172
Brockway: Fenner 45
Buhari: Gen. Alhaji Mohammed 224, 226, 227, 228, 229, 230, 231, 232, 233, 234, 246, 247, 253, 278, 279, 288
Buxton: Sir Thomas 45

## C

Callaghan: James 200
Carter: President Jimmy 262
Conway: Monsignor Dominic 166

## D

Dambazua: Alhaji Lawan 257
Denard: Col. Robert 171
Diete-Spiff: Commander 172

Dike: Dr. Kenneth 167
Dikko: Alhaji Umaru 228, 229, 253
Dimka: Isaac 197, 198, 199, 200, 201, 234

# E

Edoja: Maj. G. T. 239
Effiong: Maj. Gen. Phillip 178, 180
Elias Dr. T. Oladele 104, 192 193
Emir: of Kano 128 220
Enahoro: Chief Anthony 56, 86, 131, 168, 169, 170, 252 256
Eusene: Col. 172

# F

Faulgues: Brig. Rene 171
Fawehimi: Gani 261
Fergusson: Brig. Sir Bernard 185

# G

Garbar: John 177
Gomwalk: Police Commissioner 201
Gussing: Nils-Goran 184 185

# H

Hananiya: Maj. Gen 229

# I

Ibrahim: Alhaji Waziri 209, 211
Idiabong: Brig. Babtunde 231 233
Ifeajuna: Emmanuel 99, 101, 103, 106, 107, 148, 161, 163, 277 164
Ikoku: S.G. 211
Ironsi: Maj. Gen. Aguti 104, 106, 107, 109, 113, 114, 115, 116, 118, 119, 121, 122, 123, 124, 127, 128, 129, 132, 135, 139, 146, 161, 182, 277

# J

Jadande: Alhaji Lateef 72, 249 230 251

## K

Kano: Alhaji Aminu  211 257
Kingibe: Dr.  249, 251
Kuti: Dr. Beko Ransome  10, 231, 262

## M

Mandela: Nelson  270, 271, 288
Marwa: Maitasine Mohammed  220
Mbanefo: Sir Louis  168, 169, 170, 178
Mbu: Matthew  240
Milroy: Maj. Gen. W.A.  184
Mugabe: Robert  269
Mukoro: Maj. S. D.  239
Musa: Balarabe  220

## N

Nzeribe: Chief Arthur  242
Nzeribe: Dr. Ben  211

## O

Obasenjo: Brigadier  174
Obote: President Milton  168
Odugwu: Bernard  181
Ogon: Michael  219
Ohabanu: Dr. Cyril  194
Ojukwu  116, 128, 129, 130, 131, 132, 134, 135, 138, 139, 140, 142, 145, 146, 147, 148, 149, 150, 151, 153, 154, 155, 159, 160, 161, 162, 163, 165, 166, 167, 169, 170, 171, 172, 174, 175, 177, 178, 180, 189, 221, 236, 245, 252
Okonkwo: Major  163
Olkiewizc: Col. Alfons  184
Olumono: Adebiyi  256
Omeruah: Capt. Emeka  230
Onaguruwa: Dr. Olu  249, 251
Orka: Maj. Gideon Gwarzo  239, 249

## R

Raad: Maj. Gen. Arthur  184
Rifkind: Malcolm  284

Rimi: Abba Abubakar 220
Robertson: Sir James 74, 75 284
Rocheau: Monsignor Georges 166
Rowlands: Edward 200

## S

Saro-Wiwa: Ken 264
Selassie: Emperor Haile 165
Shagari: Alhaji Shehu 210 212
Shonekan: Chief Ernest 240
Showinka: Wole 252
Smith: Arnold 167
Smith: Ian 159

## T

Tegegne: Brig.Gen.Negga 184
Thant: U 185
Thompson-Akpabio: Dr. 231
Thomson: George 167
Tofa: Alhaji Bashir 240

## U

Udoma: Mr Justice 207, 208
Ugo: Sylvester 241

## V

Vasta: Gen. Mamman 234

## W

Wachuku: Dr. Jaja 219
Waziri: Alhaji 214
White: Mr. Justice Karabi 253
Williams: Chief Rotimi 195

## Y

Ya'r Adua: Brig. 200
Yar'adua: Gen. 241
Yaro: Jushua Dogon 233